lonely planet

BEST ROAD TRIPS

SOUTHWEST USA

ESCAPES ON THE OPEN ROAD

ANTHONY HAM, HUGH MCNAUGHTAN, AMY C BALFOUR,
STEPHEN LIOY, CAROLYN MCCARTHY, CHRISTOPHER PITTS,
RYAN VER BERKMOES, BENEDICT WALKER

Contents

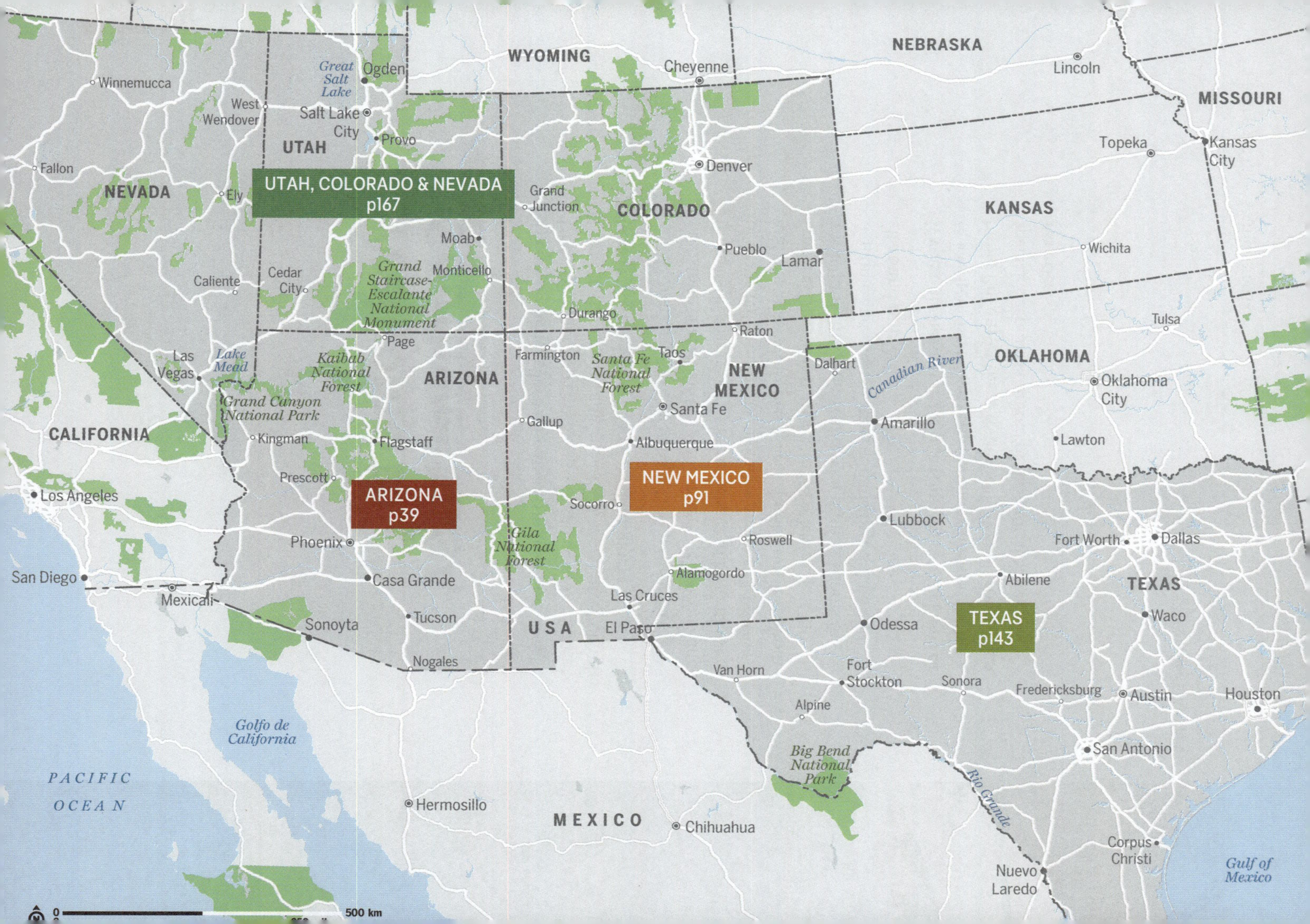

UTAH, COLORADO & NEVADA p167
ARIZONA p39
NEW MEXICO p91
TEXAS p143
NEVADA
UTAH
WYOMING
NEBRASKA
MISSOURI
KANSAS
COLORADO
CALIFORNIA
ARIZONA
NEW MEXICO
OKLAHOMA
TEXAS
USA
MEXICO
PACIFIC OCEAN
Golfo de California
Gulf of Mexico
Great Salt Lake
Lake Mead
Canadian River
Rio Grande
Grand Canyon National Park
Kaibab National Forest
Grand Staircase-Escalante National Monument
Santa Fe National Forest
Gila National Forest
Big Bend National Park
Winnemucca
Fallon
West Wendover
Ely
Caliente
Las Vegas
Ogden
Salt Lake City
Provo
Moab
Monticello
Cedar City
Page
Grand Junction
Durango
Cheyenne
Denver
Pueblo
Lamar
Lincoln
Topeka
Kansas City
Wichita
Tulsa
Oklahoma City
Lawton
Raton
Taos
Farmington
Santa Fe
Gallup
Albuquerque
Socorro
Roswell
Alamogordo
Las Cruces
El Paso
Dalhart
Amarillo
Lubbock
Odessa
Abilene
Fort Worth
Dallas
Waco
Austin
Houston
San Antonio
Fredericksburg
Sonora
Fort Stockton
Van Horn
Alpine
Corpus Christi
Nuevo Laredo
Chihuahua
Hermosillo
Kingman
Flagstaff
Prescott
Phoenix
Casa Grande
Tucson
Nogales
Sonoyta
Mexicali
San Diego
Los Angeles
0
500 km

Welcome to Southwest USA

There's no better place for a road trip than Southwest USA. Whether you're drawn to Route 66 or the Grand Canyon, the astonishing breadth of experiences on offer here is like the US writ large in all its glory.

The 32 road trips in this book take you through the sandstone charms of Utah, the deserts of Arizona and the artistic sparkle of New Mexico. Or the wildflowers of Texas Hill Country, Colorado's ancient cliff towns and Nevada's wide open spaces. But it's not just about scenery. Dinosaur tracks, Old West towns, kitschy attractions, BBQ joints and wine-tasting rooms in dynamic and diverse cities add history, drama and all-round fun.

If you only have time for one trip, you can pick one of our writers' best-loved trips of the Southwest in this book. But any of these routes will take you somewhere special, deep into the soul of the United States of America.

Vermilion Cliffs (p50)
MARINA POUSHKINA/SHUTTERSTOCK ©

Our Picks

BEST CLASSIC DRIVES

For decades, Americans have been driving Route 66 or through Monument Valley – or any way they can – to get to the Grand Canyon. The classic drives we cover here are their own road movies, pilgrimages of a sort, and there's something reassuring about joining generations of road-trippers out there. These trips are destinations in themselves, although they come with the bonus of taking you to some of the most beautiful places in the country.

JUST OFF SEASON

Consider driving these routes in late spring or early fall to avoid the summer crowds.

1

Route 66: The Southwest

Get kitschy along the Mother Road in Texas, New Mexico and Arizona on the ultimate American road trip.

P28

2

Zion & Bryce Canyon National Parks

Drive amid red rock grandeur in two stunning national parks that showcase the best of natural Utah.

P170

3

Four Corners Cruise

Loop past the Southwest's biggest and boldest sights from Nevada to New Mexico and everywhere in between.

P20

4

Fantastic Canyon Voyage

All roads lead to the Grand Canyon on this journey through Arizona's cowboy country.

P54

5

High & Low Roads to Taos

Drive over mountains and down canyons between iconic destinations like the Rio Grande and Sangre de Cristos.

P94

DRIVERS LICENSE

Foreign visitors can legally drive a car in the US for up to 12 months using their home driver's license.

LYNN YEH/SHUTTERSTOCK ©

Seligman (p34) Route 66: The Southwest

INTERNATIONAL DRIVING PERMIT

Carrying an International Driving Permit (IDP) is helpful if your license doesn't have a photo or isn't in English.

Bryce Canyon (p175)
Zion & Bryce Canyon National Parks

CAR RENTAL & INSURANCE

Car-rental companies provide liability insurance, but most charge extra. Optional collision damage waiver or loss damage waiver also costs extra.

Our Picks

BEST SCENIC DRIVES

The open roads of the Southwest take you through some of America's most recognizable landscapes: sandstone canyons, big skies, saguaro-dotted deserts and twisty mountain ridges. Some roads take you to some pretty spectacular places, none more so than the Grand Canyon. But the routes here are in themselves jaw-droppingly beautiful. Plan to take longer than you expect: you'll pull over to the side of the road so often that you'll take ages to get anywhere.

DON'T LEAVE HOME WITHOUT IT

Don't put the key into the ignition if you don't have travel insurance, which is legally required.

1

Highway 50: The Loneliest Road

In spring, this highway across the white-hot belly of Nevada is flanked to the east by snowcapped peaks.

P204

2

Big Bend Scenic Loop

With the Marfa Lights and a renegade Prada store, things get weird on this superb loop.

P154

JSPANNHOFF/SHUTTERSTOCK ©

Silverton (p196) San Juan Skyway & Million Dollar Highway

3

San Juan Skyway & Million Dollar Highway

Thar's gold in them thar views on your way through beautiful Colorado from Mesa Verde to Telluride.

P194

4

Fantastic Canyon Voyage

Curve over mountains and roll past red rocks and pine trees on your way through Arizona to the Grand Canyon.

P54

5

Scenic Byway 12

Arguably Utah's most stunning drive, this route takes in sculpted slickrock and razor-thin ridgebacks, and climbs an 11,000ft-tall mountain.

P176

Scenic Byway 12 (p176)

Our Picks

BEST OLD WEST DRIVES

Ancient civilizations left behind dwellings that merge with the mountains, gunslingers left bullet holes and the heroes of the Alamo left legends to fill a hundred books. The Southwest is fertile terrain for the myths of the Wild West, and, of course, Native American stories of great pride and poignancy infuse every corner of the region. Building your trip around these stories makes for some fabulous journeys.

WATCH FOR WILDLIFE

Signs urge caution where wild animals frequent roadsides. Take these signs seriously, particularly at dusk and dawn.

1

A Taste of the Old West

Boothill Graveyard and the OK Corral spotlight mining town lore in Tombstone.

P42

2

Southwest Indian Nations Sojourn

Petroglyphs provide clues about prehistoric lifestyles while museums cover cultural treasures.

P86

3

High & Low Roads to Taos

Santa Fe recently celebrated its 400th birthday, but Taos Pueblo is older by 200-plus years.

P94

WINTER TIRES

Where winter driving is an issue, many cars are fitted with steel-studded snow tires, while snow chains are sometimes required.

HANNATOR/SHUTTERSTOCK ©

Monument Valley (p186)

4

Hill Country

Remember the Alamo then learn about President Lyndon Johnson at his ranch and boyhood home.

P146

5

Monument Valley & Trail of the Ancients

Red-rock sandstone buttes shelter cliff ruins and astonishing desert views in this Western classic.

P186

WATCH FOR LIVESTOCK

In deserts and range country, livestock sometimes graze next to unfenced roads. These areas are signed as 'Open Range.'

San Francisco de Asís, Taos (p96)

Our Picks

BEST WILD WEST DRIVES

The Southwest can seem like a family playground, offering everything from quirky sideshows to landscapes ripe for exploration. Myths and legends swirl through the region and following their trail can make for the best history lesson the kids will ever have. The Grand Canyon, dinosaurs, outlaw heroes and Geronimo: whether you're looking for a quiet escape or an adventurous deep dive into the drama-filled terrain, there's something here for every family.

RED LIGHT!

Unless signs prohibit it (that's you, New York), you may turn right at a red light after first coming to a full stop.

1

A Taste of the Old West

Ride a stagecoach, watch a shootout and explore an old copper mine.

P42

2

Las Cruces to Carlsbad Caverns

Enjoy livestock-milking demos, sled rides down a sand dune and a cavernous wonderland.

P118

3

Moab & Southeastern National Parks

Kids keep busy with junior ranger programs at two national parks and there's low-key rafting and hiking.

P180

HANDS-FREE

In many states, it's illegal to talk on a handheld cell phone while driving; use a hands-free device instead.

NICK FOX/SHUTTERSTOCK ©

Tombstone (p44) A Taste of the Old West

4

Dinosaur Diamond Prehistoric Byway

Dinosaur bones and footprints are bait for budding paleontologists in Utah and Colorado.

P190

5

Billy the Kid Trail

Travel what might be the oldest road in America and follow in the footsteps of Geronimo and Billy the Kid.

P136

Our Picks

BEST FOOD & WINE LOVERS' DRIVES

The Southwest has a cuisine all its own, blending Mexican and American influences with results that many people will cross the country just to sample. From green-chile cheeseburgers to vegan BLTs and hefty Navajo tacos, Native American dishes to the urban hot pot of Phoenix or Las Vegas, Texan barbecue to the subtleties of fusion cooking Colorado-style – eating in the Southwest is as diverse as the views you can enjoy while eating.

INTERSECTIONS

At four-way stop signs, cars should proceed in order of arrival; when two cars arrive simultaneously, the one on the right has the right of way.

1

A Taste of the Old West

Oh, Tucson, we love how you eat: Sonoran hotdogs, breakfast burritos and *nuevo*-Mexican masterpieces.

P42

2

Southwest Indian Nations Sojourn

Savor American Indian dishes at Kai, give fry bread a try in Phoenix and enjoy lamb-and-hominy stew on the Hopi Reservation.

P86

3

El Camino Real & Turquoise Trail

Cheeseburger topped with Hatch's famous green chiles? A match made in New Mexico.

P100

PAYING FOR FUEL

Many gas stations have fuel pumps with credit-card pay screens. Most ask for your zip code. Foreign travelers will have to pay inside before pumping gas

BRENT HOFACKER/SHUTTERSTOCK ©

Sonoran hotdogs

4

Hill Country

In Texas, the emphasis is on barbecue, and in Hill Country, the fun is in sampling the sauce.

P146

5

Southern Desert Wanderings

A special microclimate encourages fine grapes around Sonoita and Elgin, one of the most surprising finds in the Southwest.

P70

When to Go

Desert heat in the Southwest states can be fierce. But summer road trips are an American rite of passage.

I LIVE HERE

I LOVE DRIVING HERE

Anthony Ham, writer @AnthonyHamWriter

The first time I ever drove across the American Southwest, it was May and it was magnificent. The sky was a perfect, steely blue, an incredible backdrop to red rock and red deserts. The air was crisp and clear, and visibility stretched all the way to the high, snowcapped peaks of Colorado. The further I drove, the more I felt like I was writing my very own road movie, passing through a glorious landscape so recognizably American that I could only have been in the splendid Southwest.

In summer, Colorado's mountain roads are cleared of snow, and all roads, visitor centers, accommodations and attractions are open. It's also when some of the country's best festivals happen.

But summer is also when half the US seems to be en route to the Grand Canyon, and while your car may have air-conditioning, in Utah, New Mexico and Nevada in particular, summer temperatures can be brutal. Most outdoor activities will only be possible early morning and late afternoon.

Spring or fall can be a clever alternative, with cool festivals and blooming wildflowers in places like Texas' Hill Country.

KAREN GRIGORYAN/SHUTTERSTOCK ©

Horseshoe Bend (p49)

Weather Watch (Denver)

JANUARY	FEBRUARY	MARCH	APRIL	MAY	JUNE
Avg daytime max: **46°F (8°C)**	Avg daytime max: **48°F (9°C)**	Avg daytime max: **57°F (14°C)**	Avg daytime max: **64°F (18°C)**	Avg daytime max: **72°F (22°C)**	Avg daytime max: **84°F (29°C)**
Days of rainfall or snowfall: **4**	Days of rainfall or snowfall: **4**	Days of rainfall or snowfall: **6**	Days of rainfall or snowfall: **7**	Days of rainfall or snowfall: **9**	Days of rainfall or snowfall: **6**

©MELAND/SHUTTERSTOCK

International Balloon Fiesta

SUNSHINE & RAIN

The sunniest city in the US appears to be Yuma, Arizona, with an average of 242 sunny days a year. This is followed by Phoenix, Arizona, with 211 days, and Las Vegas with 210.

Accommodations

Prices vary considerably by season, but festivals are one example where otherwise innocuous dates can see hotels, motels and RV parks booked out months in advance for sky-high prices. The same applies to most national parks in summer. Moving your trip even a few weeks either side of the logjam can make all the difference.

A CLIMATE OF EXTREMES

The world's hottest-ever air temperature was recorded at Furnace Creek, in Death Valley in the Mojave Desert on July 10, 1913: 134°F (57°C). Remarkably, just six months earlier, on January 8, 1913, Death Valley's coldest-ever temperature was also recorded, also at Furnace Creek: 15°F (-10°C).

THE BIG FESTIVALS

South by Southwest Austin, TX, turns into ground zero for one of the biggest music (and film) festivals in North America. **March**

Burning Man Festival Some 70,000 revelers, artists and free spirits descend on Nevada's Black Rock Desert. **September**

Telluride Film Festival Draws some of the biggest names and films from Hollywood. **September**

Great American Beer Festival In Denver, a craft beer version of Oktoberfest. **September or October**

QUIRKY FESTIVALS

Historic Route 66 Fun Run A vintage car rally dedicated to the US's most famous road. **May**

Santa Fe Fiesta & Burning of Zozobra Has a candlelit procession and the torching of Zozobra, an effigy of 'Old Man Gloom'. **September**

International Balloon Fiesta Takes to the skies over Albuquerque, New Mexico. The balloons are a wonderful sight. **October**

Houston Art Car Parade Sees car devotees paint their vehicles in weird and wacky ways then drive through Houston. **April**

JULY	AUGUST	SEPTEMBER	OCTOBER	NOVEMBER	DECEMBER
Avg daytime max: **88°F (31°C)**	Avg daytime max: **86°F (30°C)**	Avg daytime max: **79°F (26°C)**	Avg daytime max: **66°F (19°C)**	Avg daytime max: **54°F (12°C)**	Avg daytime max: **46°F (8°C)**
Days of rainfall or snowfall: **6**	Days of rainfall or snowfall: **5**	Days of rainfall or snowfall: **4**	Days of rainfall or snowfall: **5**	Days of rainfall or snowfall: **4**	Days of rainfall or snowfall: **4**

Get Prepared for Southwest USA

Useful things to load in your bag, your ears and your brain

Clothing

Wear what you want: In the US just about anything goes, and you'll rarely feel uncomfortable because of what you're wearing. Knowing the kind of trip you're planning will help in preparing you wardrobe. Will you be hiking? Are you traveling in summer or winter? Will you be eating in nice restaurants? Do you plan to go to the beach down on the Gulf Coast?

Mountain appropriate: If you're traveling in mountain regions, you should carry some warm clothes. In winter (when many mountain roads are closed) in Colorado, this may mean a full set of ski gear. In high summer, take a warm jacket for cooler high-altitude temperatures.

Sun protection: In the deserts of the Southwest, don't forget sunglasses and a broad-brimmed sun hat.

Hiking gear: If you're planning on hiking, especially in the mountains, make that jacket waterproof and make sure you're wearing hiking boots. Otherwise, good walking shoes should be fine for most walks.

Something for going out: Many upmarket restaurants, and certainly most upscale bars or clubs, have quite strict dress codes. It's worth bringing along dressier attire (smart casual) for those times when you decide to go somewhere nice.

WATCH

Butch Cassidy & the Sundance Kid
(George Roy Hill; 1969) Follows the adventures of two real-life outlaws who hid out in Utah.

National Lampoon's Vacation
(Harold Ramis; 1983) Chevy Chase on a classic summer road trip, including through the Southwest.

Thelma & Louise
(Ridley Scott; 1991) Two gal pals run from the law and into stunning Southwest scenery.

Forrest Gump
(Robert Zemeckis; 1994) Forrest stopped his cross-country run in Monument Valley, which straddles the Utah–Arizona line.

The Hangover
(Todd Phillips; 2009) It's a bachelor party gone wrong – or right – in Las Vegas.

TUPUNGATO/SHUTTERSTOCK ©

Canyonlands National Park (p180)

Words

To ride shotgun: To travel in the passenger seat.

RV: Stands for 'recreation vehicle' and refers to a motorhome or caravan.

Airstream: A specific kind of motorhome that looks like an expensive metal tube.

BLM: The Bureau of Land Management, the government department responsible for public lands where you can park with an RV.

KOA: A popular chain of family-friendly campgrounds.

Rig: A word for motorhome or RV.

SP: Stands for 'state park'.

Hit the road: To start driving or get back on the move.

Spring break: When students take advantage of school or college holidays, hit the road and head for a party area – stay off the roads.

Snowbirds: These semi-nomad people spend their summers in the north and winters in the south and are always chasing the warm weather.

Wallydocking: The practice of parking overnight at a Walmart parking to avoid paying for camping.

LISTEN

America
(Simon & Garfunkel; 1968) Young lovers hitchhiking in search of America.

The Freewheelin' Bob Dylan
(Bob Dylan; 1963) Early classic road music from this Nobel Prize winner.

Carried to Dust
(Calexico; 2008) This ethereal Tucson band jams on vivid images from the Southwest.

This American Life
(thisamericanlife.org) Podcast offering endearing, quirky and often powerful snapshots from US life.

READ

On the Road
(Jack Kerouac; 1957) A journey through post-WWII America, including Colorado and Utah.

Desert Solitaire
(Edward Abbey; 1968) Lyrical essays about the Southwest and industrial tourism by no-holds-barred eco-curmudgeon.

Blue Highways
(William Least Heat-Moon; 1982) A classic of American travel writing and the ultimate road trip.

American Zion
(Betsy Gaines Quammen; 2020) A fascinating journey through the American West and its contested open spaces.

ROAD TRIPS

Tucumcari (p30)

NICK FOX/SHUTTERSTOCK ©

Contents

01

Four Corners Cruise

BEST FOR OUTDOORS

Angels Landing Trail in Zion National Park.

DURATION	DISTANCE	GREAT FOR
10 days	1593 miles / 2564km	Family, outdoors

BEST TIME TO GO	Spring and fall for thinner crowds and pleasant temperatures.

Las Vegas

Everything about this trip demands superlatives – from the Grand Canyon to Vegas, Zion and beyond, it's a procession of some of the biggest, boldest items on many a bucket list. The rugged buttes and mesas of Monument Valley are mesmerizing, an alluring mix of the familiar and otherworldly, and it's a captivating spell – but by no means the only one cast along this Four Corners Cruise.

Link your trip

11 High & Low Roads to Taos

Take the high or the low road between Santa Fe and Taos, with fine craftwork, historic churches and mountain scenery.

27 Moab & Southeastern National Parks

From Monument Valley drive north on US 163 to US 191, continuing north to Moab and sandstone arches.

01 LAS VEGAS

Take in Sin City's synthetic charms on a morning walk past the iconic casinos and hotels of the Strip, then spend the afternoon downtown at the **Mob Museum** (themobmuseum.org), a three-story collection examining organized crime in America and its connection to Las Vegas. One block south, zip-line over Fremont St from the 11th-story launchpad of **Slotzilla** (vegasexperience.com/slotzilla-zip-line), then end the night with an illuminated stroll at the **Neon Museum** (neonmuseum.org).

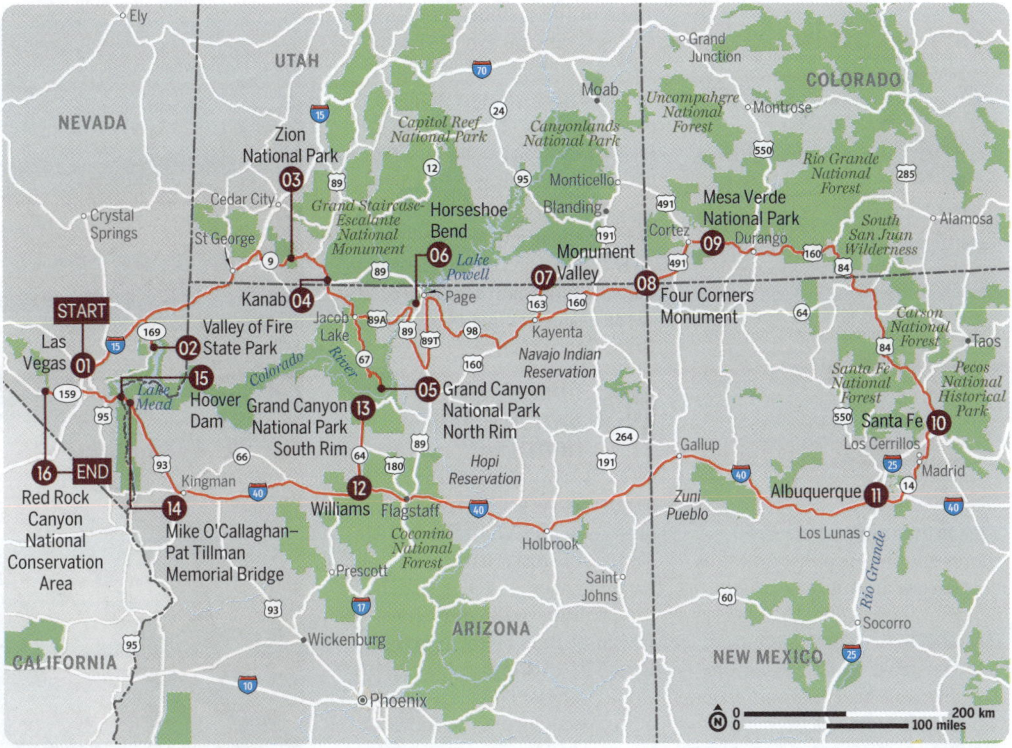

The giant pink stiletto in the lobby of Vegas' **Cosmopolitan** (cosmopolitanlasvegas.com) is an eye-catcher. Designed by Roark Gourley, the 9ft-tall shoe was supposed to be treated with the reverence due a piece of art, but its protective ropes were soon pushed aside by partygoers seeking 'unique' selfies. In response, the Cosmopolitan removed the ropes and in 16 months the outsized footwear got so much love it needed to be sent out for repairs.

THE DRIVE
Follow I-15 north for 34 miles then take exit 75. From here, Hwy 169/Valley of Fire Hwy travels 18 miles to the park.

02 VALLEY OF FIRE STATE PARK

Before losing yourself in the sandstone sculpture-gardens of Utah, swing through this masterwork of desert scenery to prime yourself for what's ahead. It's an easy detour, with the Valley of Fire Hwy and Hwy 169 running through **Valley of Fire State Park** (parks.nv.gov/parks/valley-of-fire) and passing close to the psychedelically shaped red-rock formations. From the visitor center, take the scenic side road out to **White Domes**, an 11-mile round trip. En route you'll pass Rainbow Vista and the turn-off to **Fire Canyon** and **Silica Dome** (where Captain Kirk perished in *Star Trek: Generations*).

Spring and fall are the best times to visit; avoid summer when temperatures typically exceed 100°F (37°C).

THE DRIVE
Return to I-15 north, cruising through Arizona and into Utah. Leave the highway at exit 16 and follow Hwy 9 east for 32 miles.

03 ZION NATIONAL PARK

The climb up **Angels Landing** in **Zion National Park** (nps.gov/zion) may be the best day hike in North America. From Grotto Trailhead, the 5.4-mile round trip crosses the Virgin River, hugs a towering cliffside, squeezes through a narrow canyon, snakes up Walters Wiggles, then traverses

WHY I LOVE THIS TRIP

Hugh McNaughtan, writer

Epic, grandiose and utterly beguiling, this trip is nothing less than a crash course in the glories of America's Southwest. While Vegas is a global byword for sin and frivolity, there are plenty of opportunities to make peace with your soul in the wilds of the Grand Canyon's North Rim, in the peerless splendor of Zion National Park's canyons and in the sacred places of the vast Navajo Reservation.

a razor-thin ridge where steel chains and the encouraging words of strangers are your only safety net. Your reward after the final scramble to the 5790ft summit? A bird's-eye view of Zion Canyon. The hike reflects what's best about the park: beauty, adventure and the shared community of people who love the outdoors.

THE DRIVE
Twist out of the park on Hwy 9 east, driving almost 25 miles to Hwy 89. Follow Hwy 89 south to the vast, open-air movie set that is Kanab.

04 KANAB

Sitting between Zion, Grand Staircase-Escalante (p178) and the Grand Canyon North Rim, Kanab is a good spot for a base camp. Hundreds of Western movies were filmed here – John Wayne and other gunslingin' celebs really put the town on the map. Today, animal lovers know that the town is home to the **Best Friends Animal Sanctuary** (bestfriends.org), the country's largest no-kill animal shelter. Tours of the facility – home to dogs, cats, pigs, birds and more – are free, but call ahead to confirm times and to make a reservation. The sanctuary is located in Angel Canyon, also called Kanab Canyon by locals.

THE DRIVE
Continue into Arizona – now on Hwy 89A – and climb the Kaibab Plateau. Turn south onto Hwy 67 at Jacob Lake and drive 44 miles to Grand Canyon Lodge.

05 GRAND CANYON NATIONAL PARK NORTH RIM

While driving through the ponderosa forest that opens onto rolling meadows in Kaibab National Forest, keep an eye out for mule deer as you approach the entrance to the **park** (nps.gov/grca). Stop by the **North Rim Visitor Center**, beside Grand Canyon Lodge (p52; both closed during the snows of October to May), for information and to join ranger-led nature walks and nighttime programs. If it's 5 o'clock somewhere, enjoy a cocktail from the lodge terrace of the **Rough Rider Saloon** (grandcanyonforever.com) while soaking up the view.

For an easy but scenic half-day hike, follow the 4-mile (round-trip) **Cape Final Trail** through ponderosa pine forests with great canyon views. The steep and difficult 14-mile **North Kaibab Trail** is the only maintained rim-to-river trail and connects with trails to the South Rim near Phantom Ranch. The trailhead is 2 miles north of Grand Canyon Lodge. For a taste of inner-canyon hiking, walk 0.75 miles down to **Coconino Overlook** or 2 miles to the **Supai Tunnel**.

SUMIKOPHOTO/SHUTTERSTOCK ©

Grand Canyon

TOP TIP:

No Bottled Water

As a conservation measure, Grand Canyon National Park no longer sells bottled water. Instead, fill your thermos at water filling stations along the rim or at Canyon View Marketplace. Water bottles had constituted 20% of the waste generated in the park.

THE DRIVE
Track back to Jacob Lake, then head east on Hwy 89A, down the Kaibab Plateau, past blink-and-miss-it Marble Canyon and to the junction with Hwy 89. Turn left and drive 26 miles north to Page.

06 HORSESHOE BEND

The clifftop view at Horseshoe Bend will sear itself into your memory. One thousand feet below, the **Colorado River** carves a perfect U through a colossal thickness of Navajo sandstone. It's simultaneously beautiful and terrifying. There are no railings – it's just you, a sheer drop and dozens of people you don't know taking selfies on the treacherous rim. Free-range toddlers are not a good idea. From the parking lot it's a 0.75-mile one-way hike to the rim. There's a moderate hill along the way, and the trail is unshaded, so the walk can be a little strenuous in summer – but it's worth it. The trailhead is on Hwy 89, south of Page and just south of mile marker 541.

THE DRIVE
Rejoin Hwy 89 and drive north a short distance to Hwy 98. Turn right and follow 98 southeast to Hwy 160. Turn left and drive 34 miles north, passing the entrance to Navajo National Monument. In Kayenta, turn left onto Hwy 163 North and drive almost 22 miles to Monument Valley, on the Arizona–Utah border.

07 MONUMENT VALLEY

'May I walk in beauty' is the final line of a famous Navajo prayer. Beauty comes in countless forms on this vast reservation, but Monument Valley's majestic array of rugged buttes and wind-worn mesas must be its most sensational. For up-close views of the formations, drive into the **Monument Valley Navajo Tribal Park** (navajonationparks.org) and follow the unpaved 17-mile scenic loop that passes some of the most dramatic formations, such as the **East and West Mitten Buttes** and the **Three Sisters**. For a guided tour (1½/2½ hours $65/85), which will take you into areas where private vehicles cannot go, stop by one of the

MARCLSCHAUER/SHUTTERSTOCK ©

Cliff Palace, Mesa Verde National Park

kiosks in the parking lot beside the View Hotel.

THE DRIVE Follow Hwy 163 back to Kayenta. Turn left and take Hwy 160 east about 73 miles to tiny Tee Noc Pos. Take a sharp left to stay on Hwy 160 and drive 6 miles to Four Corners Rd and the Monument.

08 FOUR CORNERS MONUMENT

It's seriously remote, but you can't skip the **Four Corners Monument** (navajonationparks.org) on a road trip through the epicenter of the Southwest! Once you arrive, don't be shy: put a foot into Arizona and plant the other in New Mexico. Slap a hand in Utah and place the other in Colorado. Smile for the camera. It makes a good photo, even if it's not 100% accurate – government surveyors have admitted that the marker is almost 2000ft east of where it should be (although it remains a legally recognized border point). Half the fun here is watching the contortions performed by happy-snappers determined to straddle all four states.

THE DRIVE Return to Hwy 160 and turn left. It's a 50-mile drive across the northwestern tip of New Mexico and through Colorado to Mesa Verde. Hwy 160 becomes Hwy 491 for around 20 miles of this journey.

09 MESA VERDE NATIONAL PARK

Ancestral Puebloan sites are found throughout the canyons and mesas of **Mesa Verde** (nps.gov/meve), perched on a high plateau south of Cortez and Mancos. According to the experts, the Ancestral Puebloans didn't 'disappear' 700 years ago, they simply migrated south, developing into the American Indian tribes that live in the Southwest to this day. If you only have time for a short visit, check out the **Chapin Mesa Museum** and walk through the **Spruce Tree House**, where you can climb down a wooden ladder into a kiva.

Mesa Verde rewards travelers who set aside a day or more to take the ranger-led tours of **Cliff Palace** and **Balcony House**, explore **Wetherill Mesa** (the quieter side of canyon), linger around the museum, or participate in one of the campfire programs at **Morefield Campground** (visitmesaverde.com). The park also provides plenty of hiking, skiing, snowshoeing and mountain-biking options. Visitors can camp out or stay in luxury at the lodge.

THE DRIVE Hop back onto US 160, following it 36 miles east to Durango and then another 61 miles to join US 84 south for the 151-mile run to Santa Fe. You'll pass through Abiquiú, home of artist Georgia O'Keeffe from 1949 until her death in 1986. Continue toward Santa Fe, exiting onto N Guadalupe St to head toward the Plaza.

Photo opportunity

The glory of the Grand Canyon from the Rim Trail.

10 SANTA FE

This 400-year-old city is pretty darn inviting. You've got the juxtaposition of art and landscape, with cow skulls hanging from sky-blue walls and slender crosses topping centuries-old missions. And then there's the comfortable mingling of American Indian, Hispanic and Anglo cultures, with ancient pueblos, 300-year-old haciendas and stylish modern buildings standing in easy proximity.

The beauty of the region was captured by New Mexico's most famous artist, Georgia O'Keeffe. Possessing the world's largest collection of her work, the **Georgia O'Keeffe Museum** (okeeffemuseum.org) showcases the thick brushwork and luminous colors that don't always come through on the ubiquitous posters. Take your time to relish them here firsthand. The museum is housed in a former Spanish Baptist church with adobe walls that has been renovated to form 10 skylit galleries.

The city is anchored by the **Plaza**, which was the end of the Santa Fe Trail between 1822 and 1880.

THE DRIVE The historic route to Albuquerque is the Turquoise Trail, which follows Hwy 14 south for 50 miles through Los Cerrillos and Madrid. If you're in a hurry, take I-25 south.

11 ALBUQUERQUE

Most of Albuquerque's top sites are concentrated in Old Town, which is a straight shot west on Central Ave from Nob Hill and the University of New Mexico (UNM). Soak up the ambience on a walking tour.

The most extravagant route to the top of 10,378ft Sandia Crest

Photo Finish: Kolb Studio

Before digital photography, brothers Ellsworth and Emery Kolb were shooting souvenir photos of mule-riding Grand Canyon visitors as they began their descent down the Bright Angel Trail. The brothers would sell finished prints to the tourists returning to the rim at the end of the day. But in the early 1900s there was no running water on the South Rim – so how did they process their prints? After snapping photos from their studio window that overlooked a bend in the trail, one of the brothers would run 4.6 miles down to the waters of Indian Garden with the negatives, print the photos in their lab there and then run, or perhaps hike briskly, back up the Bright Angel to meet visitors with their prints.

is via the **Sandia Peak Tramway** (sandiapeak.com). The 2.7-mile tram ride starts in the desert realm of cholla cactus and soars to the pine-topped summit. For exercise, take the beautiful 8-mile (one-way) **La Luz Trail** (laluztrail.com) back down, connecting with the 2-mile **Tramway Trail** to return to your car. The La Luz Trail passes a small waterfall, pine forests and spectacular views. It gets hot, so start early. Take Tramway Blvd east from I-25 to get to the tramway.

THE DRIVE
From Albuquerque to Williams, in Arizona, I-40 overlaps or parallels Route 66. It's 359 miles to Williams.

12 WILLIAMS

Train buffs, Route 66 enthusiasts and Grand Canyon–bound vacationers all cross paths in Williams, an inviting small town with all the charm and authenticity of 'Main Street America.' If you only have time for a day visit to the park, the **Grand Canyon Railway** (thetrain.com) is a fun and hassle-free way to get there and back. After a **Wild West show** beside the tracks, the train departs for its 2½-hour ride to the South Rim, where you can explore by foot or shuttle. Late March through October passengers can ride in reconditioned open-air Pullman cabooses.

On Route 66 the divey **World Famous Sultana Bar**, which once housed a speakeasy, is a great place to sink some suds beneath a menagerie of stuffed wildlife.

13 GRAND CANYON NATIONAL PARK SOUTH RIM

A walk along the **Rim Trail** (nps.gov/grca) in **Grand Canyon Village** brings stunning views of the iconic canyon, as well as historic buildings, American Indian crafts and geological displays.

Starting from the plaza at **Bright Angel Trail**, walk east on the Rim Trail to **Kolb Studio**, which holds a small bookstore and an art gallery. Next door is **Lookout Studio**, designed by noted architect Mary Jane Colter to look like the stone dwellings of the Southwest's Puebloans.

Step into the 1905 **El Tovar Hotel** to see its replica Remington bronzes, stained glass, stuffed mounts and exposed beams, or to admire the canyon views from its porches.

Next door, the **Hopi House**, another Colter-designed structure, has sold high-quality American Indian jewelry and other crafts since 1904. Just east, the **Trail of Time** interpretative display traces the history of the canyon's formation. End with the intriguing exhibits and gorgeous views of the **Yavapai Geology Museum**.

THE DRIVE
Having returned to Williams, take the I-40 113 miles west to Kingman, then join US 93 north. Head north for 75 miles, crossing into Nevada, where exit 2 leads on to Hwy 172 and Hoover Dam.

14 MIKE O'CALLAGHAN–PAT TILLMAN MEMORIAL BRIDGE

This graceful span, dedicated in 2010, was named for Mike O'Callaghan, governor of Nevada from 1971 to 1979, and for NFL star Pat Tillman, who was a safety for the Arizona Cardinals when he enlisted as a US Army Ranger after September 11. Tillman was killed by friendly fire during a battle in Afghanistan in 2004.

Open to pedestrians along a walkway separated from traffic on Hwy 93, the bridge sits 900ft above the Colorado River. It's the second-highest bridge in the US, and provides a bird's-eye eye view of Hoover Dam and Lake Mead behind it.

Wild West show, Williams

THE DRIVE
Just over the bridge, turn right onto the access road and drive a short distance down to Hoover Dam.

15 HOOVER DAM

A statue of bronze winged figures stands atop **Hoover Dam** (usbr.gov/lc/hooverdam), memorializing those who built the massive 726ft concrete structure, one of the world's tallest dams. This New Deal public works project, completed ahead of schedule and under budget in 1936, was the first major dam of the Colorado River. Thousands of men and their families, eager for work in the height of the Depression, came to Black Canyon and worked in excruciating conditions – dangling hundreds of feet above the canyon in desert heat of up to 120°F (49°C). Over 100 lost their lives.

Today, guided tours begin at the visitor center, where a video screening features original footage of the construction. After the movie take an elevator ride 50 stories below to view the dam's massive power generators, each of which alone could power a city of 100,000 people.

THE DRIVE
Return to US 93, following it west then north as it joins I-515. Take exit 61 for I-215 north. After 11 miles I-215 becomes Clark County 215. Follow it just over 13 miles to Charleston Blvd/Hwy 159 at exit 26 and follow it west.

16 RED ROCK CANYON NATIONAL CONSERVATION AREA

The evidence of awesome natural forces in this **national conservation area** (redrockcanyonlv.org) can't be exaggerated. Created about 65 million years ago, the canyon is more like a valley, with a steep, rugged red rock escarpment rising 3000ft on its western edge; dramatic evidence of tectonic-plate collisions.

The 13-mile, one-way scenic drive passes some of the canyon's most striking features, where you can access hiking trails and rock-climbing routes. The 2.5-mile round-trip hike to **Calico Tanks** climbs through the sandstone and ends atop rocks offering a grand view of the desert and mountains, with Vegas thrown in for sizzle.

National park passes are accepted for admission.

02

Route 66: The Southwest

BEST 2 DAYS

The natural wonders at Petrified Forest National Park and Meteor Crater.

Wigwam Motel (p33), Holbrook

DURATION	DISTANCE	GREAT FOR
5–7 days	900 miles / 1448km	History and culture, family, food and drink

BEST TIME TO GO	
	April through September for the best conditions on the Colorado Plateau.

Concrete wigwams, neon cowboys, lumbering dinosaurs: you'll get your kitsch on Route 66 following this storied stretch of the 'Mother Road' through Texas, New Mexico and Arizona. And it draws a diverse sampling of humanity – from a busload of bleary-eyed tourists to a horde of tough-looking biker dudes.

Link your trip

10 Southwest Indian Nations Sojourn

Swap kitsch for cliff dwellings at Walnut Canyon, west of Meteor Crater.

24 Heart of Texas

Swing south to the colorful Palo Duro Canyon from Amarillo.

01 MCLEAN

Beyond the towns, the great wide open of the Texas Panhandle is punctuated only by the occasional windmill, and the distinct odor of cattle feedlots. The Mother Road cuts across this emptiness for 178 miles, and the entire route has been superseded by I-40 – but there are a few noteworthy attractions.

The sprawling grasslands of Texas and other western cattle states were once open range, where steers and cowboys could wander where they darn

well pleased. That all changed in the 1880s when the devil's rope – more commonly known as barbed wire – began dividing up the land into private parcels. The **Devil's Rope Museum** in the battered town of McLean off exit 141 has vast barbed-wire displays and a quirky little room devoted to Route 66. The detailed map of the road in Texas is fascinating. Also worth a look are the moving portraits of Dust Bowl damage and refugees from human-made environmental disaster.

THE DRIVE
I-40 west of McLean glides over low-rolling hills. The landscape flattens at Groom, home of the tilting water tower and a 19-story cross at exit 112. Take exit 96 for Conway to snap a photo of the forlorn VW Beetle Ranch, aka the Bug Ranch, on the south side of the interstate before continuing on the I-40 to Amarillo; 75 miles all told.

02 AMARILLO

This cowboy town holds a plethora of Route 66 sites: the **Big Texan Steak Ranch**, the historic livestock auction and the **San Jacinto District**, which still has original Route 66 businesses.

As for the Big Texan, this hokey but classic attraction opened on Route 66 in 1960. It moved to its current location when I-40 opened in 1971 and has never looked back. The attention-grabbing gimmick here is the 'free 72oz steak' offer – you have to eat this enormous portion of cow plus a multitude of sides in under one hour, or you pay for the entire meal ($72). Contestants sit at a raised table to 'entertain' the other diners. Less than 10% pass the challenge. Insane eating aside, the ranch is a fine place to eat, and the steaks are excellent.

THE DRIVE
Continue west on I-40. Take exit 67, about 5 miles west of the edge of downtown Amarillo, then take S Western St under the interstate to Cadillac Ranch.

History of Route 66

Launched in 1926, Route 66 stretched from Chicago to Los Angeles, linking a ribbon of small towns and country byways as it rolled across eight states. The road gained notoriety during the Great Depression, when migrant farmers followed it west from the Dust Bowl across the Great Plains. The nickname the 'Mother Road' first appeared in John Steinbeck's 1939 novel about the era, *The Grapes of Wrath*. Meanwhile, unemployed young men were hired to pave the final stretches of muddy road. They completed the job, as it turns out, just in time for WWII and the flood of soldiers and factory workers that took the road to fortune and despair. Things got a little more fun in the 1950s, when newfound prosperity prompted Americans to hit the open road. Sadly, just as things got going, the Feds rolled out the interstate system, which eventually caused the Mother Road's demise. The very last town to be bypassed by an interstate was Arizona's Williams, in 1984.

03 CADILLAC RANCH

The shells of 10 Cadillacs were planted in the deserted ground west of Amarillo in 1974 – an installation that's come to be known as Cadillac Ranch. Reportedly, it was created as a tribute to the golden age of car travel. The cars date from 1948 to 1959 – a period in which tail fins just kept getting bigger and bigger. Come prepared: the accepted practice is to leave your own mark by spray painting on the cars. It can also get quite windy.

THE DRIVE
Follow I-40 west 68 miles to the New Mexico border. Tucumcari – and its abundance of motel rooms – is 42 miles further.

04 TUCUMCARI

A ranching and farming town sandwiched between the mesas and the plains, Tucumcari is home to one of the best-preserved sections of Route 66. It's a great place to drive through at night, when dozens of neon signs – relics of the town's Mother Road heyday – cast a crazy rainbow-colored glow. Tucumcari's Route 66 motoring legacy and other regional highlights are recorded on 35 murals in downtown and the surrounding area. Pick up a map for the murals at the **visitor center** (tucumcarinm.com).

The engaging **Mesalands Dinosaur Museum** (mesalands.edu) showcases real dinosaur bones and has hands-on exhibits for kids. Casts of dinosaur bones are done in bronze (not the usual plaster of paris), which shows fine detail.

Photo opportunity

Capture the quirky concrete tipis at the Wigwam Motel in Holbrook, AZ.

THE DRIVE
West on I-40, dry and windy plains spread into the distance, the horizon interrupted by flat-topped mesas. To stretch your legs, take exit 277 from I-40 to Route 66, downtown Santa Rosa and the Route 66 Auto Museum, which has upward of 35 cars from the 1920s through the 1960s, all in beautiful condition. It's 174 miles in total to Albuquerque.

05 ALBUQUERQUE

After 1936, Route 66 was re-aligned from its original path, which linked north through Santa Fe, to a direct line west into Albuquerque. Today, the city's **Central Ave** follows the post-1937 route. It passes through **Nob Hill**, the university, downtown and **Old Town**. Stop for a walking tour of Old Town if you have time.

West of I-25, look for the spectacular tile-and-wood artistry of the **KiMo Theatre** (cabq.gov/kimo), across from the old **Indian Trading Post**. This 1927 icon of pueblo-deco architecture blends American Indian and art-deco design. It also screens classic movies like *Singin' in the Rain* and *2001: A Space Odyssey*. For prehistoric designs, take exit 154, just west of downtown, and drive north 3 miles to **Petroglyph National**

Old Town, Albuquerque

Meteor Crater

GIMAS/SHUTTERSTOCK ©

Monument (p113), which has more than 20,000 ancient rock etchings.

THE DRIVE
Route 66 dips from I-40 into Gallup, becoming the main drag, lined with beautifully renovated buildings, including the 1928 Spanish Colonial El Morro Theatre. From Gallup, it's 21 miles to Arizona. Once in Arizona, take exit 311 for Petrified Forest National Park. It's 211 miles all up.

06 PETRIFIED FOREST NATIONAL PARK

The 'trees' of the **Petrified Forest** (nps.gov/pefo) are fragmented, fossilized 225-million-year-old logs scattered over a vast area of arid grassland. Many are huge – up to 6ft in diameter – and at least one spans a ravine to form a natural bridge. The trees arrived via major floods, only to be buried beneath silica-rich volcanic ash before they could decompose. Groundwater dissolved the silica, carried it through the logs and crystallized into solid, sparkly quartz mashed up with iron, carbon, manganese and other minerals. Uplift and erosion eventually exposed the logs.

The park, which straddles I-40, has an entrance at exit 311 in the north and another off Hwy 180 in the south. A 28-mile paved scenic road, Park Rd, links the two. To avoid backtracking, westbound travelers should start in the north, eastbound travelers in the south.

THE DRIVE
Back on I-40, drive west 26 miles to Holbrook, a former Wild West town now home to rock shops and the photo-ready Wigwam Motel, which was added to the National Register of Historic Places in 2002. If someone is on the grounds before the 4pm check-in, they'll probably let you peek inside one of the wigwams. Continue west on I-40; it's another 33 miles.

WHY I LOVE THIS TRIP

Hugh McNaughtan, writer

The stretch of the world's most famous motorway from Seligman to Kingman takes you to the heart of Route 66. From the quirky Burma Shave signs outside Seligman to the nostalgia-steeped Hackberry General Store and the heritage-listed motels of Kingman, it's the Mother Road as it once was, and hopefully will be for years to come.

07 WINSLOW

Thanks to the Eagles' 1972 hit 'Take It Easy' (their first single release), lonesome little Winslow is now a popular stop on the tourist track. Pose with the life-sized bronze statue of a hitchhiker backed by a charmingly hokey trompe l'oeil mural of that famous girl in a flatbed Ford at the corner of 2nd St and Kinsley Ave.

THE DRIVE
Twenty miles west of Winslow, take exit 233 off I-40 and drive 6 miles south through cattle country, following the signs for Meteor Crater.

08 METEOR CRATER

Some 50,000 years ago an asteroid traveling at 26,000mph crashed here, blasting a hole more than 550ft deep and nearly 1 mile across. Today

GALLUP MURAL WALK

Take a walk around Gallup, an old Route 66 town on I-40 between Albuquerque and the Arizona border, and experience its 136-year-old story through art. Starting from City Hall on the corner of W Aztec Ave and S 2nd St, you'll see plenty of buildings sporting giant murals, both abstract and realist, that memorialize special events in Gallup's roller-coaster history. The city's mural painting tradition started in the 1930s as part of President Franklin D Roosevelt's Great Depression Work Projects Administration (WPA) program. It continues to this day, with 21st-century artists reimagining the story of Gallup through contemporary eyes.

the privately owned **crater** (meteorcrater.com) is a major tourist attraction with exhibits about meteorites, crater geology and the Apollo astronauts who used its lunar-like surface to train for their moon missions. You're not allowed to go down into the crater, but there are a few lookout points as well as guided one-hour rim-walking tours (free with admission). Look for the glinting piece of a plane that crashed inside the crater.

THE DRIVE
Follow I-40 to exit 204 and pick up Route 66 into Flagstaff. This is also the exit for Walnut Canyon National Monument. From the east, Route 66 passes a lengthy swath of cheap indie motels as well as the Museum Club (3404 E Rte 66), a log-cabin-style roadhouse that's been refreshing road-trippers since 1936.

09 FLAGSTAFF

This cultured college town still has an Old West heart. At the **visitor center** (flagstaffarizona.org), inside the historic train station, pick up the free Route 66 walking-tour guide. One building of note on the tour is the **Downtowner Motel**, formerly a brothel and the Grand Canyon International Hostel. Just north of Route 66 are two century-old hotels: the **Hotel Monte Vista** and the **Weatherford Hotel**. Both have plenty of character, not to mention convivial watering holes and lively ghosts. See them as part of a Flagstaff walking tour.

If you're interested in architecture, stop by **Riordan Mansion State Historic Park** (azstateparks.com/riordan-mansion), practically part of the Northern Arizona University campus. Having made a fortune from their Arizona Lumber Company, brothers Michael and Timothy Riordan built this striking log-slab mansion in 1904. Its Craftsman-style design is the work of architect Charles Whittlesey, who also designed El Tovar on the Grand Canyon's South Rim.

THE DRIVE
Continue west on I-40 and Route 66 to Williams, home of the Grand Canyon Railway and the last community along Route 66 to be bypassed by I-40. Route 66 runs one way through town, from west to east – you'll need to take parallel Railroad Ave, rejoin I-40, then leave it again at exit 139. All up, a 76-mile drive to Seligman.

STEVE LAGRECA/SHUTTERSTOCK ©

Delgadillo's Snow Cap Drive-In

10 SELIGMAN

This town takes its Route 66 heritage seriously – or with a squirt of fake mustard, thanks to the Delgadillo brothers, who for decades were the Mother Road's biggest boosters. Juan sadly passed away in 2004, but evergreen Angel and his wife still run **Angel & Vilma's Original Route 66 Gift Shop** (route66giftshop.com), where

you can poke around for souvenirs and admire license plates sent in by fans from all over the world. The much-lamented Juan used to rule prankishly supreme over **Delgadillo's Snow Cap Drive-In**, a Route 66 institution serving burgers, ice cream and pranks that's now run by his children Cecilia and John.

THE DRIVE
The Mother Road rolls northwest through dry, scrub-covered country, passing Burma Shave signs and lonely trains. After a drive of 25 miles, look for the kitsch dinosaur at mile marker 115.

11 GRAND CANYON CAVERNS & INN

An elevator drops 210ft underground to artificially lit limestone caverns and the skeletal remains of a prehistoric ground sloth at **Grand Canyon Caverns** (gccaverns.com). While there's no connection with the Grand Canyon beyond the name, this can be a cool and diverting escape from the summer heat, and is always popular with kids. And if you really want to make a night of it, $850 buys repose in the Cavern Suite. This underground 'room' has two double beds, a sitting area and multicolored lamps. If you ever wanted to cast yourself in one of those postapocalyptic survival movies, here's your chance!

Route 66 Reads

John Steinbeck's 1939 novel *The Grapes of Wrath* is the definitive tale of travel on the Mother Road during the Dust Bowl era. Woody Guthrie's *Bound for Glory*, first published in 1943, is the road-trip autobiography of the revered folk singer during the Depression. Several museums and bookshops along Route 66 stock American Indian, Old West and pioneer writing with ties to the old highway.

THE DRIVE Continue west through Peach Springs, Truxton and Valentine, for 35 miles.

12 HACKBERRY

Tiny, sleepy Hackberry is one of the few still-kicking settlements on this segment of the Mother Road's original alignment. Inside an eccentrically remodeled gas station dating to 1934 is the **Hackberry General Store** (hackberrygeneralstore.com). Originated by highway memorialist Robert Waldmire, the store is a great place to stop for a cold drink and Route 66 memorabilia. Check out the vintage petrol pumps, cars faded by decades of hot desert light, old toilet seats and rusted-out ironwork.

THE DRIVE From here, Route 66 arcs southwest, back toward I-40, then barrels into Kingman, which is 27 miles away.

13 KINGMAN

Founded in the heady 1880s railway days, Kingman is a quiet place today, but popular with Route 66 buffs for its well-preserved motels and other heyday architecture. A 1907 powerhouse holds the **visitor center** (gokingman.com) and the small but engaging **Route 66 Museum**, which really brings the glory days of the Mother Road to life. You could also check out the **former Methodist church** at 5th and Spring St, where Clark Gable and Carole Lombard eloped in 1939.

In Kingman, Route 66 is also called Andy Devine Ave, named after the hometown hero who acted in Hollywood classics like *Stagecoach*, in which he played the perpetually befuddled stagecoach driver.

THE DRIVE Route 66/Hwy 10 corkscrews 29 miles up through the rugged Black Mountains, passing falling rocks, cacti and tumbleweeds on its way over Sitgreaves Pass (3523ft) to the old mining town of Oatman.

14 OATMAN

Since the veins of ore ran dry in 1942, crusty Oatman has reinvented itself as a movie set and Wild West tourist trap, complete with staged gun fights (daily at 1:30pm, and sometimes 3:30pm) and gift stores with names like **Fast Fanny's Place** and the **Classy Ass**.

Speaking of asses, there are plenty of them (the four-legged kind, that is) roaming the streets. Placid and endearing, they're the descendants of pack animals left by the early miners. These burros may beg for food, but do not feed them your lunch leftovers; instead, buy healthier hay cubes from nearby stores. Squeezed among the shops is the 1902 **Oatman Hotel**, a surprisingly modest shack (no longer renting rooms) where Clark Gable and Carole Lombard spent their wedding night in 1939. On July 4 the town holds a sidewalk egg-frying contest; it gets quite warm here in summer.

From here, Route 66 twists down to Golden Shores and the I-40.

SCENIC DRIVE: PETRIFIED FOREST NATIONAL PARK

The leisurely Park Rd, which travels through the park (p33), has about 15 pullouts with interpretive signs and some short trails. North of I-40, enjoy sweeping views of the Painted Desert, where nature presents a hauntingly beautiful palette, especially at sunset. After Park Rd turns south, keep a lookout for the roadside display about Route 66, just north of the interstate.

The 3-mile loop drive out to Blue Mesa has 360-degree views of spectacular badlands, log falls and logs balancing atop hills with the leathery texture of elephant skin.

Two trails near the southern entrance provide the best access for close-ups of the petrified logs: the 0.6-mile Long Logs Trail, which has the largest concentration, and the 0.4-mile Giant Logs Trail, which is entered through the **Rainbow Forest Museum** (nps.gov) and sports the park's largest log.

Petrified Forest National Park

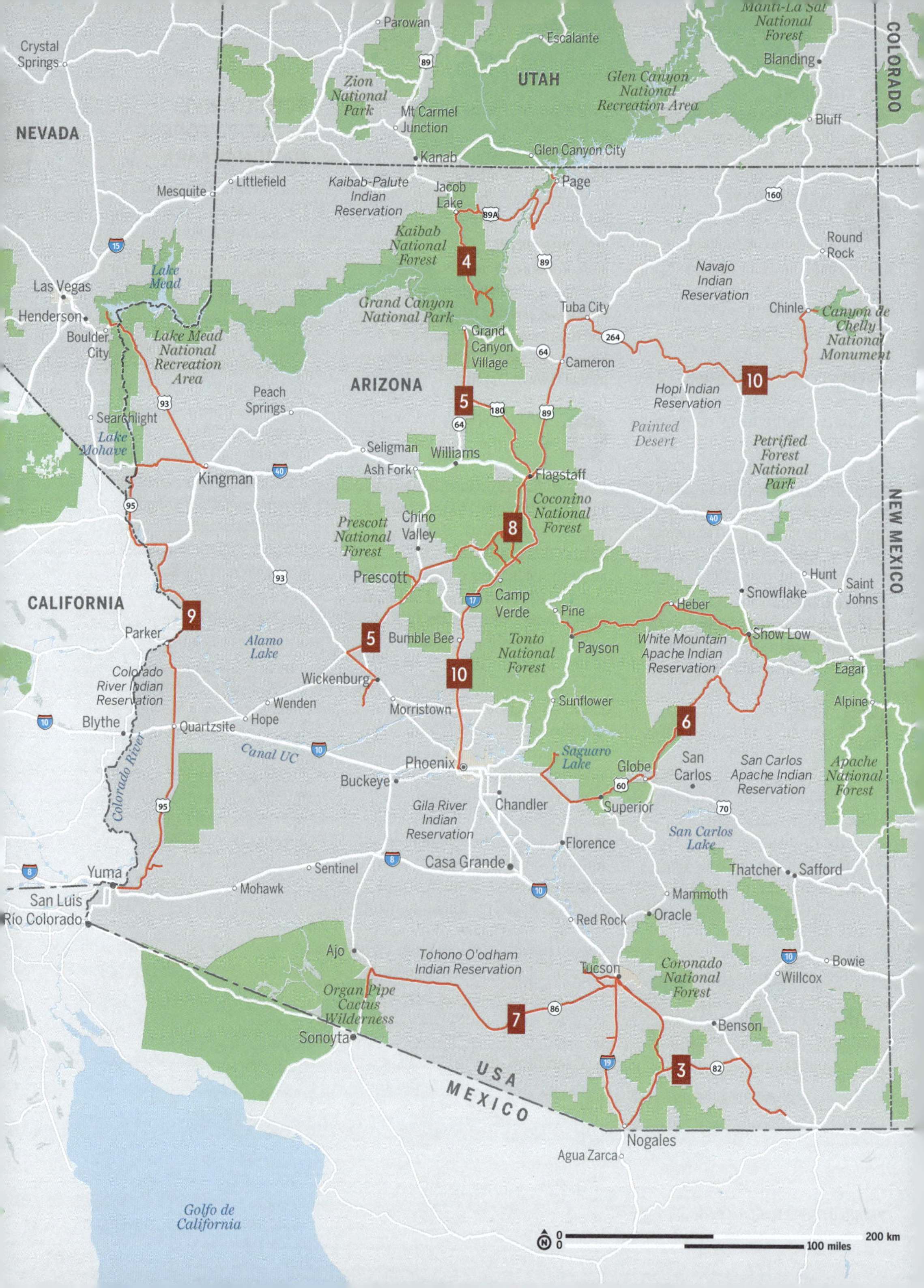

NEVADA
UTAH
ARIZONA
CALIFORNIA
COLORADO
NEW MEXICO
USA
MEXICO
Crystal Springs
Parowan
Escalante
Manti-La Sal National Forest
Blanding
Zion National Park
Mt Carmel Junction
Glen Canyon National Recreation Area
Bluff
Kanab
Glen Canyon City
Page
Mesquite
Littlefield
Kaibab-Palute Indian Reservation
Jacob Lake
Kaibab National Forest
Lake Mead
Las Vegas
Henderson
Boulder City
Grand Canyon National Park
Grand Canyon Village
Lake Mead National Recreation Area
Tuba City
Navajo Indian Reservation
Round Rock
Chinle
Canyon de Chelly National Monument
Cameron
Hopi Indian Reservation
Peach Springs
Searchlight
Lake Mohave
Seligman
Williams
Ash Fork
Kingman
Flagstaff
Painted Desert
Petrified Forest National Park
Coconino National Forest
Prescott National Forest
Chino Valley
Prescott
Camp Verde
Pine
Heber
Hunt
Snowflake
Saint Johns
Show Low
Parker
Alamo Lake
Bumble Bee
Tonto National Forest
Payson
White Mountain Apache Indian Reservation
Eagar
Colorado River Indian Reservation
Wickenburg
Morristown
Wenden
Hope
Sunflower
Alpine
Blythe
Quartzsite
Canal UC
Phoenix
Saguaro Lake
Globe
San Carlos
San Carlos Apache Indian Reservation
Apache National Forest
Colorado River
Buckeye
Gila River Indian Reservation
Chandler
Superior
San Carlos Lake
Florence
Casa Grande
Sentinel
Thatcher
Safford
Yuma
Mohawk
San Luis
Río Colorado
Mammoth
Red Rock
Oracle
Ajo
Tohono O'odham Indian Reservation
Tucson
Coronado National Forest
Bowie
Willcox
Organ Pipe Cactus Wilderness
Sonoyta
Benson
Nogales
Agua Zarca
Golfo de California
0
200 km
0
100 miles

VICHIE81/SHUTTERSTOCK ©

Antelope Canyon (p49)

Arizona

Explore
Arizona

The wide, open spaces of Arizona, the sixth-largest state in the Union, are ideal for road-trip adventures. The state's excellent road network traverses drama-filled landscapes, and, adding much personality to driving here, there's the ever-present shadow of the Wild West past. This is outlaw country. It's where Wyatt Earp took no prisoners at the OK Corral and where wily Geronimo gave the US Army fits in the Chiricahua Mountains. Elsewhere, the sinful old mining town of Jerome clings to a crumbling hillside. Through it all runs the Colorado River, which has been gouging out the Grand Canyon for six million years.

Phoenix

Everything that's good about urban Arizona is found in Phoenix, from outstanding museums to fabulous craft breweries. It also has one of the most varied tables when it comes to cuisine from Southwest USA and further afield, and is a real cultural powerhouse. As a base for exploring the region, Phoenix has the full range of accommodations that include motels and high-end resorts, historic B&Bs and boutique designer hotels. And with more than 300 days of sunshine a year, the 'Valley of the Sun' is an ideal escape for much of the year.

Flagstaff

Deep in the heart of Arizona, the largest ponderosa forest in the US surrounds Flagstaff, a city with a historic core, arboretum, museums and restless spirit. Everyone here seems to want to head out hiking or cycling. Then they all return to town for great coffee, craft beer and a surprisingly cosmopolitan culinary scene. Accommodations here run the full gamut of possibilities, from B&Bs and historic hotels to ubiquitous motels. Oh, and the Grand Canyon's not far away, too.

Tucson

One of Southwestern USA's most dynamic towns, Tucson (too-sawn), in Arizona's south, is a fun-loving college town – the University of Arizona has 45,000 students here – with a vibrant cultural calendar. Set in a flat valley hemmed in by snaggle-toothed mountains and swaths of saguaro, Arizona's second-largest city has historic, multicultural neighborhoods

WHEN TO GO

Many routes pass through desert country with some of the hottest summer temperatures in the country. It's also when half the country heads for the Grand Canyon. Fall and spring are ideal for milder temperatures and fewer crowds. Winter is good for spas and dude ranches, and for cross-country skiing in Kaibab National Forest.

with great indie and vintage shopping, a fab dining scene, fiesta-filled nightlife and all manner of wildly beautiful attractions right on the city's doorstep.

Sedona

Hunkered down amid striking red sandstone formations, Sedona's truly spectacular backdrop makes it a delightful base for exploring the Arizonan heartland. It's a popular outdoors center, with all manner of thrills to be had hiking, mountain biking and climbing amid the surrounding desert spires. It's also known for its high-end belles when it comes to accommodations. And, for those of a spiritual bent, Sedona offers something a little extra: many people believe that this area has a number of vortexes that radiate the earth's energy, and the city hosts everything from purveyors of alternative medicines to past-life workshops.

Kingman

Kingman is a road-trip town par excellence. Among Route 66 aficionados, Kingman is known as the main hub of the longest uninterrupted stretch of the historic highway, running from Topock to Seligman. It's a world of retro diners and smokin' barbecue joints, and among its early-20th-century buildings is the former Methodist church where Clark Gable and Carole Lombard eloped in 1939. Accommodations range from mountain retreats to Route 66 motel classics.

TRANSPORT

Phoenix' Sky Harbor International Airport is a major gateway to the entire Southwest; Tucson also receives its share of flights. Amtrak train connections are available from Los Angeles to Tucson and Flagstaff, Flagstaff to Albuquerque, and Tucson to El Paso. Greyhound includes these centers and Phoenix in its interstate bus network.

WHAT'S ON

M3F

In early March, local and international acts head for Phoenix for this fine music festival (m3ffest.com).

Tucson Folk Festival

This April folk music festival (tucsonfolkfest.org) brings together more than 120 acts.

Historic Route 66 Fun Run

This vintage car rally celebrates the Mother Road in Kingman (azrt66.com) on the first weekend in May.

Navajo Nation Fair

Established in 1946, this fun fair is held in early September in Window Rock.

WHERE TO STAY

There's fantastic diversity of sleeping options in Arizona, from lushly watered resorts glittering like oases in the desert, to free dispersed camping in huge swaths of untrammeled ponderosa forest. Expect accommodations in and around the Grand Canyon to book out long in advance in peak (summer) months – the same period that sees prices and demand plummet further south as temperatures soar. Tucson in particular offers a quintessentially Arizonan mix, with historic hotel, a ranch and B&Bs to go with the ubiquitous motels. Kingman is good for Route 66 kitsch, while Scottsdale, a satellite of Phoenix, is very high end.

Resources

Arizona Office of Tourism (visitarizona.com) Comprehensive planning information, covering sights, activities, accommodations, current trends and more. It also has a useful app.

Arizona Department of Transportation (az511.gov) Statewide travel and traffic information, including precise journey times.

National Park Service (nps.gov) Essential resource for Arizona's national parks.

03

ARIZONA

A Taste of the Old West

BEST FOR WESTERN FANTASIES

The saguaro-swaddled outdoor movie set that is Old Tucson Studios.

Old Tucson Studios

DURATION	DISTANCE	GREAT FOR
3 days	129 miles / 207km	History and culture, food and drink, family

BEST TIME TO GO	While the higher stops are cooler, and accessible year-round, Tucson really roasts in the summer months.

There are three certainties in southern Arizona: big skies, boisterous saloons and endless forests of the iconic saguaro cactus, marching away to the horizon and Mexico. And one quick stroll around Boothill Graveyard outside Tombstone tells you everything you need to know about living – and dying – in Western mining towns in the late 1800s. Though legend may exceed reality, 'Arizona Territory' was a true frontier.

Link your trip

7 Southern Desert Wanderings
From Fairbank travel west on Hwy 82 to Sonoita for wine tasting and high-country wandering.

18 Into the Gila
Drive north from Tombstone to I-10 east for some green chile in southwestern New Mexico.

01 TUCSON

Tucson's Old Western roots go deep: the **Presidio Historic District** is a throwback to the Spanish military presence in the 18th century. For an engaging primer on Arizona's Old West history, visit the **Arizona History Museum** (arizonahistoricalsociety.org) beside the University of Arizona's 1885 campus. The Arizona Mining Hall exhibit is a walk-through replica of an old copper mine. The Geronimo exhibit displays the Apache warrior's rifle and an 1880s photograph of his

negotiations with United States Army General George Crook, taken by Tombstone photographer CS Fly.

Lined with charismatic bars and indie businesses, **4th Avenue** (fourthavenue.org) is 1 mile west of here. For more art and history, try a Tucson walking tour.

THE DRIVE
Drive north two blocks to E Speedway Blvd and turn left. Continue 9 miles as Speedway becomes W Gates Pass Rd and swoops into Tucson Mountain Park. Watch for cops and cyclists. As you climb toward the pass, look for a one-way sign. Turn right here. If you miss it, turn around at the next parking lot.

02 GATES PASS SCENIC OVERLOOK

Named for Thomas Gates, who was looking for a short cut through the Tucson Mountains to his carbonate mine, this **overlook** offers a mountain-flanked view of western Arizona. On a clear day you can see 36 miles across the desert to 6875ft **Kitt Peak**, home of the Kitt Peak National Observatory (p75). There are trails, interpretive signs and stunning forests of saguaro. It's a delightful place to watch the sunset.

THE DRIVE
Continue west until Gates Pass Rd ends. Turn left onto S Kinney Rd.

03 OLD TUCSON STUDIOS

Nicknamed 'Hollywood in the Desert,' this **old movie set** (oldtucson.com) of 1860s Tucson was built in 1939 for the filming of *Arizona* (1940). Hundreds of flicks followed, bringing in a galaxy of stars. Now a Wild West theme park, it caters mainly to families hankering for shoot-outs, stagecoach rides, saloons, sheriffs and stunts (but no roller coasters or similar rides). The **museum** displays movie and TV memorabilia, including clothing worn by Clint Eastwood in *Joe Kidd* (1972) and Michael Landon in *Little House on the Prairie* (1974). The surrounding saguaro-studded mountainsides are a stunning spectacle in their own right.

THE DRIVE Follow S Kinney Rd south to Hwy 86 E. Drive east to I-19, following it north to I-10 east. Continue 21 miles to exit 281 for Hwy 83 south. Pick up Hwy 82 east and cross the San Pedro River. The Fairbank turnoff is just ahead on the left. The total drive is around 87 miles.

04 FAIRBANK HISTORIC SITE

It's the silence that grabs you on a stroll through the ghost town of **Fairbank**, on Hwy 82, just east of San Pedro River, where a handful of old buildings cluster near the road and the river. Established in 1881 to serve the New Mexico & Arizona Railroad, Fairbank was a transportation hub for nearby mining towns, quickly reaching a population of 15,000. The last residents left in the 1970s. Today, there's a **visitor center** with displays in the restored 1920s schoolhouse; if it's closed, pick up the walking-tour brochure from the kiosk. The tour loops past abandoned houses, a stable and an 1882 mercantile building.

THE DRIVE Drive east on Hwy 82 to Hwy 80. Turn right and drive south about 3 miles.

05 BOOTHILL GRAVEYARD

Boot Hill was a name commonly given to graveyards for gunslingers and those who died violent deaths; ie they died with their boots on. For a list of the graves – and causes of death – of those buried in this **cemetery**, buy the brochure at the entrance. The graves of Billy Clanton and Tom and Frank McLaury, all killed at the shoot-out at the OK Corral, are on Row 2. The marker for Lester Moore, a Wells Fargo agent, may be the most famous: 'Here lies Lester Moore, Four slugs from a .44, No Les, no More.'

THE DRIVE Turn left onto Hwy 80, which becomes E Fremont St in Tombstone, about 0.25 miles ahead.

06 TOMBSTONE

On October 26, 1881, Wyatt Earp, brothers Virgil and Morgan and their friend Doc Holliday gunned down outlaws Billy Clanton and Tom and Frank McLaury at the **OK Corral** (ok-corral.com). Today, the corral is the heart of Tombstone. It has models of the gunfighters and other exhibits, including CS Fly's early photography studio and a re-created 'crib,' the term for rooms used by hard-working, low-paid prostitutes. The town earned its name from first-on-the-scene prospector Ed Schieffelin, who was told all he would find in the dangerous region was his own tombstone.

The **Bird Cage Theater** (tombstonebirdcage.com) was a saloon, a dance hall, a gambling parlor and a home for 'negotiable affections' in the 1880s. Today it's filled with bullet holes and dusty artifacts like Doc Holliday's old Faro gaming table. Doc Holliday's girlfriend's bar **Big Nose Kate's** (bignosekates.info) is also full of Wild West character.

For a less sensational look at the town's past, visit the informative **Tombstone Courthouse State Historic Park** (azstateparks.com/tombstone).

THE DRIVE Follow Hwy 80 southeast for 25 miles through desert scrub and the Mule Mountains.

07 QUEEN MINE TOUR

Could you have worked in the dark confines of an Arizona copper mine? Test your mental toughness on a tour of the **Queen Mine** (queenminetour.com) near downtown Bisbee. Visitors wear miners' garb, carry lanterns and ride a mine train 1500ft into one of the area's deepest copper mines. In the early 20th century this was the most productive mine in Arizona, famous for particularly deep-shaded turquoise rocks known as Bisbee Blue. The tour, which lasts about an hour, is fun for kids.

The **Bisbee Visitor Center** (discoverbisbee.com) is also here.

THE DRIVE Drive half a mile south on Hwy 80.

08 LAVENDER PIT

The 'Scenic View' sign for this immense, stepped gash in the earth might not seem accurate to all sightseers when confronted with this violent but undeniably impressive earthly scar. An open-pit mine, it produced about 600,000 tons of copper between 1950 and 1974.

THE DRIVE Follow Hwy 80 north to Tombstone Canyon Rd, which leads into downtown Bisbee.

09 BISBEE

Bisbee built its fortune on ore found in the surrounding **Mule Mountains**. Between 1880 and 1975, underground and open-pit mines coughed up copper in sumptuous

Tombstone

ENTER HERE
O.K. CORRAL®
GUNFIGHT SITE
"WALK WHERE THEY FELL"
TOMBSTONE
HISTORAMA
OLD TIME PHOTOS
OPEN
OUTLAW
T's BOOKS & MORE

Bisbee

NICK FOX/SHUTTERSTOCK ©

proportions, generating more than $6 billion worth of metals. By 1910 the population had climbed to 25,000, and nearly 50 saloons and bordellos crammed notorious **Brewery Gulch**.

As the local copper mines began to fizzle in the 1970s, hippies and artists arrived. The interweaving of the new creative types and the old miners has produced a welcoming bunch of eccentrics clinging to the mountainside.

The **Bisbee Mining & Historical Museum** (bisbeemuseum.org) does an excellent job documenting the town's past and the changing face of mining. From there, wander the galleries and indie shops on **Main St**, with a side trip into Brewery Gulch, where the 100-year-old St Elmo's always attracts a boisterous crowd. Or try the nearby **Old Bisbee Brewing Company** (oldbisbeebrewingcompany.com), an easy-going watering hole that crafts a lip-smacking variety of brews, including root beer.

DETOUR

Chiricahua National Monument

Start: 09 Bisbee

Pronounced 'cheery-cow-wha,' this remote **national monument** (nps.gov/chir) is a wonderland of whimsical rock formations and ponderosa-fringed gulches. Rearing up from the surrounding seas of arid grassland, it's a 'sky island' of volcanic rocks shaped by the elements into fluted pinnacles, mighty bridges, balancing boulders and soaring spires. The remoteness made Chiricahua a favorite hiding place of Apache warrior Cochise and his men. Today, the same quality attracts birds and wildlife.

From Bisbee, take Hwy 80 then Double Adobe Rd west, turn north on Central Hwy to join Hwy 191, then take 181 to Chiricahua: all up 71 miles. The paved **Bonita Canyon Scenic Drive** climbs 8 miles to Massai Point at 6870ft, where you'll see thousands of spires positioned on the slopes like some petrified army. To explore in greater depth, hit the trails. A free hikers' shuttle bus leaves daily from the **visitor center** (nps.gov) at 8:30am or 9am, heading up to Massai Point. Hikers usually return by foot.

If you're short on time, hike the **Echo Canyon Trail** at least half a mile to the **Grottoes**, an amazing 'cathedral' of giant boulders.

Photo opportunity

A mountain-framed view of the Sonoran Desert at Gates Pass Scenic Overlook.

04

ARIZONA

Grand Canyon North Rim & Lake Powell

BEST FOR OUTDOORS

Hiking the wooded Widforss Trail along the edge of the Canyon's North Rim.

DURATION	DISTANCE	GREAT FOR
3 days	159 miles / 256km	Outdoors

BEST TIME TO GO	
	May to October when the North Rim is open.

Antelope Canyon

Want the Grand Canyon without the crowds? The Arizona Strip is the Land that Time Forgot. Look around as you glide over Navajo Bridge. Below, the Colorado River cracks apart the earth. To the north, the Vermilion Cliffs rear up like the crest of some petrified crimson tide. To the south, windblown desert scrub sweeps unendingly toward the horizon. And overhead? California condors swoop from their nests.

Link your trip

25 Zion & Bryce Canyon National Parks

Leave the Kaibab Plateau on Hwy 89A and continue to Hwy 9, which makes a stunning red rock descent into Zion.

26 Scenic Byway 12

Swing north from Monument Valley for Ancestral Puebloan ruins.

01 GLEN CANYON DAM & LAKE POWELL

The 720ft-tall **Glen Canyon Dam** (glencanyonnha.org) is a concrete ode to America's ingenuity and can-do spirit. Completed in 1963, it's the nation's highest concrete arch dam (Hoover Dam to the west is 16ft taller, but is technically a different kind of structure). Guided, 45-minute tours, departing from the **Carl Hayden Visitor Center** (nps.gov/glca), drop deep inside the dam via elevators. Displays and videos in the visitor center tell the story of the dam's construction and provide technical insights into its operation.

The adjacent sparkling swath of blue is **Lake Powell**, part of the **Glen Canyon National Recreation Area** (nps.gov/glca). The 186-mile-long lake was named for John Wesley Powell, the one-armed Union veteran who led the groundbreaking Colorado River expedition through the Grand Canyon in 1869. The lake straddles the Utah–Arizona border, its shoreline fringed with striking red rocks. Rent kayaks ($50 per day) at Wahweap Marina at the **Lake Powell Resort** (lakepowell.com).

THE DRIVE
Page is just three miles southeast. Take Hwy 89 south past Navajo Dr. For an expansive view of the dam, turn right onto Scenic View Rd, following it to the viewpoint parking area.

02 PAGE

Established to house the workers who built Glen Canyon Dam, Page today is a great base camp for exploring the area. It's also the place to join a tour of the stunning **Antelope Canyon**, a slot canyon on the Navajo Reservation accessible only on Navajo-led tours. In the more popular upper canyon, about a quarter-mile long, water and wind have carved the sandstone into an astonishingly sensuous temple of nature. Tours can feel like cattle crushes, especially at noon when the perfect light in the canyon makes tours most popular, but the beauty of the site makes it worthwhile. Try **Roger Ekis' Antelope Canyon Tours** (antelopecanyon.com).

THE DRIVE
Follow Hwy 89 south out of Page. Continue 2 miles south after the junction of Hwy 89 and Hwy 98.

03 HORSESHOE BEND

For a short hike with a dramatic payoff, it's hard to beat **Horseshoe Bend**. Here, a 0.75-mile, one-way path leads to a lofty view of the Colorado River, where it's cut a 1000ft-deep horseshoe bend through sandstone for aeons. Though it's short, the sandy, shadeless trail and moderate incline can be a slog in hot weather. And watch your step – there are no guardrails at the viewpoint and the canyon lip can be treacherous. If you're afraid of heights, or don't trust your toddler-wrangling skills, stop at the covered hilltop shelter – the view is still mighty impressive.

THE DRIVE
Follow Hwy 89 21 miles south to Bitter Springs, where the 89A branches northwest toward the scanty settlement of Marble Canyon, 15 miles farther.

04 MARBLE CANYON

Hwy 89A crosses the Navajo Bridge over the Colorado River at Marble Canyon. Actually, there are two bridges: a modern one for motorists that opened in 1995, and the historical one dating to 1929. Walking across the latter you'll enjoy fabulous views down Marble Canyon to the northeast lip of the Grand Canyon. The

Navajo Bridge Interpretive Center (nps.gov/glca) on the west bank has good background information about the bridges and the area. Keep an eye out for California condors.

THE DRIVE
Return to Hwy 89A and turn right. Turn right again, almost immediately, onto Lees Ferry Rd. Follow it 6 miles.

05 LEES FERRY

Lees Ferry is the premier put-in for Grand Canyon rafting trips on the Colorado River. It's also a very popular spot for fly-fishing. The area, which is a fee site within Glen Canyon National Recreation Area, was named for John D Lee, the Mormon leader of the 1857 Mountain Meadows Massacre, in which 120 emigrants from Arkansas were murdered by Mormon and Paiute forces. To escape prosecution, Lee moved his wives and children to this remote outpost where they lived at the **Lonely Dell Ranch** and operated the area's only ferry service. Lee was tracked down and executed in 1877, but the ferry operated until the Navajo Bridge opened in 1929. You can still walk around the ranch, and even sample the fruits of its orchards.

THE DRIVE
Head back along the 36km on SH4 and SH49. Take a right onto Hwy 89A and continue about 3 miles. This region, along the Colorado River north of the national park, is called Marble Canyon.

06 LEES FERRY LODGE

This scrappy roadside bar, not actually at Lees Ferry, is one of those joints where you're never quite sure who's going to roar off the highway and push through the door – rebel motorcyclist, park ranger, retired academic with a passion for lonely places – but they'll surely have a good story. There's a pool table and an impressive selection of beer.

THE DRIVE
Take 89A west, and turn right onto the graded House Rock Valley Rd (BLM Rd 1065) at the base of the Kaibab Plateau. Drive 3 miles further for a 25-mile total journey to get to the Condor Viewing Site.

07 VERMILION CLIFFS

To increase your chances of spotting a California condor, stop at the **Condor Viewing Site** (blm.gov/az), near their release point. The birds, whose ancestors patrolled the skies in prehistoric times, were almost driven to extinction by the 1980s. The remaining condors were placed in captive breeding programs – six were released here in 1996, and more are released each year. Today, a good proportion of the entire global population of wild California condors can be found here.

THE DRIVE
Return to Hwy 89A as it climbs 5000ft through the Kaibab National Forest to the lakeless outpost of Jacob Lake. All told, a quick 13-mile hop.

DETOUR
The Wave
Start: 07 Vermilion Cliffs

The Wave is a trail-free expanse of slick rock that ends at a smooth, orange-and-white striped rock, shaped into a perfect wave. This sinuous sandstone swirl, which is located in the **Paria Canyon-Vermilion**

Horseshoe Bend (p49)

Photo opportunity

The titanic U-curve of the Colorado River at Horseshoe Bend.

Cliffs Wilderness, is a favorite of photographers.

A hike to the Wave requires a North Coyote Buttes permit ($7 for human and dog alike), which can be tough to obtain in spring and fall. To order a permit online, visit blm.gov and search for 'Coyote Buttes.' They're available four months in advance. The website also provides details about walk-up permits, awarded by lottery at the Grand Staircase–Escalante National Monument Visitor Center in Kanab, UT (p178). If you win a spot, your permit is good for the following day. The Wave is around 5.5 miles from the trailhead at Wire Pass, reached by continuing north on House Rock Rd for 18 miles past the Condor Viewing Site, into Utah. Plan for a six-hour hike.

08 JACOB LAKE

In these lonesome parts, Jacob Lake is the closest thing to a metropolis – and all it offers is a gas station, a handful of campgrounds, an inn with a bakery and restaurant, and the USFS **Kaibab Plateau Visitor Center** (fs.usda.gov). The bakery at the Jacob Lake Inn Restaurant is known for its homemade cookies.

THE DRIVE
The 44 miles between Jacob Lake and the Grand Canyon Lodge via Hwy 67 south is one of the Southwest's finest drives. It rolls through hills of ponderosa forest that open onto lush meadows in Kaibab National Forest. It is, however, closed between November and May.

09 GRAND CANYON LODGE

For immediate inspiration, walk through the stunning sunroom at the Grand Canyon Lodge to the narrow, quarter-mile path that leads to **Bright Angel Point** (nps.gov). Here you'll enjoy huge, unobstructed views into the canyon and across to the South Rim. On clear days, look for the San Francisco Peaks, more than 80 miles south.

At 8200ft, the North Rim is about 10°F (6°C) cooler than the South, which is 1000ft lower – even on summer evenings you'll need a sweater. Park admission is $30 per vehicle and the lodge and all services close from mid-October through mid-May.

THE DRIVE
Follow Hwy 67 2.7 miles north from the Lodge, passing the North Rim Campground. Continue about 1 mile west on the Point Sublime Access Rd.

10 WIDFORSS TRAIL

Pick up a sack lunch (remember to order the night before) at the **Grand Canyon Lodge Dining Room** (grandcanyonforever.com), then spend the morning hiking through meadows and aspen on this 10-mile round-trip trail. Following the edge of a forested plateau, it's a pleasant, pine-shaded walk with great rim-side views. It ends at 7811ft-high **Widforss Point**, with awe-inspiring canyon views. It's a particularly pretty hike in September and October, when the trees turn golden.

THE DRIVE
Drive north a quarter mile on Hwy 67 to Cape Royal Rd. Turn right, after around 5 miles turn left onto Point Imperial Rd, then continue a further 3 miles.

11 POINT IMPERIAL

Point Imperial is the highest overlook on the North Rim, at 8803ft. Soak up the view of Nankoweap Creek, the Vermilion Cliffs, Marble Canyon and the Painted Desert.

THE DRIVE
Return to Cape Royal Rd and turn left, passing viewpoints at Vista Encantada, Roosevelt Point and Walhalla Overlook. It's about 12 miles to the Cape Royal Overlook.

12 CAPE ROYAL

At the end of the road follow the 0.6-mile paved trail that passes Angel's Window, a natural arch, before ending at Cape Royal Point and its stupendous views of the canyon.

DON'T MISS:

Horseshoe Bend

If you're a sucker for a gobsmacking view, stroll to this cliffside perch to peer down at the Colorado River – 1000ft below.

Bright Angel

05

ARIZONA

Fantastic Canyon Voyage

DURATION	DISTANCE	GREAT FOR
4–5 days	235 miles / 378km	History and culture, food and drink

BEST TIME TO GO	Visit in fall and spring, to beat the heat and summer crowds.

The Old West meets the New on this scenic sojourn to the Grand Canyon. Visit cowboy country and mining towns, wineries and red rocks, before the grand finale at the Big Ditch. It's pretty, it's wild and it carries a decent whack of Arizona's rough-and-tumble history. But this route isn't all about the past: a burgeoning wine scene and great contemporary dining add 21st-century allure.

Link your trip

08 Highway 89A: Red Rock Country

For close-up views of stunning red-rock scenery, explore Sedona along Hwy 89A.

10 Southwest Indian Nations Sojourn

From Grand Canyon National Park, follow Hwy 64 east to Wupatki National Monument to learn about early residents.

01 WICKENBURG

With its saddle shops and Old West storefronts, Wickenburg looks like it fell out of the sky – directly from the 1890s. At the ever-popular **Desert Caballeros Western Museum** (westernmuseum.org), the artwork celebrates the West and the lives of those that won it. The Hays *Spirit of the Cowboy* collection examines the raw materials behind the cowboy myth, showcasing rifles, ropes and saddles. The *Cowgirl Up!* exhibit and sale in March and April is a fun and impressive tribute to an eclectic array of Western women artists.

RUSTY TODARO/SHUTTERSTOCK ©

The Jail Tree

BEST FOR HISTORY & CULTURE

Push through the swinging doors of history in Wickenburg, Prescott and Jerome.

Scattered across downtown are statues of the town's founders and colorful characters. One of the latter was George Sayers, a 'bibulous reprobate' who was chained to the **Jail Tree** on Tegner St in the late 1800s. Press the button to hear his tale, then head over the road to the locally loved **Nana's Sandwich Shoppe** for a feed.

Wickenburg is pleasant anytime but summer, when temperatures regularly top 110°F (43°C).

THE DRIVE
Head west on Hwy 60, turn left onto Vulture Mine Rd. Saguaros and cattle guards mark the lonely 14-mile drive to the mine.

02 VULTURE MINE ROAD

At the remote and dusty **Vulture Mine** (vultureminetours.com), Austrian immigrant Henry Wickenburg staked his claim and made his fortune. The site holds the main shaft, where $30 million worth of gold was mined; the blacksmith shop and other decrepit old buildings; and the Hanging Tree. You can visit by guided tour on Saturday mornings between late October and May.

On the way back into town, consider spending the night at the **Flying E Ranch**, where guests can sign up for two-hour trail rides.

THE DRIVE
From downtown Wickenburg, pick up Hwy 93 north and drive 5 miles to 89N. Continuing north, the route leaves the Sonoran Desert and tackles the Weaver Mountains, climbing 2500ft in 4 miles. It's 59 miles to Prescott.

03 PRESCOTT

Fire raged through Whiskey Row in downtown Prescott ('press-kit') on July 14, 1900. Quick-thinking locals saved the town's most prized possession: the 24ft-long Brunswick Bar that anchored the **Palace Saloon** (whiskeyrowpalace.com). After lugging the solid oak bar onto **Courthouse Plaza**, they grabbed their drinks and continued the party. Prescott's cooperative spirit lives on, infusing the city with a welcoming vibe.

The Palace is at the centre of Prescott's **Historic Downtown and Whiskey Row**, where 40 drinking establishments once supplied suds and sour mash to rough-hewn cowboys, miners and wastrels.

To learn more about Prescott, which was Arizona's first territorial capital, visit the engaging **Sharlot Hall Museum** (sharlot.org), named for its 1928 founder, pioneer woman Sharlot Hall. The city is also home to the **World's Oldest Rodeo** (worldsoldestrodeo.com), which dates to 1888 and is held the week before July 4.

THE DRIVE
From the County Courthouse downtown, drive west on Gurley St, which turns into Thumb Butte Rd, an overall drive of just 4 miles.

04 THUMB BUTTE

Prescott sits in the middle of the Prescott National Forest, a 1.2-million-acre playground bursting with scenic slopes, lakes and ponderosa pines. The **Prescott National Forest Office** (fs.usda.gov/prescott) has information about local hikes, drives, picnic areas and campgrounds. A day-use fee is required - and payable - at many area trailheads. Intra-agency passes, including the America the Beautiful pass, cover this fee.

For a short hike, head to the hard-to-miss Thumb Butte. The 1.75-mile **Thumb Butte Trail #33** is a moderate workout and offers nice views of the town and mountains. Leashed dogs are OK.

Photo opportunity

The Grand Canyon from Mather Point.

THE DRIVE
Follow Hwy 89N out of Prescott, passing the Granite Dells rock formations on the 11-mile drive. Granite Dells Rd leads to a trail through the granite boulders on the Mile High Trail System (prescott-az.gov).

05 PHIPPEN MUSEUM

Strutting its stuff like a rodeo champ, the thoroughly engaging **Phippen Museum** (phippenartmuseum.org) ropes in visitors with an entertaining mix of special exhibits spotlighting cowboy and Western art. Named for the late George Phippen, a local, self-taught artist who helped put Western art on the map, it's worth a stop to see what's brewing. As you'll discover, Western art is broader than oil paintings of weather-beaten faces under broad hat brims - although you might see some of those as well.

THE DRIVE
Just north, leave Hwy 89 for Hwy 89A. This 27-mile serpentine road brooks no distraction as it approaches hillside Jerome, tucked in the Mingus Mountains. If you dare, glance east for stunning glimpses of the Verde Valley.

JAY YUAN/SHUTTERSTOCK ©

Mather Point (p61), Grand Canyon

06 JEROME

As the road snakes down steep Cleopatra Hill, it can be hard to tell whether the buildings are winning or losing their battle with gravity. Just take the **Sliding Jail** – it's waaaay down there at the bottom of town.

Now shabbily chic, this resurrected ghost town was known as the 'Wickedest Town in the West' during its late-1800s copper-mining heyday. In those days it teemed with brothels, saloons and opium dens. When the mines petered out in 1953, Jerome's population plummeted. Then came the '60s, when scores of hippies snapped up crumbling, atmospheric buildings for pennies, more or less restored them and injected the town with a groovy joie de vivre.

Join the party with a stroll past the galleries, indie shops, old buildings and wine-tasting rooms that are scattered up and down the hillside. Local artists sell their work at the **Jerome Artists Cooperative Gallery** (jeromecoop.com), while burly but friendly-enough bikers gather at the **Spirit Room Bar** (spiritroom.com).

THE DRIVE
Follow Main St/Hwy 89A out of downtown then turn left onto Douglas Rd.

07 AUDREY HEADFRAME PARK & JEROME STATE HISTORIC PARK

Jerome's darkly humorous embrace of its industrial past is clear at this former minehead, which boasts the largest surviving timber framehead in the state. The

Old Town District, Cottonwood

glass platform covering the mining shaft at **Audrey Headframe Park** (jeromehistoricalsociety.com) isn't your everyday roadside attraction: it's death staring you in the face. If the cover shattered, the drop is 1910ft – a mere 650ft longer than from atop the Empire State Building.

Sufficiently disturbed? Chill out next door at the excellent **Jerome State Historic Park** (azstateparks.com), which explores the town's mining past. The museum is inside the 1916 mansion of eccentric mining mogul Jimmy 'Rawhide' Douglas. The folksy video is worth watching before you explore the museum.

EGROY/SHUTTERSTOCK ©

THE DRIVE
Hwy 89A drops to tranquil Clarkdale. At the traffic circle, take the second exit onto the Clarkdale Pkwy and into town. Follow Main St east to S Broadway then turn left onto Tuzigoot Rd, a total drive of just 7 miles.

08 TUZIGOOT NATIONAL MONUMENT

Squatting atop a ridge east of Clarkdale, **Tuzigoot National Monument** (nps.gov/tuzi), a pueblo built by the prehistoric Sinaguan people (Spanish for 'without water'), is believed to have been inhabited from 1000 to 1400CE. At its peak as many as 225 people lived in its 110 rooms. Stop by the informative visitor center to examine tools, pottery and arrowheads, then climb a short, steep trail (not suitable for wheelchairs) for memorable views of the Verde Valley.

THE DRIVE
Return to S Broadway and follow it south into Old Town Cottonwood, just 3 miles south of Tuzigoot.

09 COTTONWOOD

Cottonwood has kicked up its cool quotient, particularly around the pedestrian-friendly **Old Town District**. On this low-key strip there are loads of good restaurants and wine-tasting rooms, and several interesting indie stores. The inviting tasting room **Arizona Stronghold** (azstronghold.com) has welcoming staff, comfy couches, and live music on Friday nights. Enjoy a few more wine samples across the street at the chocolate-and-wine-pairing **Pillsbury Wine Company** (pillsburywine.com). For wet-and-wild wine tasting in Cottonwood, join a Water to Wine kayak tour ($97) with **Sedona Adventure Tours** (sedonaadventuretours.com) on the Verde River to **Alcantara Vineyards** (alcantaravineyard.com).

THE DRIVE
Follow Main St south to reconnect with Hwy 89A, then drive a further 20 miles to Sedona. At the roundabout at the junction of Hwy 89A and Hwy 179, called the Y, continue into uptown Sedona. The main visitor center sits at the junction of Hwy 89A and Forest Rd.

10 SEDONA

The stunning red rocks here have an intensely spiritual pull for many visitors. Some New Age believers even think that the sandstone

WHY I LOVE THIS TRIP

Hugh McNaughtan, writer

Yes, the landscape's spectacular, but much of this state's charm lies in how it's translated a rough-and-ready past into a characterful and appealing present. Central Arizona is packed with former mining, railroad and lumber towns that have taken the demise of traditional industries in their stride, developing wine, food and cultural scenes that keep the lifeblood pumping. Enjoy Prescott, Jerome, Cottonwood, Flagstaff and Sedona on your way to the canyon.

formations hold 'vortices' that vibrate to the frequencies of the 'deepest earth energies.' Judge for yourself atop **Airport Mesa** (Airport Rd), the vortex most convenient to downtown. Here, a short scramble leads to a lofty view of the surrounding sandstone monoliths, which blaze a psychedelic red and orange at sunset. To get to the viewpoint, drive up Airport Rd for half a mile and look for a small parking area ($3) on the left.

Another arresting site is the **Chapel of the Holy Cross** (chapeloftheholycross.com), a church tucked between spectacular red-rock columns 3 miles south of town. This modern Catholic chapel was built by Marguerite Brunwig Staude in the tradition of Frank Lloyd Wright.

THE DRIVE
Follow Hwy 179 9 miles south, past Bell Rock, through the village of Oak Creek to the Red Rock Country Visitor Center.

11 RED ROCK COUNTRY VISITOR CENTER

Outdoor adventurers love the super-scenic hiking and biking trails in and around Sedona. The US Forest Service provides the helpful and free *Recreation Guide to Your National Forest,* which has brief descriptions of popular trails and a map pinpointing their routes and trailheads. Pick one up at the **Red Rock Country Visitor Center** (redrockcountry.org), just south of the village of Oak Creek. Staff can guide you to less populated trails, or those best suited to your interests.

THE DRIVE
Hwy 89A rolls north through the riparian greenery of scenic Oak Creek Canyon, where red cliffs and pine forest rear spectacularly from either side of the road. Once out of the canyon pick up I-17 north. The total drive to Flagstaff is 39 miles.

12 FLAGSTAFF

Flagstaff's charms are myriad, from its pedestrian-friendly historic downtown to high-altitude pursuits like skiing and hiking. **Humphrey's Peak** (fs.usda.gov), the highest point in the state, provides an inspiring backdrop. Start at the downtown **visitor center** (flagstaffarizona.org), which has free brochures for walking tours, including a guide to Flagstaff's haunted places.

The fascinating **Lowell Observatory** (lowell.edu), built in 1894 and site of the first official sighting of Pluto (in 1930), sits on a hill just outside downtown. During the day you can take a guided tour, while at night, weather permitting, there's stargazing. Flagstaff's microbreweries are the stars on the one-mile **Flagstaff Brewery Trail** (craftbeerflg.com). But if walking seems too pedestrian, climb aboard the **Alpine Pedaler** (alpinepedaler.com), a 14-passenger 'party on wheels' that brakes for bars and breweries.

THE DRIVE
The next morning – and mornings are best for the 90-mile trip – take Hwy 180 west and enjoy the views of the San Francisco Peaks through the treetops. When you reach Hwy 64 at the town of Valle, turn right and drive the remainder of the journey north on the broad uplands of the Coconino Plateau.

13 TUSAYAN

This little town, sitting 1 mile south of the Grand Canyon's South Entrance on Hwy 64, is basically a half-mile strip of canyon-focused hotels and restaurants. Stop at the **National Geographic Visitor Center & IMAX Theater** (explorethecanyon.com) to prepay the $30-per-vehicle park fee and save yourself what could be a long wait at the entrance. Always screening in the IMAX theater is the terrific 34-minute film *Grand Canyon – The Hidden Secrets*. With exhilarating river-running scenes and virtual-reality drops off canyon rims, the film plunges you into the history and geology of the canyon through the eyes of ancient American Indians, first explorer John Wesley Powell and a soaring eagle.

In summer, you can leave your car here and catch the Tusayan shuttle into the park.

THE DRIVE
Follow Hwy 64 1 mile north to the park entrance. Admission to the national park is $30 per vehicle, $25 for motorcycles or $15 for pedestrians or bikes, and is good for seven days. All up, it's a serene 7 miles to Mather Point.

DON'T MISS:

Audrey Headframe Park

Stand on a piece of glass over a 1910ft mining shaft. Look down, if you dare.

14 MATHER POINT & GRAND CANYON VISITOR CENTER

Park at the **visitor center** (nps.gov/grca) but don't go inside. Not yet. Walk (or run) directly to **Mather Point**, the first overlook after the South Entrance. It's usually packed elbow-to-elbow with a global array of tourists, but even with the crowds there's a sense of communal wonder that keeps things civil. You'll see – the sheer immensity of the canyon just grabs you, then holds you as you scan the endless details – rugged mesas, sculpted spires and an almost overwhelming sense of scale.

Once your sense of wonder is surfeited, head back to the main visitor center, with its theater and bookstore. On the plaza, bulletin boards and kiosks display information about ranger programs, the weather, tours and hikes. Inside is a ranger-staffed information desk and a lecture hall, where rangers offer daily talks on a variety of subjects. The theater screens a 20-minute movie, *Grand Canyon: A Journey of Wonder*, on the hour and half-hour.

From here, explore the park via park shuttle, a **bike** (bikegrandcanyon.com) or your own four wheels. In summer, parking can be a challenge in Grand Canyon Village.

THE DRIVE
The Village Loop Rd leads into Grand Canyon Village. Pass El Tovar, Kachina and Thunderbird Lodges on the 2-mile drive to Bright Angel Lodge. The Bright Angel Trailhead is just west of the lodge

Grand Canyon

Bright Angel trail

THOMAS BLANCK/SHUTTERSTOCK ©

DETOUR

Desert View Drive

Start: 14 Mather Point & Grand Canyon Visitor Center

This scenic road meanders 25 miles to the East Entrance on Hwy 64, passing some of the park's finest viewpoints, picnic areas and historic sites. **Grand View Point** marks the trailhead where miner Peter Berry opened the aptly named Grand View Hotel in 1897 – it really is one of the Grand Canyon's most stunning viewpoints. Another captivating view awaits at **Moran Point** (nps.gov/grca), named for the landscape painter whose work helped secure the Grand Canyon national monument status in 1908. Further along is **Tusayan Museum & Ruin**, where you can walk around the remains of an excavated Puebloan village dating to 1185. At the end of the road is the **Desert View Watchtower**, designed by Mary Jane Colter and inspired by Ancestral Puebloan structures – the terrace provides panoramic views of the canyon and river. The circular staircase inside leads past Hopi murals to 360-degree views on the top floor.

15 GRAND CANYON VILLAGE

The **Bright Angel Trail** is the most popular of the South Rim corridor trails, and its steep and scenic 8-mile descent to the Colorado River has four logical turn-around points: Mile-and-a-Half Resthouse, Three Mile Resthouse, Indian Garden and Plateau Point. Summer heat can be crippling and the climb is steep. Day hikers should turn around at one of the two resthouses (a 3- to 6-mile round trip).

If you're more interested in history and geography than strenuous hiking, follow the easy **Rim Trail** east from here. Heading west, the Rim Trail passes every overlook on the way to **Hermits Rest** (nps.gov/grca), offering spectacular views. The Hermits Rest shuttle runs parallel to the trail, so hike until you're tired, then hop aboard to continue or return. But be sure to hop off for the sunset, which is best at **Hopi Point** (which draws crowds) or **Pima Point**.

DON'T MISS:

Airport Mesa

It's an easy scramble to a sweeping 360-degree view of Sedona's monolithic red rocks.

06

ARIZONA

Mogollon Rim Country

BEST FOR HISTORY

Learning the tragic history of the Indian Wars at Fort Apache National Historic Park.

Woods Canyon lake, Mogollon Rim

DURATION	DISTANCE	GREAT FOR
3–5 days	271 miles / 436km	Outdoors, history and culture

BEST TIME TO GO	Spring for wildflowers and fall for the colorful cottonwoods and aspens.

Natural wonders and quirky towns dot the Mogollon Rim, an oft-overlooked 200-mile swath of forested cliffs at the southern edge of the Colorado Plateau. After the verdant hush of the pines atop the Mogollon Rim (pronounced 'muggy-own'), the stark, twisting drop into Salt River Canyon comes as a shock. But it's these dramatic changes that make this trip such a varied feast for the senses.

Link your trip

2 Route 66: The Southwest

From Payson, follow Hwy 87 north to 'Take It Easy' corner in Winslow.

18 Into the Gila

Hankerin' for pie? Drive east on Hwy 60 to Pie Town, NM.

01 TONTO NATURAL BRIDGE STATE PARK

The drive from Flagstaff to Hwy 87 on S Lake Mary Rd is gorgeous, passing ponderosa pines and glinting lakes as it mounts the Mogollon Rim at the southern edge of the Colorado Plateau. The Rim was named for Don Juan Ignacio Flores Mogollon, a Spanish governor of the province of New Mexico in the 1700s. When you reach Hwy 87, turn right and continue to **Tonto Natural Bridge State Park** (azstateparks.com/tonto). The Park's precipitous entrance road ends at the eponymous bridge – at 183ft high and straddling a 150ft-wide canyon, it's

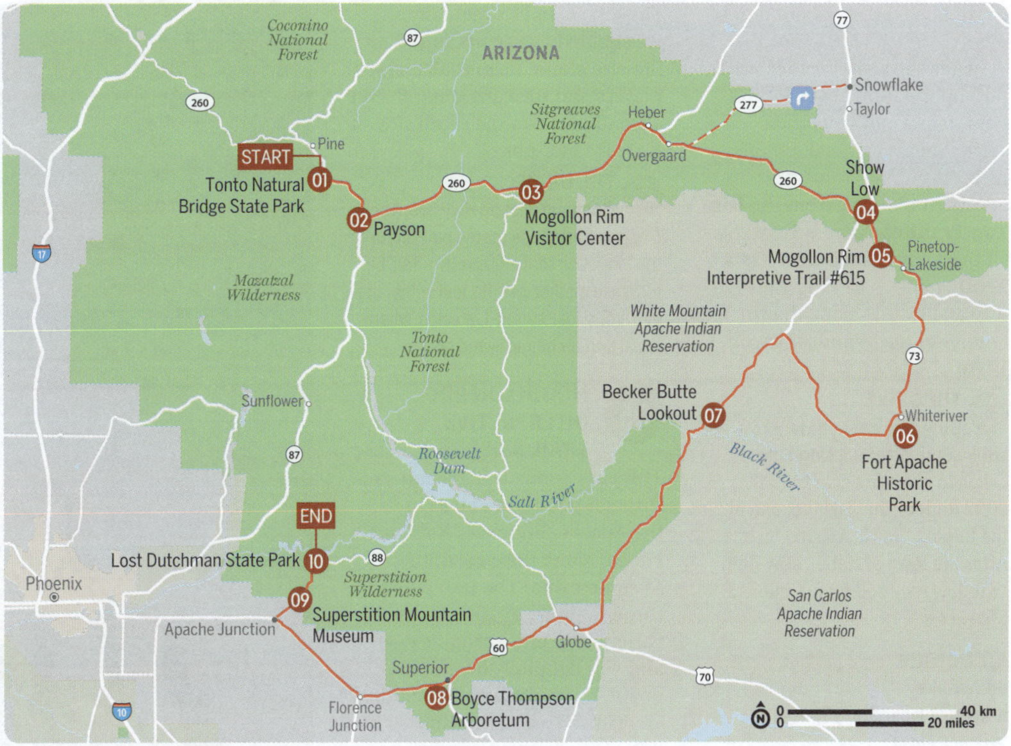

the world's largest natural travertine bridge. It formed through countless centuries of attrition, as Pine Creek gradually worked its way through a massive dam of calcium carbonate. You can view it from multiple angles, and steep trails descend into the canyon for close-ups.

THE DRIVE
Return to Hwy 87 and head south to Payson, all up a drive of 14 miles.

02 PAYSON

Founded by gold miners in 1882, Payson's real riches turned out to be above ground. Vast pine forests fed a booming timber industry, ranchers ran cattle along the Mogollon Rim and down to the Tonto Basin, and wild game was plentiful. Today, Payson is a recreation and retirement destination for Phoenix citizens, with hunting and fishing in the nearby forests, lakes and streams.

Exhibits at the **Rim Country Museum** (rimcountrymuseums.com), viewed on docent-led tours, illustrate the native, pioneer and mining history of the region. Highlights include a replica of a blacksmith shop and a walk-through of the Zane Grey Cabin, faithfully rebuilt here after the author's original homestead burned in the tragic 1990 conflagration known as the Dude Fire. Tours can be shortened if you have limited time.

THE DRIVE
Heading east, Hwy 260 cuts through a vast blanket of lofty pines, where 'Elk Crossing' and 'Watch for Elk' signs will keep you on your toes as you drive the 30 miles to the next stop.

03 MOGOLLON RIM VISITOR CENTER

For expansive views of southern forests and lakes, stop at the **Mogollon Rim Visitor Center** (fs.usda.gov). Its deck looks over the Mogollon Rim, a dramatic geological break a couple of thousand feet high between the high desert of the Colorado Plateau and the low desert to the south. The Rim contains the world's largest contiguous forests of ponderosa pine.

Inside the visitor center you'll find information about local flora, fauna and recreation. There are also animal mounts, including a full-grown bear. Several trails leave from the **Rim Top Trailhead** across Hwy 260. Of these, the **Rim Lakes Vista Trail** crosses back over the highway and travels along the rim for 3 miles to the **Woods Canyon Vista**.

THE DRIVE
Continue east on Hwy 260. Look south after passing Forest Lakes to see a fire scar from the 2002 Rodeo-Chediski fire, one of the largest fires in Arizona history. After the town of Heber, stay right to follow Hwy 260 for 60 miles to Show Low.

DETOUR
Snowflake
Start: 03 Mogollon Rim Visitor Center

Snowflake is the northernmost city of Rim Country. The town gets an occasional light dusting of snow, but is really named after the founders: a Mr Snow and a Mr Flake. Seriously. Settled by Mormon pioneers in the late 1800s, there are more than 100 historic homes here, many with handsome red brick and white trim. From Heber-Overgaard, take Hwy 277 east, around 120 miles out and back.

04 SHOW LOW

Back in 1876, a 100,000-acre ranch was at stake in a marathon card game. As daybreak approached, the players agreed that whoever could 'show low' would take the prize. One player flipped over the deuce of clubs. The town that arose here took the name Show Low and its main drag was named Deuce of Clubs St. A life-size statue memorializing the players and the card game sits on a small plaza on the south side of E Deuce of Clubs.

THE DRIVE
Continue east on Hwy 260. About 6 miles ahead, look for the pull-off for the Mogollon Rim Interpretive Trail, before mile marker 348. It's just within the city limits for Pinetop-Lakeside, where you'll find restaurants and hotels.

05 MOGOLLON RIM INTERPRETIVE TRAIL #615

This easy 1-mile trail meanders through ponderosa pines in the Apache-Sitgreaves National Forest, along the edge of the Mogollon Rim. The trail passes through forest of great botanical variety; you may see mule deer, and will definitely hear (and hopefully see) a variety of birds. You'll also pass an unusual sight: a Douglas fir beside an alligator juniper, two plants rarely seen together because they have different climatic requirements. And the view from the Rim? Picture rolling waves of trees. The

DON'T MISS:
Superstition Mountain Museum

Small and old-school, but a charmer; check out its wacky wildlife dioramas, treasure maps and the likely looting gear of a stagecoach robber.

Salt River (p68)

Photo opportunity

The grandeur of the Salt River Canyon from along Hwy 60.

first half mile of the trail is paved and wheelchair accessible.

THE DRIVE
Follow Hwy 260 east to Hon-Dah Resort-Casino on the northern edge of the White Mountain Apache Tribe Reservation. Turn right onto Hwy 73, driving south through ponderosa forest and mountain meadows. The view opens up at Whiteriver. About 5 miles south of town, turn left onto Indian Rte 46 to complete the 33-mile leg.

06 FORT APACHE NATIONAL HISTORIC PARK

Bounded by the Mogollon Rim to the north and the Salt River to the south, the White Mountain Apache Tribe Reservation covers 2627 sq miles, most of which is forest. Head for the Nohwike' Bágowa Cultural Center and Museum at **Fort Apache Historic Park** (wmat.nsn.us), an Army post between 1870 and 1922, where you'll find a thorough introduction to the White Mountain Apache world.

A self-guided tour leads to the fort's historic buildings. An exhibit inside an 1871 officers' quarters highlights Apache scouts and explains why tribal members helped the US Army subdue other American Indian tribes in the Indian Wars. The **Theodore Roosevelt Boarding School** was established here in 1923 and is still in operation.

Admission includes entry to the **Kinishba Ruins**, a pre-Columbian stone pueblo that once had hundreds of rooms. At the museum, pick up a guide to the ruins, which are at the end of a well-graded dirt road that begins 4 miles west off Hwy 73: they're well worth a stop.

THE DRIVE
From the ruins, turn right onto Hwy 73 and drive 24 miles to US 60. Turn left for a twisting descent through the stunning Salt River Canyon. As you drop into the canyon, watch for the overlook parking lot between mile markers 298 and 297.

07 BECKER BUTTE LOOKOUT

Pull over, pull over, pull over! You've got to see the view from this stone-walled overlook, which is perched above the

DOUG MACLEOD/SHUTTERSTOCK ©

Superstition Mountains

majestic **Salt River Canyon**, a 2000ft gash carving its way through the imposing landscape. The river, unhampered by dams, runs wild below the juniper-covered buttes. Hwy 60 runs through the **White Mountain Apache Tribe Reservation** north of the Salt River, and a recreational permit is required to explore beyond the overlooks (see wmatoutdoor.org). South of the river, the highway runs through the **San Carlos Apache Tribe Reservation**. For recreational permit information here, see sancarlosrecreationwildlife.com.

THE DRIVE
Hwy 60 passes more viewpoints as it drops to the Salt River. After crossing the river the highway climbs out of the canyon. Continue west through Globe, which makes a good lunch stop, and Superior, where copper country rises toward rim country. It's 92 miles from the Hwy 60 junction to the next stop.

08 BOYCE THOMPSON ARBORETUM

This lovely **arboretum** (ag.arizona.edu/bta) covers nearly 400 acres and is a living museum with flora species from arid regions around the world. During the spring bloom, which peaks March though early May, the park is vibrant with color and smells as sweet as a candy factory. Saguaros bloom in May and June. Leashed pets are welcome.

THE DRIVE
Follow US 60 west around 24 miles to W Mountain View Rd. Turn right and drive north about 4.5 miles to North Apache Trail/AZ 88 and turn right again.

09 SUPERSTITION MOUNTAIN MUSEUM

The thoroughly delightful **Superstition Mountain Museum** (superstitionmountainmuseum.org) welcomes guests with mesmerizing dioramas of wild animals trying to kill each other – again. But most impressive is the wall of treasure maps, all purporting to lead to the Lost Dutchman Mine, where 19th-century German prospector Jacob Waltz, the 'Dutchman,' allegedly struck gold in these parts. On his deathbed, Waltz supposedly revealed the whereabouts of the source of ore, but it's never been found – despite the efforts of thousands.

Outside, you'll find the Elvis Memorial Chapel from the Elvis movie *Charro!* (1969). It was moved here after surviving a devastating fire at Apacheland Movie Ranch.

THE DRIVE
Drive 1 mile northeast on N Apache Trail, passing the Goldfield Ghost Town (goldfieldghosttown.com), an unabashed tourist trap that is also, well, kind of fun.

10 LOST DUTCHMAN STATE PARK

The sought-after gold mine it's named after is the main claim to fame of this **state park** (azstateparks.com), but this striking place is really a treasure itself, with a surreal massif of the Superstition Mountains dominating the terrain. Enjoy easy and moderate trails and perhaps pitch for the night in the very pretty campground. Look for vast blooms of desert wildflowers here, especially after a wet winter.

The Truth is Out There

One of the USA's most famous cases of putative alien abduction took place in Rim Country. Logger Travis Walton claims he was abducted near Snowflake by an alien craft in 1975. What makes his story interesting is that there were eyewitnesses, and a police manhunt failed to turn up Walton for two days – time on the mother ship, he says. According to the Forest Service, the telephone booth that Walton called for help from after his abduction is still there and makes a nice photo op. For more details, visit Walton's website, travis-walton.com, or check out the 1993 movie *Fire in the Sky*, based on his story.

07

ARIZONA

Southern Desert Wanderings

BEST FOR FLORA & FAUNA

Wander past coyotes and cacti at the Arizona-Sonora Desert Museum.

DURATION	DISTANCE	GREAT FOR
3–4 days	321 miles / 517km	Outdoors, family, food and drink

BEST TIME TO GO	October to March, to avoid the desert heat.

Arizona-Sonora Desert Museum

You'll swoosh past saguaros on this loop through the Sonoran Desert. Striding in serried ranks across broad, cloud-dappled plains and up sweeping mountain flanks, these giant cacti make a stunning impression on the eye. But saguaros aren't the only attractions of this delightful desert drive: mountaintop observatories, rippling wine country and moody Spanish missions await.

Link your trip

3 A Taste of the Old West

Follow Hwy 82 east from Sonoita to a ghost town and the OK Corral.

9 Highway 95: Yuma to Lake Mead

Feeling the need to see water after all that desert? Take Hwy 85 north to I-10 then head west to the Colorado River.

01 SAGUARO NATIONAL PARK (WEST)

If you're standing beside a docent at this **cacti-filled park** (nps.gov/sagu), do not refer to the limbs of the saguaro (sah-wah-ro) as branches. As you'll quickly learn, a saguaro has 'arms,' not mere branches – a distinction that makes sense when you consider the human-like features of these silent scarecrows of the Sonoran Desert. A vast army of these majestic, ribbed sentinels is protected within the park.

The park is divided into two halves, separated by 30 miles and the city of Tucson. In the western Tucson Mountain District, the **visitor center** (nps.gov/sagu) sits beside the short **Cactus Garden Trail** where signage identifies desert plants. The nearby **Scenic Bajada Loop Drive** is a 6-mile graded dirt road through cactus forest.

THE DRIVE
Watch for cyclists on N Kinney Rd as you drive 3 miles south.

02 ARIZONA-SONORA DESERT MUSEUM

Home to cacti, coyotes and tiny hummingbirds, this fascinating **place** (desertmuseum.org) is one part zoo, one part botanical garden and one part museum – a trifecta that can keep young and old entertained for easily half a day. All sorts of desert denizens, from cantankerous coatis to playful prairie dogs, make their home in natural enclosures hemmed in by invisible fences. The grounds are thick with desert plants, and docents are on hand to answer questions and give demonstrations.

Wear a hat and walking shoes, and remember that the big cats are most active in the morning.

THE DRIVE
Continue south to Hwy 86. Drive east to I-19, taking it north to I-10 east. Leave I-10 east at exit 281 for Hwy 83 south to Sonoita at Hwy 82, a total journey of 61 miles. To get to Elgin, cross Hwy 82 and continue on Hwy 83 a further 4 miles to Elgin Rd.

03 SONOITA & ELGIN

Ah, what a view: long vistas of lush, windswept high grassland; dark, knobby forest mountains; and slow upland streams in the creases in between. Sonoita and tiny Elgin, in the southern grasslands, were once important railway stops, but since the line closed in 1962, tourism, viticulture and the arts have been their bread and butter.

The valleys here occupy a special microclimate amenable to wine grapes, making the region a center for Arizona's burgeoning wine industry. For tastings, start at **Callaghan Vineyards** (callaghanvineyards.com) in Elgin, traditionally one of the most highly regarded wineries in the state. Return to Sonoita for **Dos Cabezas Wineworks** (doscabezas.com), a rustically pretty, family-run operation near the crossroads of Hwys 82 and 83.

THE DRIVE
Return to Hwy 82 and follow it southwest to Patagonia, which is sandwiched between the Mexican border, the Santa Rita Mountains and the Patagonia Mountains; a drive of 22 miles all up.

04 PATAGONIA

Sitting almost 5000ft above sea level, Patagonia is cool and breezy. The town borders Sonoita Creek, part of a riparian green zone that draws migrating birds and sharp-eyed birders.

A few gentle trails meander through the **Patagonia-Sonoita Creek Preserve** (nature.org/arizona), an enchanting willow and cottonwood forest managed by the Nature Conservancy. It supports seven distinct vegetative ecosystems, four endangered species of native fish and more than 300 species of birds, including rarities from Mexico. The peak migratory seasons are April and May, and late August to September. Join guided nature walks on Saturday mornings at 9am.

THE DRIVE
Follow Hwy 82 southwest, passing Patagonia Lake State Park on the 18 miles to the border town of Nogales. Here, pick up I-19 north to complete the 36-mile leg.

05 TUMACÁCORI NATIONAL HISTORICAL PARK

This pink-and-cream **edifice** (nps.gov/tuma) shimmers on the desert air like a missionary's dream. In 1691 Father Eusebio Kino and his cohort arrived at the Tumacácori settlement and quickly founded a mission to convert the local American Indians. However, repeated Apache raids and the harsh winter of 1848 drove the priests out, leaving the complex to crumble for decades. Start self-guided tours of the hauntingly beautiful ruins at the visitor center.

Just south, pick up spices, salsa and fantastic homemade chile pastes at **Santa Cruz Chili & Spice** (santacruzchili.com), in business since the 1950s.

THE DRIVE
Continue north on I-19. Exit 34 leads to Tubac, a former Spanish garrison town now home to a cluster of 100 or so galleries and shops selling art and high-end crafts. Continue north to exit 69 to complete the 26-mile leg.

06 TITAN MISSILE MUSEUM

The **Titan Missile Museum** (titanmissilemuseum.org) is where the obliteration of humanity becomes frighteningly real. At this original Titan II missile site, a crew stood ready 24/7 to launch a nuclear warhead within seconds of receiving a presidential order. The Titan II was the first liquid-propelled intercontinental ballistic missile (ICBM) that could be fired from below ground and could reach its target – halfway around the world – in 30 minutes or less. The facility was on constant alert from 1963 to 1986. The 75-minute tours are both creepy and fascinating, and reservations are advised.

THE DRIVE
Rejoin I-19 north and drive to exit 92 for the next 18-mile hop.

07 MISSION SAN XAVIER DEL BAC

The dazzling white towers of this **mission** (patronatosanxavier.org) bring an otherworldly glow to the desert. Nicknamed 'White Dove of the Desert,' the original mission was founded by Jesuit missionary Father Eusebio Kino in 1700, but was mostly destroyed in the Pima uprising of 1751. Its successor was gracefully rebuilt in the late 1700s in a harmonious blend of Moorish, Byzantine and Mexican Renaissance styles. Carefully restored in the 1990s and still religiously active, it's one of the best-preserved and most beautiful Spanish missions in the country.

TELLES FAMILY SHRINE

On Hwy 82 south of Patagonia, just beyond mile marker 16, look east for a pull-off and historic plaque. The latter spotlights **John Ward's Ranch**, established here in 1858. Behind the plaque, stairs climb to a protected shrine built inside a rock face. The shrine was created in the 1940s by Juanita and Juan Telles, who promised to keep its candles burning if their sons returned safely from WWII. Their sons came home, and the candles still burn.

Mission San Xavier del Bac

Photo opportunity

Frame a towering saguaro against the sky in the western section of Saguaro National Park.

Organ Pipe Cactus National Monument

LHBLLC/SHUTTERSTOCK ©

The wall-sized, carved, painted and gilded retable behind the altar, in the moody, candlelit interior, tells the story of creation in dizzying detail. The faithful line up to pray to a reclining wooden figure of St Francis, the mission's patron saint.

THE DRIVE
Follow San Xavier Rd west to S Mission Rd, go north to W Valencia Rd, then west 9 miles to Hwy 86 south. Continue just over 25 miles. Turn left onto Hwy 386 and climb to Kitt Peak – a twisty drive with ravishing views across the desert. It's a total of 49 miles.

08 KITT PEAK NATIONAL OBSERVATORY

Dark and clear night skies make **Kitt Peak** (kpno.noirlab.edu) a perfect site for one of the world's largest observatories. Just east of Sells, this 6875ft-high mountaintop is stacked with two radio telescopes and 22 optical telescopes. The access road was closed after a fire in June 2022, but at the time of writing it was due to reopen in October 2023.

THE DRIVE
Take Hwy 386 north back to Hwy 86. Drive 81 miles west on Hwy 86 to Why and the junction with Hwy 85. Follow Hwy 85 south 22 miles to the Kris Eggle Visitor Center in Organ Pipe Cactus National Monument.

09 ORGAN PIPE CACTUS NATIONAL MONUMENT

Along the Mexican border, this remote **national park** (nps.gov/orpi) is a gorgeous, forbidding land. It's home to an astonishing number of animals and plants, including 28 species of cacti – first and foremost its namesake organ-pipe. A giant columnar cactus, it differs from the more prevalent saguaro in that its arms radiate from the base. Organ-pipes are common in Mexico but very rare north of the border. Animals that have adapted to this arid climate include bighorn sheep, coyotes, kangaroo rats, mountain lions and the pig-like javelina.

Winter and early spring, when Mexican gold poppies and purple lupines blanket the barren ground, are the most pleasant seasons to visit. Summers are shimmering hot (routinely above 100°F/37°C) and bring monsoon rains between July and September.

The 21-mile **Ajo Mountain Drive** leads northeast from the visitor center through a spectacular landscape of steep-sided jagged cliffs and burned-red rocks.

08

ARIZONA

Highway 89A: Red Rock Country

DURATION	DISTANCE	GREAT FOR
2 days	61 miles / 98km	Outdoors, food and drink

BEST TIME TO GO	Temperatures are most pleasant fall through spring.

This gorgeous drive is like entering an animated landscape painting, from the lush greenery of Oak Creek to the fiery brilliance of the Red Rock Scenic Byway. A 61-mile lasso loop, this trip was designed to maximize gawping, punctuated with a few easy stops that get you close to those magnetic red rocks. Once you've driven the main loop, choose a path, join a tour or pinpoint another petroglyph site for further exploration.

Link your trip

5 Fantastic Canyon Voyage

Continue north on Hwy 89A from Oak Creek Vista to charismatic Flagstaff.

10 Southwest Indian Nations Sojourn

From V-Bar-V drive north on I-17 to the cliff dwellings at Walnut Canyon National Monument.

01 OAK CREEK VISTA

With its dramatic canyon walls and riparian lushness, **Oak Creek Canyon** is certainly stunning. But what makes this 14-mile stretch of Hwy 89A really special is the hint of the untamed, the lure of nature's bounty not yet captured and commodified. See for yourself at Oak Creek Vista, about 14 miles south of Flagstaff. From this towering perch, the pine-draped canyon whooshes ahead like an unruly child just released from Mother Nature's time out. American Indian vendors sell jewelry beside the parking lot.

BEST FOR OUTDOORS

Wheee! Whoosh over red-rock waterfalls at Slide Rock State Park.

Slide Rock State Park

THE DRIVE Hwy 89A twists into the canyon then rolls along Oak Creek past Pine Flat and Cave Springs campgrounds in the Coconino National Forest. The trailhead for the popular West Fork Trail, which follows the creek for 7 miles, soon beckons on the right.

02 SLIDE ROCK STATE PARK

On a hot summer day you're likely to get caught in a traffic jam at **Slide Rock State Park** (azstateparks.com/parks/slro), where swimmers come in droves to swoosh down the creek on rock-lined chutes and watery slides. Come early or late in the day to avoid the worst congestion. If things get too crowded, you can always wait until you reach **Grasshopper Point** (fs.usda.gov), south of Oak Creek Visitor Center.

THE DRIVE Continue south past Manzanita Campground; it's three sinuous, scenic miles to the next stop.

03 OAK CREEK VISITOR CENTER

The pull-off for this small **visitor center** (fs.usda.gov) is a nice place to stretch your legs. A lovely little coffee and sandwich shop, **Indian Gardens Cafe & Market** (indiangardens.com), can be found here, as well as the long-established **Garland's Indian Jewelry** (garlandsjewelry.com) selling jewelry, kachinas, baskets and pottery.

THE DRIVE Continue south on Hwy 89A, passing a great swimming hole, Grasshopper Point (car day-use fee $8), before rolling into Sedona's 'city' center, called Uptown. Four miles in total.

04 UPTOWN SEDONA

Compact and busy (particularly around March and April), Uptown is where you'll find reservation desks for tour companies hoping to take you deeper into the stunning red-rock country around Sedona.

Jeep tours here are a fun, if bumpy, way to see the sights, but it can be hard to distinguish between the companies. One thing to check is backcountry accessibility; the companies have permits for different routes and sites, so if there's a specific formation you want to see, check around. The hard-to-miss **Pink Jeep Tours** (pinkjeeptours.com) run 15 different thrilling and funny off-road and hiking tours lasting from about two hours (adult/child from $59/54) to four hours (from $154/139).

Sedona's **visitor center** (visitsedona.com), great for info on hikes and other activities in red-rock country, is at the corner of Hwy 89A and Forest Rd.

THE DRIVE

Take Hwy 89A a short distance south to the roundabout at its junction with Hwy 179, known locally as the Y. Take 179 south and turn right almost immediately.

DETOUR

Palatki & Honanki Heritage Sites
Start: 04 Uptown Sedona

Thousand-year-old Sinaguan cliff dwellings and rock art are great reasons to brave a 9-mile dirt road leading to two archaeological sites on the edge of the wilderness. At **Palatki Heritage Site** (fs.usda.gov) there's a small visitor center and three easy trails (not amenable to wheelchairs, unfortunately). To manage crowds, reservations are required. True ruin groupies should ask here about the ruins at **Honanki Heritage Site** (fs.usda.gov), another 3 miles north. To get to Palatki, follow Hwy 89A west 10 miles from the Y then turn right onto dirt FR 525 (Red Canyon Rd) and follow it about 6 miles to FR 795. Take FR 795 for 1.5 miles. Both sites require a Red Rock Pass.

05 TLAQUEPAQUE VILLAGE

This **shopping village** (tlaq.com) is a series of Mexican-style interconnected plazas that are home to dozens of high-end art galleries, shops and restaurants. It's easy to lose a couple of hours meandering through this maze. If you're peckish, head a little further down Hwy 179 to the lip-smacking Mexican **Elote Cafe** (elotecafe.com).

THE DRIVE

Return to the Y and pick up Hwy 89A south. Chimney Rock and Coffee Pot Rock glow to the north. After passing Arroyo Pinon Dr, turn left onto upper Red Rock Loop Rd. The junction is 4 miles west of the Y.

06 RED ROCK LOOP ROAD

Any time is a good time to drive the winding 7-mile Red Rock Loop Rd, which is paved except for one short section. If you're in a mood to take photographs, turn left after 1.5 miles for the **Red Rock Crossing/Crescent Moon Recreation Area**. A small army of photographers usually gathers at the crossing at sunset to record the dramatic light show unfolding on iconic **Cathedral Rock**.

Continue driving through the blaze of sandstone glory to the aptly named **Red Rock State Park** (azstateparks.com/red-rock). Not to be confused with Slide Rock State Park, this far more low-key place includes an environmental education center, a visitor center, picnic areas and 5 miles of well-marked trails in a riparian environment boasting gorgeous scenery. Ranger-led activities include nature walks, bird walks and full-moon hikes during warmer months.

TOP TIP:
Red Rock Passes

To park at many trailheads and recreational areas in the Coconino National Forest, you'll need to buy a Red Rock Pass ($5/15 per day/week) from visitor centers, ranger stations or vending machines at some trailheads and picnic areas. Passes go on your dashboard. Federal Interagency passes are valid. Applicable areas are plastered with signs, which you can ignore if stopping briefly for a photograph. Check the *Recreation Guide to Your National Forest*, available at National Forest visitor centers or online, to determine where the passes are required. Currently, passes are required at most recreational sites beside Hwy 89A in Oak Creek Canyon and beside Hwy 179 between Chapel Rd and the Bell Rock Pathway trailhead in the village of Oak Creek.

Cathedral Rock

Photo opportunity

Cathedral Rock looks mighty majestic from Red Rock Crossing.

Montezuma Castle

DON'T MISS:

Pondering Petroglyphs

Solar calendars? The art of shamans? Or simply prehistoric graffiti? See for yourself in central Arizona.

DAVID BYRON KEENER/SHUTTERSTOCK ©

THE DRIVE
Rejoin Hwy 89A, turn left and drive 7 miles southwest to N Page Springs Rd.

07 PAGE SPRINGS CELLARS

The vineyards, wineries and tasting rooms lining Hwy 89A and I-17 are bringing a dash of energy and style to central Arizona's Verde Valley. Several wineries with tasting rooms hug a scrubby stretch of Page Springs Rd, east of Cornville – one of the best is **Page Springs Cellars** (pagespringscellars.com). This busy spot has welcoming, knowledgeable staff and a cozy back porch overlooking Oak Creek. It's a thoroughly enjoyable place to savor the bruschetta and Rhône-style Arizona wines.

THE DRIVE
Turn right onto Page Springs Rd and drive south to Cornville Rd, which you'll follow south 8 miles to I-17. Drive north to exit 298 and FR 618. Drive east about 3 miles, passing Beaver Creek Campground. The total drive is just over 20 miles.

08 V-BAR-V HERITAGE SITE

More than 1000 petroglyphs – most attributed to the southern Sinaguan people who lived at nearby **Montezuma Castle** – have been identified at this well-protected Forest Service **site** (fs.usda.gov). A short trail from the **visitor center** to the rock site runs parallel to a tributary of the **Verde River**. During the Sinaguan period (between 1150 and 1400 CE) the site was probably used by shamans and in part as a solar calendar. See if you can find the depiction of a female shaman. And the embracing stick-figure couple? Not dancing. A Red Rock Pass is required.

THE DRIVE
Follow FR 618 northwest, crossing I-17. The Red Rock Scenic Byway (Hwy 179) begins three miles from here and continues for the rest of the final, 10-mile leg. Enjoy the show.

09 VILLAGE OF OAK CREEK

Now that the scenic driving is done, stop at the Red Rock Country Visitor Center (p60), just south of the village of Oak Creek, for more information about places you want to explore further. Pick up the free *Recreation Guide to Your National Forest*, which has a great map of hiking and biking trails in greater Sedona and along Oak Creek. The map also shows camping spots and picnic areas.

A great cycling route is the easy but beautiful **Bell Rock Pathway** just north on Hwy 179. The pathway is across the street from **Sedona Bike & Bean** (bike-bean.com), a blissful combo of coffee bar and bike-rental place. The 7-mile round trip crosses lots of other hiking and biking paths, and it's easy to spend a day exploring. Hwy 179 takes you north back to Uptown Sedona.

09

ARIZONA

Highway 95: Yuma to Lake Mead

DURATION	DISTANCE	GREAT FOR
3 days	312 miles / 502km	Outdoors

BEST TIME TO GO	
	Fall to spring for gem shows and to avoid the searing summer heat.

In western Arizona the scenery comes with a few quirky sides: a notorious prison, a tiny chapel, a lonely ghost town and the actual London Bridge. There are some lonely stretches in this dessicated part of the state, it can't be denied. But, in between, there's plenty to savor, and some classic highway towns in which to hang your hat and kick up your heels. Plus, you can marvel at one of the greatest engineering feats in the USA.

Link your trip

1 Four Corners Cruise

From Hoover Dam, drive northwest 33 miles on Hwy 93 to Sin City to kick off a classic Southwest loop.

2 Route 66: The Southwest

North of Lake Havasu, leave I-40 W at exit 1, join Route 66 then climb to see the begging burros of Oatman.

01 YUMA

This sprawling city at the confluence of the Gila and Colorado Rivers was home to Arizona's notorious **territorial prison** (azstateparks.com), which was nicknamed 'Hellhole of the West,' in part because of the city's blazing temperatures. Between 1876 and 1909, 3069 convicts were incarcerated here for crimes ranging from murder to 'seduction under the promise of marriage.'

Today, the prison is Yuma's star attraction. Walking around the yard, behind iron-grille doors and

SERGII FIGURNYI/SHUTTERSTOCK ©

Hoover Dam (p84)

into cells crowded with stacked bunks, you might get retroactively scared straight. And that's without mentioning the Dark Cell, a cave-like room where troublesome prisoners were locked together in a 5ft-high metal cage. Step inside and tremble. To delve deeper into Yuma's frontier history make time for the nearby **Yuma Quartermaster Depot State Park** (azstateparks.com/yuma-quartermaster).

A new trail system along the adjacent Colorado River links the prison with downtown's **Gateway Park** and the restored **Yuma East Wetlands**.

THE DRIVE
Jump onto US 95 N, following the railroad tracks and sandy hills to complete the 17-mile drive to the next stop.

02 PAUSE-REST-WORSHIP CHURCH

Northeast of Yuma, a tiny white-and-blue **chapel** (S Ave 13E) sits modestly on a patch of nondescript farmland. The 8ft-by-12ft structure seats about 12 and has stained-glass windows. A local farmer built the original in 1995 as a memorial to his wife, Loren Pratts; when a freak storm destroyed it in 2011, the local community rallied to rebuild it. If you're feeling contemplative, pull over, step inside and ponder the meaning of neighborliness.

THE DRIVE
Continue north on Hwy 95. After 25 miles turn right onto Castle Dome Mine Rd (mile marker 55) and drive 10 miles, the last seven of which are unpaved but well maintained. The drive takes you south of the Yuma Proving Ground, where the US Army tests weapon systems and munitions, and then into the Kofa National Wildlife Refuge.

03 CASTLE DOME MINE

Meticulously reconstructed using as many original artifacts as possible, the remote **museum** (castledomemuseum.org) here showcases an evocative mining town that was founded in 1864 during a silver boom.

There are about 50 buildings in all, many of them retrieved from nearby mines. As you walk from the saloon to the blacksmith shop you can read about the people who used to live here. Also displayed is the world's oldest pair of Levi's, dating from 1890. A separate walking tour passes mine shafts and an old cemetery. Cash or check only.

THE DRIVE
Return to Hwy 95 and continue north 50 miles to the I-10. Cross the interstate, turn left on W Main St and follow it about a mile.

04 QUARTZSITE

The desert here floods with RVs in January and February, when visitors arrive for rock and mineral shows. Quartzsite's most curious monument is a small stone pyramid topped by a metal camel in the town graveyard. This memorial is for Haiji Ali, a Syrian camel driver who arrived in 1856 to help with a US Army experiment using camels to transport goods across the desert. The experiment didn't work but Ali, nicknamed Hi Jolly, became a prospector. He died here in 1902.

THE DRIVE
Hwy 95 N enters the Colorado River Indian Reservation 25 miles north of Quartzsite. Buy gas and fast food in Parker. To drive over Parker Dam (the world's deepest dam, with 73% of its 320ft height beneath the riverbed) turn left onto Parker Dam Rd about 15 miles north. Return to Hwy 95 N to finish the 57-mile leg.

05 BILL WILLIAMS NATIONAL WILDLIFE REFUGE

Abutting **Cattail Cove**, where the Bill Williams River meets Lake Havasu, is this calm **wildlife refuge** (fws.gov/refuge/bill-williams-river), which helps protect the unique transition zone between the Mojave and Sonoran desert ecosystems. On a finger of land pointing into the lake, there's a 1.4-mile interpretive trail through a botanic garden of native flora, with shaded benches and access to fishing platforms. Endangered birds like to roost in the largest cottonwood/willow grove along the entire length of the Colorado River. The entrance is between miles 161 and 162.

Photo opportunity
Hoover Dam from the Mike O'Callaghan–Pat Tillman Memorial Bridge.

THE DRIVE
With Lake Havasu to the west, drive north 24 miles to Lake Havasu City.

06 LAKE HAVASU CITY

Gracefully arched, Georgian-era **London Bridge** may be one of Arizona's most incongruous tourist sites, but it's also among its most popular. It's a bona fide original, having spanned the Thames from 1831 to 1967, when it was quite literally falling down (as predicted in the nursery rhyme). Purchased by a developer, it was dismantled and reassembled in the Arizona desert. Day-trippers come by the busload to walk across it and soak up faux British 'heritage' in the kitschy-quaint **English Village**.

The lake is the other major draw. Formed in 1938 by the construction of Parker Dam, it's beloved by water rats, especially students on spring break (roughly March to April) and summer-heat refugees from Phoenix and beyond.

The helpful **visitor center** (golakehavasu.com) sits at the northeastern corner of the bridge.

THE DRIVE
Drive north to I-40 W. From I-40, continue west to Needles, just over the California border, and join Hwy 95 to complete the 66-mile northern run.

07 BULLHEAD CITY & LAUGHLIN

Named for a rock that resembled the head of a snoozing bull (now under Lake Mojave), Bullhead City began as a construction camp for Davis Dam, built in the 1940s. The town survives today primarily because of the casinos across the Colorado River in Laughlin, which has a little more sizzle. The twin town was founded in 1964 by gaming impresario Don Laughlin (a high-school dropout from Minnesota) and is a good stop for a cheap sleep and a little gambling action.

THE DRIVE
Follow Hwy 95 N to Hwy 68 E. It's not the quickest route but it leads through a glorious, rocky pass to Route 66 hot spot Kingman, where museums, vintage motels and good food await. From Kingman, take Hwy 93 N. After crossing into Nevada, take exit 2 for NV 172, the dam-access road. The distance is 103 miles all up.

08 HOOVER DAM

Completed in 1936, this mighty **dam** (usbr.gov/lc/hooverdam), on the Arizona–Nevada border, created Lake Mead, which has 700 miles of shoreline. The 726ft concrete structure was the Colorado River's first major dam, and its graceful curve and art-deco style contrast superbly with the stark landscape.

Guided-tour options include the 30-minute power-plant tour or the more in-depth, one-hour Hoover Dam tour. Tickets for both are sold at the visitor center. If you're interested in history and construction facts, spring for the longer tour. Tickets for the power-plant tour can also be purchased online.

The nearby **Mike O'Callaghan–Pat Tillman Memorial Bridge** (p26) features a pedestrian walkway with perfect views upstream of Hoover Dam. Nearby **Boulder City** is a pleasant place to spend the night.

THE DRIVE

Return to Hwy 93 W. Drive about 1.5 miles to Lakeshore Dr and turn right.

09 LAKE MEAD

Lake Mead and Hoover Dam are the most visited sites within the **Lake Mead National Recreation Area** (nps.gov/lake), which encompasses 110-mile-long Lake Mead, 67-mile-long Lake Mohave and many miles of desert around the lakes. The excellent **Lake Mead Visitor Center** (nps.gov/lake), halfway between Boulder City and Hoover Dam, has information on recreation and desert life. Here, hikers and cyclists can pick up a map of the **River Mountains Loop Trail** (rivermountainstrail.com), which offers 32 miles of trails around the lake. From there, North Shore Rd winds around the lake and makes a great scenic drive.

DETOUR

Valley of Fire State Park

Start: 09 Lake Mead

For a scenic drive with an even more scenic end point, follow **Lakeshore Scenic Dr** northwest from the Alan Bible Visitor Center to Northshore Rd, heading northeast along Lake Mead.

At Hwy 169, turn left for the **Valley of Fire State Park** (parks.nv.gov/parks/valley-of-fire), a fantasyland of wondrous shapes carved in vibrant red sandstone by the erosive forces of wind and water. Hwy 169 runs past the visitor center, which displays excellent desert-life exhibits, sells books and maps, and has information about hikes and ranger-led activities.

London Bridge, Lake Havasu City

10

ARIZONA

Southwest Indian Nations Sojourn

DURATION	DISTANCE	GREAT FOR
3–4 days	345 miles / 555km	Outdoors, history and culture, food and drink

BEST TIME TO GO	Navajo rodeos are held most weekends May through September; the Navajo Nation Fair is in September.

American Indian history is the draw on this busy trip that rolls north from Phoenix to cliff dwellings, a lava field and trading posts before ending at remote and beautiful Canyon de Chelly. Here, indigenous cultures flourished between 100 and 1400 CE. Their cliff dwellings, irrigation canals and petroglyphs stretch from the Phoenix area north into the Navajo Nation. The descendants of these peoples occupy their land to this day.

Link your trip

1 Four Corners Cruise

On the Navajo Reservation, take Hwy 160 east from Tuba City to link to the incomparable Monument Valley.

5 Fantastic Canyon Voyage

From Cameron, Hwy 64 rolls west to the South Rim of the Grand Canyon National Park.

01 PHOENIX

For a fascinating introduction to the American Indian nations of the Southwest, visit Phoenix's wonderful **Heard Museum** (heard.org). The sheer imagination and craftsmanship of the kachina (Hopi spirit doll) collection is particularly memorable. More somber but equally unforgettable is the 'Boarding School Experience,' a permanent display recounting the controversial federal policy of removing American Indian children from their families and sending them to remote boarding schools to 'Americanize' them.

SERGII FIGURNYI/SHUTTERSTOCK ©

BEST FOR HISTORY

Phoenix's Heard Museum – a glorious trove of Southwestern Indian artifacts.

Navajo hogans (p89)

Explore Phoenix's Scottsdale neighborhood on a walking tour.

THE DRIVE
Take I-17 93 miles north on the first leg. Fort Verde State Historic Park at exit 287 is the site of an 1873 US Army fort, built during the Indian Wars. Further north, exit 289 and W Middle Verde Rd lead half a mile east to Montezuma Castle Rd.

02 MONTEZUMA CASTLE NATIONAL MONUMENT

This stunningly well-preserved Sinagua **cliff dwelling** (nps.gov/moca) dates back 1000 years. The name refers to its castle-like location high on a cliff – early explorers thought the five-story-high pueblo was Aztec and dubbed it Montezuma. A museum interprets the archaeology of the site, which is visible from a short, wheelchair-accessible trail (which doesn't lead up to the protected site itself).

If you're interested in prehistoric irrigation techniques (and who isn't?) drive north to exit 293 to see the **Montezuma Well** (nps.gov/moca), a 470ft-wide sinkhole surrounded by Sinaguan and Hohokam dwellings.

THE DRIVE
Return to I-17 and drive north. At exit 298, FR 618 leads east to petroglyphs at V-Bar-V Heritage Site. Just south of Flagstaff, on the brink of the lushly wooded Colorado Plateau, turn right onto I-40 and drive to exit 204, then follow Walnut Canyon Rd for 3 miles. All up, a 70-mile drive.

03 WALNUT CANYON NATIONAL MONUMENT

With so many big-name attractions nearby, the beautiful and strangely peaceful **Walnut Canyon** (nps.gov/waca) calmly sidesteps the limelight. The Sinaguan cliff dwellings here are set in the nearly vertical walls of a small limestone butte amid a forested canyon of supreme beauty. The mile-long **Island Trail** steeply descends 185ft (beware – this means more than 200 stairs) and passes 25 rooms built under the natural overhangs of the curvaceous butte. The shorter, wheelchair-accessible **Rim Trail** is still worth the effort, offering several views of the cliff dwellings from across the canyon.

THE DRIVE
Follow Walnut Canyon Rd across I-40 and turn left onto Route 66. Follow Route 66 west to Hwy 89, from where it's about 12 miles to Park Loop Rd, and only a little further to Sunset Crater.

04 SUNSET CRATER VOLCANO NATIONAL MONUMENT

Some time around 1064CE a volcano erupted here, spewing ash over 800 sq miles, spawning the Kana-A lava flow and leaving behind the 8029ft, soot-black Sunset Crater. The eruption forced farmers to vacate lands they had cultivated for 400 years, as subsequent fulminations continued for more than 200 years.

Covered by a single entrance fee ($20 for one car, valid for seven days), both Sunset Crater Volcano and Wupatki National Monument lie along Park Loop Rd, a well-marked, 35-mile circuit east of Hwy 89.

The **Sunset Crater Volcano National Monument Visitor Center** (nps.gov/sucr) houses a seismograph and other exhibits pertaining to volcanology. Viewpoints and a 1-mile interpretive trail through the buckled landscape of the **Bonito lava flow** (formed c 1180) spotlight volcanic features. There's also a 0.3-mile, wheelchair-accessible loop.

THE DRIVE
Continue 16 miles north on Park Loop Rd to the Wupatki National Monument Visitor Center.

05 WUPATKI NATIONAL MONUMENT

The first eruptions here enriched the soil, and ancestors of today's Hopi and Zuni people returned to farm the land in the early 1100s. By 1180, thousands were living here in advanced multistory buildings, but by 1250 their pueblos stood abandoned.

About 2700 of these structures lie within **Wupatki** (nps.gov/wupa), though only a few are open to the public (others can be visited by those organized enough to secure a place on one of the National Park Service tours). A short self-guided tour of the largest dwelling, **Wupatki Pueblo**, begins behind the visitor center.

THE DRIVE
Return to Hwy 89 N, which enters the Navajo Reservation just beyond Gray Mountain. Cameron Trading

SMARTYUNKNOWN/SHUTTERSTOCK ©

Wupatki National Monument

Post, which has a huge selection of American Indian crafts, is just north of the junction with Hwy 64. Continue on Hwy 89 N for almost 16 miles. Turn right onto Hwy 160 and drive another 10 miles to Tuba City.

06 TUBA CITY & MOENKOPI

Tuba City, named for 19th-century Hopi chief Tuve (or Toova) is the largest single community in the Navajo Nation. To the southeast is the village of Moenkopi, a small Hopi enclave surrounded by Navajo land. For details about cultural protocol, visit explorenavajo.com, and remember that alcohol is not permitted on the reservation.

Tuba City is home to the interesting **Explore Navajo Interactive Museum** (explorenavajo.com), where you'll discover why the Navajo call themselves the 'People of the Fourth World,' and learn about the tragic Long Walk. Contemporary Navajo life is also explored.

Next door, and included in your entry fee, is a small museum about the Navajo Code Talkers, who provided invaluable service to the American effort in WWII. Visits wrap up in the historic Tuba City Trading Post, which dates to the 1870s. For more information about exploring the Navajo Reservation and obtaining the permits required for hiking and camping, visit navajonationparks.org.

THE DRIVE
Drive east 64 miles on Hwy 264 to Second Mesa.

DETOUR
Navajo National Monument
Start: 06 Tuba City & Moenkopi

The sublimely well-preserved Ancestral Puebloan cliff dwellings of **Betatkin** and **Keet Seel** are protected at the **Navajo National Monument** (nps.gov/nava) and can only be reached on foot. The site, administered by the National Park Service, is 9 miles north of Hwy 160 at the end of paved Hwy 564.

For a distant glimpse of Betatkin follow the easy **Sandal Trail** about half a mile from the visitor center. Betatkin is reached on a ranger-led 3-mile round-trip hike from the visitor center. Carry plenty of water, especially if setting off on the steep and strenuous 17-mile round-trip hike to the beautiful Keet Seel. The trail, open late May to early September, is limited to 20 people daily and requires a backcountry permit. Make reservations starting in late January.

Photo opportunity
The ancient cliff-hugging adobe houses of Montezuma Castle.

07 HOPI NATION

Three rocky, sand-colored hilltops, named First, Second and Third Mesa, form the heart of the Hopi Nation, which is completely surrounded by the much larger **Navajo Nation**. Descendants of the Ancestral Puebloans, the Hopi are one of the most untouched tribes in the US. Their village of Old Oraibi may be the oldest continuously inhabited settlement in North America.

On Second Mesa, the **Hopi Cultural Center** provides food and lodging, and is the home of the small **Hopi Museum**, with walls full of historical photographs and cultural exhibits. The Hopi have a deep and distinguished tradition of decorative arts and crafts.

Be aware that photographs, sketching and recording are not allowed on the reservation.

THE DRIVE
Drive 57 miles east on Hwy 264 to Hwy 191. If you continue a further 36 miles along Hwy 264, you come to the Navajo capital of Window Rock, where the excellent Navajo Nation Museum is located. For Canyon de Chelly, follow Hwy 191 north to Chinle and turn right onto Indian Rte 7 to complete this 91-mile leg.

08 CANYON DE CHELLY NATIONAL MONUMENT

Inhabited for 5000 years, the sacred and beautiful Canyon de Chelly (pronounced 'd-shay') shelters prehistoric rock art and 1000-year-old Ancestral Puebloan dwellings. Navajo families still farm the narrow strip of land at the canyon's base.

The national monument is on private Navajo land, but is run by the National Park Service. The 16-mile **South Rim Drive** runs along the canyon's scenic lip and has the most dramatic viewpoints. It dead-ends at the spectacular **Spider Rock Overlook**. For the most part the **North Rim Drive** follows a side canyon called **Canyon del Muerto**. Viewpoints at the **Antelope House Overlook** offer lofty cliff-top views of a natural rock fortress and cliff dwellings.

Only enter hogans (traditional homes) with a guide and don't take photographs without permission. To travel inside the canyon, choose a guide from the list provided by the **visitor center** (nps.gov/cach); it's also on the park website.

UTAH
COLORADO
Walsenburg
Alamosa
South San Juan Wilderness
Ute Mountain Indian Reservation
Trinidad
Comanche National Grassland
25
Shiprock
Chama
Raton
Capulin Volcano National Monument
Gorbernador
Latir Peak Wilderness
Des Moines
Farmington
Carson National Forest
Maxwell
Clayton
Navajo Indian Reservation
Taos
Springer
Rita Blanca National Grassland
Newcomb
13
11
15
412
Kiowa National Grassland West
Naschitti
Chaco Culture National Historical Park
Cuba
Los Alamos
Santa Fe National Forest
491
550
Wagon Mound
14
Santa Fe
Gallup
San Ysidro
Las Vegas
Thoreau
40
Laguna Pueblo
Variadero
Logan
19
Ramah
285
Tucumcari
Zuni Pueblo
El Morro
Albuquerque
Santa Rosa
San Jon
Correo
Cuervo
Zuni Pueblo
Acoma Pueblo
Isleta Pueblo
54
ARIZONA
Belen
Vaughn
Fort Sumner
Clovis
60
Quemado
12
Cibola National Forest
Datil
Portales
Socorro
NEW MEXICO
Mesa
Luna
380
Kenna
Apache Kid Wilderness
Rio Grande
Gila National Forest
Carrizozo
Capitan
18
Lincoln
Elephant Butte Lake
Roswell
Chloride
17
Ruidoso
20
Tatum
Gila Wilderness
Truth or Consequences
Tularosa
Silver City
Caballo
White Sands National Park
16
Hope
Artesia
Lovington
Alamogordo
Hobbs
Hatch
Lincoln National Forest
62
Carlsbad
Lordsburg
Eunice
Orogrande
Las Cruces
Whites City
Malaga
Deming
10
Carlsbad Caverns National Park
Rodeo
USA
Guadalupe Mountains National Park
Kermit
El Paso
MEXICO
Ciudad Juarez
Coronado National Forest
Pecos
TEXAS
Van Horn
0 200 km
0 100 miles

SEAN PAVONE/SHUTTERSTOCK ©

Albuquerque (p102)

New Mexico

Explore

New Mexico

New Mexico is Southwestern USA at its best, with landscapes on a grand scale haunted by some truly legendary historical figures. The technicolor landscapes here inspired Georgia O'Keeffe, and you'll drive within reach of adobe villages tucked beneath the 13,000ft Sangre de Cristo range and over juniper-speckled plains that roll to infinity. You'll also drive what might be the oldest road in the US and follow in the footsteps of Geronimo and Billy the Kid. You're never far from great hiking and camping or platters of equally legendary New Mexico cuisine. And when you're done, you may want to turn around and experience it all again.

Santa Fe

Santa Fe has a beguiling character all its own. Part of that comes from its historical story and the adobe architecture of its neighborhoods. Or the full calendar of fun festivals. Or Santa Fe's famously artsy inclinations. Or its cooling altitude at over 7000ft above sea level. Or the eclectic museums. Then there's the extraordinary array of activities you can join, accommodations for every budget and from every genre, and simply fabulous restaurants. What's not to like?

Albuquerque

There's something about Albuquerque. A bustling desert crossroads, Albuquerque is the right mix of urban and wild: the pink hues of the Sandia Mountains at sunset, the Rio Grande's cottonwood bosque, or the city's Route 66 diners. Excellent hiking and mountain-biking trails surround Albuquerque, it's an emerging cultural powerhouse, and it's a fine place to order a plate of red chile enchiladas and a local craft beer. Best of all, you can still hear the coyotes howl when the sun goes down.

Las Cruces

In New Mexico's far south, beneath the fluted Organ Mountains and standing at the crossroads of the I-10 and I-25, Las Cruces offers convenience, beautiful surrounds and year-round sunshine. Spicy New Mexican cooking dominates menus here, and there are numerous places to stay, glassy blue skies, flowering cacti, and a backdrop of rippling red mountains and desert lowlands.

WHEN TO GO

New Mexico is best from mid-August to October, with gorgeous weather, sunflowers and fiestas as you bask in the sunshine. Other US states would die to have New Mexico's weather from May to July, so they're also great months to drive here. You can ski the Sangre de Cristos in December, but driving the high passes can be problematic.

Taos

Few places capture the magic of New Mexico quite like Taos. A quieter alternative to Santa Fe in the state's north, Taos remains forever under the spell of the powerful landscape that surrounds it: 12,300ft snow-capped peaks rise behind town, while a sage-speckled plateau unrolls to the west before plunging 800ft straight down into the Rio Grande Gorge. And then there are the sunsets, classic mud-brick buildings, fabulous museums, quirky cafes, character-filled accommodations and excellent restaurants.

Silver City

Once a frontier silver mining hub, now a university town, quirky Silver City has a historic downtown area awash in Victorian and red adobe buildings. The whole place still reeks of the Wild West: Billy the Kid spent some of his childhood here, and some of his haunts still lurk amid the new coffee shops and art galleries. Silver City also lies on the cusp of 15 mountain ranges, four rivers, the City of Rocks State Park and the Gila National Forest. With historic hotels and decent restaurants, it's a fine place to rest from life on the road.

TRANSPORT

Most travelers fly into Albuquerque International Sunport (ABQ), but some flights also land in Santa Fe (SAF). Amtrak train services include the Southwest Chief, between Chicago and Los Angeles, stopping in Lamy (for Santa Fe), Albuquerque and Gallup. A fast and amazingly inexpensive light-rail system, the Rail Runner, connects Albuquerque and Santa Fe.

WHAT'S ON

Fiestas de Taos

New Mexican music, parades and dance fill the streets of Taos in mid-July.

Santa Fe Fiesta & Burning of Zozobra

This 10-day Santa Fe celebration in early September includes concerts, a candlelit procession, Pet Parade and unmissable effigy torching.

International Balloon Fiesta

The world's largest balloon festival happens in Albuquerque in October. You haven't lived until you've seen a three-story-tall Tony the Tiger land in your hotel courtyard.

WHERE TO STAY

For places to stay with more than a veneer of historic charm, try Taos or Silver City. For somewhere with a lot more choice, there are larger cities like Santa Fe and Albuquerque. Otherwise, New Mexico's best sleeping options range from national forest campgrounds and backcountry yurts to simple cabins, peaceful hot-spring resorts and the occasional ranch property. If you're road-tripping, you'll have no trouble finding well-known chains for all budgets in even the smallest towns. But there is also a sprinkling of historic hotels and boutique B&Bs if you plan ahead.

Resources

New Mexico State Parks (emnrd.nm.gov) Info on state parks, with a link to campsite reservations.

New Mexico Tourism (newmexico.org) Information on destination planning, activities and events.

Recreation.gov (recreation.gov) Reservations for national park and forest campsites and tours.

National Park Service (nps.gov) Lots of info about New Mexico's national parks.

11

NEW MEXICO

High & Low Roads to Taos

BEST FOR CULTURE

The 'miracle church' – and the chile – in Chimayó.

DURATION	DISTANCE	GREAT FOR
1–4 days	150 miles / 241km	History and culture, food and drink

BEST TIME TO GO	June to March, when temps are not too hot.

El Santuario de Chimayó

Santa Fe. Taos. The Rio Grande. The Sangre de Cristos. And all the adobe villages, galleries, Spanish Colonial churches and burrito stands in between make this loop a classic. You'll rise from scrub-and-sandstone desert into ponderosa forests until you reach the Taos Plateau. Then head back south through the ruggedly sculpted Rio Grande Gorge, with the river coursing alongside you.

Link your trip

12 El Camino Real & Turquoise Trail
A natural segue south from Santa Fe along the historic Rio Grande road.

15 Enchanted Circle & Eastern Sangres
Loop north from Taos, over the mountains and back again.

01 SANTA FE

Walking among the historic adobe neighborhoods, and even around the tourist-filled plaza, there's no denying that 400-year-old Santa Fe has a timeless, earthy soul. Known as 'the city different,' it seamlessly blends historical and contemporary styles and casts a spell that's hard to resist: it's the second-oldest city in the US, the oldest state capital, and throws the oldest annual party (Fiesta). It also boasts the second-largest art market in the nation, plus gourmet restaurants, world-class museums, opera, spas and more. At 7000ft above sea

level, Santa Fe is also the highest state capital in the US, and a fantastic base for hiking, mountain biking, backpacking and skiing. The plaza area has the highest concentration of sights but it's also worth a trip to Museum Hill, where you'll find the fantastical **Museum of International Folk Art** (internationalfolkart.org) and the excellent **Museum of Indian Arts & Culture** (indianartsandculture.org), among others.

THE DRIVE
For this 28-mile leg, take Hwy 84/285 north, then exit right onto Hwy 503 towards Nambé. Turn left onto Juan Medina Rd, toward the Santauario de Chimayó.

02 CHIMAYÓ

Tucked into this little village is the so-called 'Lourdes of America,' **El Santuario de Chimayó** (holychimayo.us), one of the most important cultural sites in New Mexico. In 1816, this two-towered adobe chapel was built over a spot of earth said to have miraculous healing properties. Even today, the faithful come to rub the *tierra bendita* (holy dirt) from a small pit inside the church on whatever hurts; some mix it with water and drink it. The walls of the dirt room are covered with crutches, left behind by those healed by the dirt. During Holy Week, about 30,000 pilgrims walk to Chimayó from Santa Fe, Albuquerque and beyond in the largest Catholic pilgrimage in the US. The artwork in the church is worth the trip on its own.

Chimayó also has a centuries-old tradition of producing some of the finest weavings in the area and has a handful of family-run galleries. Irvin Trujillo, a seventh-generation weaver, whose carpets are in collections at the Smithsonian in Washington, DC, and the Museum of Fine Arts

High/Low Road Festivals

Try to catch – or avoid, if you hate crowds – some of the highlights from around the year on the High and Low Roads. Check websites for exact dates each year:

Easter (Chimayó) – March/April

Taos Pueblo Pow-Wow (taos.org/events/annual-event/taos-pueblo-pow-wow) – July

International Folk Art Market (folkartmarket.org; Santa Fe) – July

Spanish Market (spanishcolonial.org; Santa Fe) – July

Indian Market (swaia.org; Santa Fe) – August

Santa Fe Fiesta (santafefiesta.org) – September

High Road Art Tour (highroadnewmexico.com; Hwy 76 to Peñasco) – September

Dixon Studio Tour (dixonarts.org) – November

Christmas on Canyon Rd – December

in Santa Fe, works out of his gallery **Centinela Traditional Arts** (chimayoweavers.com). Naturally dyed blankets, vests and pillows are sold, and you can watch the artists weaving on handlooms.

THE DRIVE
Follow Hwy 76 east for a few miles, and take the right-side turnoff to Córdova.

03 CÓRDOVA

Down in the Rio Quemado Valley, this little town is best known for its unpainted, austere *santos* (saints) carvings created by local masters such as George Lopez, Jose Delores Lopez and Sabinita Lopez Ortiz – all members of the same artistic family. Stop and see their work at the **Sabinita Lopez Ortiz shop** – one of a few galleries in town.

THE DRIVE
Hop back on Hwy 76 north, and climb higher into the Sangre de Cristo Mountains, for about 4 miles.

04 TRUCHAS

Rural New Mexico at its most sincere is showcased in Truchas, originally settled by the Spaniards in the 18th century. Robert Redford's *The Milagro Beanfield War* was filmed here (but don't bother with the movie – the book it's based on, by John Nichols, is waaaay better). Narrow roads, many unpaved, wend between century-old adobes. Fields of grass and alfalfa spread toward the sheer walls and plunging ridges that define the western flank of the Truchas Peaks. Between the rundown homes are some wonderful art galleries, which double as workshops for local weavers, painters, sculptors and other artists. The best place to get an overview of who's painting/sculpting/carving/weaving what is the **High Road Marketplace**, a cooperative art gallery with a huge variety of work by area artists.

THE DRIVE
Continue north on Hwy 76 for around 8 miles, transecting the little valleys of Ojo Sarco and Cañada de los Alamos.

05 LAS TRAMPAS

Completed in 1780 and constantly defended against Apache raids, the **Church of San José de Gracia** is considered one of the finest surviving 18th-century churches in the USA and is a National Historic Landmark. Original paintings and carvings remain in excellent condition, and self-flagellation bloodstains from Los Hermanos Penitentes (a 19th-century religious order with a strong following in the northern mountains of New Mexico) are still visible. On your way out of town, look right to see the amazing irrigation aqueduct, carved from tree trunks!

THE DRIVE
Continue north on Hwy 76, through lovely Chamisal. At the T, turn right onto Hwy 75 and stay on it through Peñasco and Vadito. At Hwy 518, turn left toward Taos. At the end of the road, turn right on Paseo del Pueblo Sur/Hwy 68 and take it on into Taos – around 32 miles in total.

06 TAOS

Taos is a place undeniably dominated by the power of its landscape: 12,300ft often-snowcapped peaks rise behind town, a sage-speckled plateau unrolls to the west before plunging 800ft straight down into the Rio Grande Gorge. The sky can be a searing sapphire

NATURE CALLS

Want to see the scenery without a pane of glass in front of your face? Off the High Road, take a stroll on the **Santa Barbara Trail**, which follows a trout-filled creek through mixed forest into the Pecos Wilderness; it's pretty flat and easygoing. To reach the trailhead, take Hwy 73 from Peñasco and follow the signs.

Off the Low Road, turn onto Hwy 570 at Pilar and check out the **Orilla Verde Recreation Area**, where you can hang out or camp along the Rio Grande (or tube or fish in it). Hike up to the rim on Old 570, a dirt road blocked by a landslide, with expansive vistas of the Taos Plateau and the Sangre de Cristos.

Some of the best views in the state are from the top of **Lake Peak** (12,409ft), which can be reached on a day hike starting at the Santa Fe Ski Basin.

From Taos Ski Valley, you can day hike to the top of **Wheeler Peak** (13,161ft), New Mexico's highest summit (the views are pretty good up there, too). For trail maps and more information, go to the **Travel Bug** (mapsofnewmexico.com) bookshop in Santa Fe or the Taos **Visitor Center** (taos.org).

Church of San José de Gracia

WHY I LOVE THIS TRIP

Christopher Pitts, writer

If you had to pick one trip that would make you want to immediately pack your bags and move to New Mexico, this would be it: the state's two most enchanting cities, the historic Taos Pueblo, the cultural legacy of El Santuario de Chimayó and the unique, piquant flavor of rural life and New Mexican cuisine – all set against a continuous panorama of spellbinding landscapes.

blue or an ominous parade of rumbling thunderheads. And then there are the sunsets…

The pueblo here is one of the oldest continuously inhabited communities in the United States and it roots the town in a long history with a rich cultural legacy – including conquistadors, Catholicism and cowboys. Taos remains a relaxed and eccentric place, with classic mud-brick buildings, quirky cafes and excellent restaurants. It's both rural and worldly, and a little bit otherworldly.

Photo opportunity

Capture the gorge and mountains at once, from Hwy 68 near Taos.

The best thing to do is walk around the plaza area soaking in the aura of the place. But you also won't want to miss **Taos Pueblo** (taospueblo.com). Built around 1450 and continuously inhabited ever since, it's the largest existing multistoried pueblo structure in the USA and one of the best surviving examples of traditional adobe construction. Also well worth a visit is the **Millicent Rogers Museum** (millicentrogers.org), filled with pottery, jewelry, baskets and textiles from the private collection of a model and oil heiress who moved to Taos in 1947 and acquired one of the best collections of American Indian and Spanish Colonial art in the USA.

Taos Pueblo

DON'T MISS:

Santuario de Chimayó

This adobe church built in 1816 is home to miracle healings and is the site of the largest Catholic pilgrimage in the US.

THE DRIVE

On this 26-mile leg, cruise the Low Road back toward Santa Fe by taking Hwy 68 south. Just before the road drops downhill, there's a large pullout with huge views, so hop out and see what you're leaving behind. Then head down into the Rio Grande Gorge. Go left on Hwy 75 to Dixon.

07 DIXON

This small agricultural and artistic community is spread along the gorgeous Rio Embudo valley. It's famous for its apples but plenty of other crops are grown here too, including some of the grapes used by two award-winning local wineries, **Vivac** (vivacwinery.com) and **La Chiripada** (lachiripada.com), both of which have tasting rooms. In summer and fall, there's a farmers market on Wednesday afternoons, with food fresh from the fields. Our favorite art gallery is actually on Hwy 68, in Rinconada, just north of Hwy 75: **Rift Gallery** (saxstonecarving.com) features masterful ceramics and stonework. On the first weekend in November, local artists open their homes and studios to the public in New Mexico's oldest studio tour. In summer, ask at the local food co-op and some kind soul might point you to the waterfalls, up a nearby dirt road.

THE DRIVE

Back on Hwy 68, head south along the river, through Embudo (a great lunch stop) and out of the gorge. Continue through Española, where you'll meet Hwy 84/285, which you can take back to Santa Fe. This leg is around 47 miles.

ROSCHETZKY PHOTOGRAPHY/SHUTTERSTOCK ©

Taos mountains

WINTER THRILLS

Some of the biggest winter draws to this part of New Mexico are skiing and snowboarding, and **Taos Ski Valley** (skitaos.org) is the premier place to hit the slopes. There's just something about the abundant powder, wicked steeps and laid-back atmosphere that makes this mountain a wintery heaven-on-earth – that is, if heaven has a 3274ft vertical drop.

Offering some of the most difficult terrain in the US, it's a fantastic place to zip down steep tree glades into untouched powder bowls. Seasoned skiers luck out, with more than half of the 70-plus trails at the Taos Ski Valley ranked expert; but there's also an award-winning ski school, so complete beginners thrive here too. The resort has a peak elevation of 12,481ft and gets an average of more than 300in of snowfall annually. The resort also has a skier-cross obstacle course at its popular terrain park.

That said, **Ski Santa Fe** (skisantafe.com) is no slouch. Less than 30 minutes from the Santa Fe plaza, it boasts the same fluffy powder (though usually a little less), with an even higher base elevation (10,350ft). Briefly admire the awesome desert and mountain vistas, then fly down chutes, steep bump runs or long groomers. The resort caters to families and expert skiers alike with its varied terrain. The quality and length of the ski season can vary wildly from year to year depending on how much snow the mountain gets (you can almost always count on a good storm in late March).

12

NEW MEXICO

El Camino Real & Turquoise Trail

DURATION	DISTANCE	GREAT FOR
3–4 days	295 miles / 475km	History and culture, food and drink

BEST TIME TO GO	September until December is best for festivals.

Historic sights, hot springs, wildlife sanctuaries and well-known cities line this route first established over 400 years ago – the Royal Road. The trip mostly follows New Mexico's main arteries north. Except when you're driving a dirt road through a section of desert called the *Jornada del Muerto* (Journey of Death). Or meandering through a bird sanctuary. Or winding past the Ortiz Mountains along the legendary Turquoise Trail.

Link your trip

11 High & Low Roads to Taos

Continue north from Santa Fe on this classic route into the soul of New Mexico.

13 Georgia O'Keeffe Country

From Santa Fe, head 48 miles northwest on Hwy 84 to Abiquiú for the state's most colorful trip.

01 LAS CRUCES

New Mexico's second-largest city, Las Cruces isn't much of a charmer, but before you hit the road take a stroll around the **Old Mesilla plaza**, which still exudes a sense of history even if it's only 160 years old. Billy the Kid was sentenced to death in the courthouse here.

THE DRIVE

Take I-25 north to exit 32, then turn right onto dirt County Rd 71/72 and follow it for 5.2 miles. Then, turn left at an intersection, heading north on CR E 070 toward Engle.

BEST FOR BIRDERS

Cranes and more at Bosque del Apache.

Elk, Bosque del Apache (p102)

Go 14 miles, driving around the aptly named Point of Rocks, to Yost Escarpment. It's 45 miles in all.

DETOUR
Hatch
Start: 01 Las Cruces

The town of Hatch, 40 miles north of Las Cruces up I-25, is known as the 'Chile Capital of the World,' sitting at the heart of New Mexico's chile-growing country. New Mexican chiles didn't originate here – most have centuries-old roots in the northern farming villages around Chimayó and Española – but the earth and irrigation in these parts proved perfect for mass production. Recent harvests have declined sharply, as imported chile is encroaching on the market, but the town still clings to its title. Even if you miss the Labor Day Weekend **Chile Festival** (hatchchilefest.com), pull off the interstate at exit 41 and pop into **Sparky's Burgers** (sparkysburgers.com) for what might be the best green chile cheeseburger in the state, served with casual pride.

To get here, when driving north from Las Cruces, skip exit 32 to the Jornada del Muerto and continue another 8.5 miles on I-25 to Hatch. Then, after getting your chile fix, head back to the Jornada exit and continue along the route – or blow off the desert road and continue on I-25 to rejoin the drive in Truth or Consequences.

02 JORNADA DEL MUERTO

This 90-mile, waterless stretch of desert was the most feared section of the Camino Real. Over the years, hundreds perished while crossing it. Travelers back then would cover as much ground as possible at night, but you'll want to see the desert basin dotted with creosote bushes and the angular uplift of the San Andres Mountains. Pull over at Yost Escarpment and walk an easy 1.5-mile (one-way) trail into the Jornada that takes you along the actual Camino Real route. There are interpretive signs along the way. In summer, try to avoid midday.

TURQUOISE TRAIL GEMS

Along with the main stops on the Turquoise Trail, you won't want to miss the **Tinkertown Museum** (tinkertown.com) – one of the weirdest in the state. Huge, detailed hand-carved dioramas of Western towns, circuses and other bizarre scenes come alive with a quarter, and signs encourage visitors to 'eat more mangoes naked.' It's just outside Cedar Crest on Hwy 536.

But wait, there's more: one of our favorite restaurants ever. The **San Marcos Cafe** feels like a country home. Aside from some of the best red chile you'll ever taste, turkeys strut and squabble outside and the whole place is connected to a feed store, giving it genuine Western soul.

THE DRIVE
Continue north from the Yost Escarpment parking lot for just over 4 miles to the entrance to Spaceport America at County Rd A39.

03 GENESIS STATUE AT SPACEPORT AMERICA

You can't just drop by **Spaceport America** (spaceport america.com), the world's first commercial spaceport, for a look around – guided tours are the only way to visit. But you can check out the simple but striking **Genesis statue** in the roundabout just before the entrance gate. Created by sculptor Otto Rigan, the arc-shaped sculpture is 40ft across and 5ft deep. Studded with glass in a configuration that mimics the constellations overhead on a summer night, the statue sparkles in the moonlight as it bends toward the heavens.

THE DRIVE
Return to A13 and continue north. At Engle, turn left to Truth or Consequences on Hwy 51 – which curves around 300ft-high Elephant Butte Dam and the drought-shrunken lake behind it. It's about 30 miles from the statue to Truth or Consequences.

04 TRUTH OR CONSEQUENCES

This quirky town met a challenge posed by a radio game show in 1950 and changed its name to that of the show, hoping to raise publicity for itself. Popular with retirees and with a growing New Age subculture, T or C is best known for two things: its hot springs and the Spaceport. Hot-spring spas with pools for day-use cluster near the Rio Grande.

If the Genesis statue sparked your curiosity about the Spaceport, head to the **Geronimo Trail Scenic Byway Visitor Center** (geronimotrail.com) downtown to sign up for a guided tour of the facility – but note that reservations should be made well in advance and tours typically depart only on weekends. Spaceport America was funded in part by Sir Richard Branson, who launched some 53 miles into space on his Virgin Galactic passenger rocket from this isolated patch of desert in 2021. Tour highlights include a ride in a swirling G-force machine, an opportunity to climb aboard hi-tech fire trucks and posing for photos on the 2.7-mile-long 'spaceway.' Tours leave from the visitor center, and the round-trip experience takes about three hours.

THE DRIVE
Take I-25 north from T or C for 35 miles to exit 115, then turn right onto Hwy 1, following it north for 20 or so hilly miles.

05 BOSQUE DEL APACHE NATIONAL WILDLIFE REFUGE

A surprising oasis of water and wildlife, the **Bosque del Apache** (fws.gov/refuge/bosque_del_apache) covers over 57,000 acres along the Rio Grande, with forested wetlands at its heart. Though a menagerie of mammals, reptiles and amphibians can be spotted, birds are the big draw: 371 species roost here by the tens of thousands, mainly from November to February. The stars of the avian show are the sandhill cranes, who even get their own festival (mid-November). It's worth driving the 12-mile loop through the refuge any time of year.

THE DRIVE
Head north on Hwy 1 to San Antonio, then west on Hwy 380, then north on I-25, 98 miles in total.

06 ALBUQUERQUE

New Mexico's largest city was founded in 1706 and for centuries centered on the Old Town Plaza, which is where you'll find many of Albuquerque's sights and attractions. The area around the plaza is worth a stroll. Though its gritty charm can sometimes be hard to spot, the neighborhoods around the University of New Mexico and Nob Hill are hipper than ever. And some fantastic museums can be found here, including the **National Museum of Nuclear**

Spaceport America

Photo opportunity

Late-afternoon glow on an adobe wall in Santa Fe.

Adobe house, Santa Fe

BRENT COULTER/SHUTTERSTOCK ©

Science & History (nuclearmuseum.org), with engaging exhibits on the development of nuclear weapons, energy, medical technology and more.

THE DRIVE
On this 43-mile leg we diverge from the Camino Real to hop on the more scenic Turquoise Trail. Take I-40 east to exit 175, where you'll take Hwy 14 north.

07 MADRID

This former company-owned mining village has transformed into a quirky gallery town that looks cute on the surface but still has an unruly edge underneath. Hop out and browse a while.

THE DRIVE
Continue north on Hwy 14 for 3 miles, then turn left into Cerrillos.

08 CERRILLOS

This little village was at the center of the turquoise trade in Spanish colonial times. To see an erratic display of historical memorabilia, stop into the **Turquoise Mining Museum** (casagrandetradingpost.com). A mile north of town, amid scrubby desert hills pockmarked with historic mining sites, **Cerrillos Hills State Park** (emnrd.nm.gov) holds 5 miles of hiking trails.

THE DRIVE
Continue north on Hwy 14, which will turn into one of Santa Fe's main commercial drags, Cerrillos Rd, 24 miles total.

09 SANTA FE

Though spurs of El Camino Real continued on up to Taos and beyond, the main trail ended here, at the Santa Fe plaza, once the Spanish chose this spot as the capital of New Mexico in 1610. It's worth taking the time to walk around the plaza, but to get the best sense of what life might have been like during the days when El Camino Real was the main route into the city, head to Santa Fe's southern outskirts, where you'll find **Rancho de las Golondrinas** (golondrinas.org). Once an overnight stopping place on the trail, it's now a 200-acre living museum, carefully reconstructed and populated with historical re-enactors. You can watch bread baking in a *horno* (traditional adobe oven), and visit the blacksmith, the molasses mill or traditional crafts workshops. There are orchards, vineyards and livestock, and festivals are held throughout the summer. To get here, take I-25 south to exit 276, then follow the signs.

DON'T MISS:

Canyon Road

The heart of the Santa Fe art scene, with over 100 galleries plus fine dining and the oldest tavern in town (El Farol).

13

NEW MEXICO

Georgia O'Keeffe Country

BEST FOR DRIVERS

Hwy 96 is one of the most beautiful roads in the state.

Shiprock (p108)

DURATION	DISTANCE	GREAT FOR
2–3 days	327 miles / 526km	History and culture, outdoors

BEST TIME TO GO May to October, for the best light.

From Chaco Canyon's architecture and the multicolored cliffs that inspired O'Keeffe to the intricate textiles of Navajo weavers, topography and creativity are inseparable here. The first part of this trip just might cover our favorite stretches of road in the state – the colors and the light blend into pure eye candy. Then strike out through the badlands of the Navajo Nation, where the earth and sky converge with raw, elemental intensity.

Link your trip

10 Southwest Indian Nations Sojourn

From Toadlena, skip state lines to check out more of the Navajo Nation, crossing the Chuska Mountains via Hwy 134 to Canyon de Chelly.

19 Highway 53 to Acoma

From Toadlena, head south to Gallup on Hwy 491 to check out ancient pueblos, lava flows and wolves.

01 ABIQUIÚ

Founded in 1754 through a Spanish land grant, the tiny town of Abiquiú near the Chama River has a few galleries and a lovely church, but is most famous as the home of painter Georgia O'Keeffe. After returning to the area many times in the 1930s and '40s, she bought an old adobe fixer-upper in 1945, restored it, and moved in in 1949. She lived between there and her place up the road at Ghost Ranch for the next 35 years. You can visit her Abiquiú house on the **Georgia O'Keeffe Home & Studio**

Tour (okeeffemuseum.org). Enclosed by a mud-brick wall, this Spanish Colonial hacienda blends into the landscape and remains much as it was when she lived here. You must make reservations for the tour, which leaves from the Tour Office next to the Abiquiú Inn. Of course, if you're in Santa Fe you should also check out the **Georgia O'Keeffe Museum** (p25).

THE DRIVE

Taking Hwy 84 north for 14 miles, force yourself to keep your eyes on the road as you drive around the jewel-like Abiquiú Lake, ringed by multicolored cliffs. Turn right at the sign for Ghost Ranch.

02 GHOST RANCH

If you're familiar with O'Keeffe's work, you may feel like you've been here before. Some of her most celebrated pieces were inspired by the sensual forms and colors of the cliffs, canyons and mesalands around **Ghost Ranch** (ghostranch.org). Though her home here is closed to the public, you can explore the area on hiking trails, guided horseback adventures or a van tour that includes stops at vistas immortalized in O'Keeffe's paintings. There are also small museums and various lodging options.

THE DRIVE

Backtrack 6 miles south on Hwy 84, then turn right onto Hwy 96, which takes you through a pastel geological wonderland. When you reach Hwy 550, near Cuba, turn right (north); before Nageezi turn left onto County Rd 7900, then right onto the washed-out dirt County Rd 7950, following signs for Chaco Culture National Historical Park. It's 130 miles total.

DETOUR

Monastery of Christ in the Desert

Start: 02 Ghost Ranch

It's hard to imagine a more peaceful place for spiritual contemplation. Set 13 miles down a dirt road, surrounded by the majestic Chama River Wilderness, you'll find the **Monastery of Christ in the Desert** (christdesert.org). This Benedictine Abbey welcomes visitors as day or overnight guests;

you can go into the unique church that combines elements of Japanese and New Mexican design, attend prayer services, or stay in a small, simple guesthouse (average suggested donation $90 per night). In tune with the aura of the place, quiet is requested.

To get here from Ghost Ranch, head north on Hwy 84 for 2.5 miles, then turn left onto Forest Rd 151. The drive is spectacular: some of the cliffs are purple! There are plenty of places to hang out by the river, and a few campsites. When you're done with this detour, retrace your steps back to Hwy 96 and pick up the drive there.

03 CHACO CANYON

About 1000 years ago, Chaco Canyon was the center of an Ancestral Puebloan (Anasazi) civilization that spread across the San Juan Basin and beyond, linked together by a carefully engineered network of 30ft-wide roads. Today, Chacoan culture is famed for the impressive architecture it left behind: Great Houses intricately pieced together, stone by stone, and oriented with remarkable accuracy to solar and lunar events as well as the cardinal directions.

You can walk through some Great Houses and other structures at **Chaco Culture National Historical Park** (nps.gov/chcu). The biggest attraction is Pueblo Bonito, which towered four to five stories tall and may have had 600 to 800 rooms and kivas. Though none of Chaco's sites have been reconstructed, plenty of rockwork is still intact. A loop road connects the main archaeological sites, hiking trails head off into the surrounding area, and there's an informative visitor center and a campground. But there's no food, gas or other supplies (water is available only at the visitor center). The closest towns with accommodations are Farmington, Aztec and Cuba. The last stretch of dirt road on the way here is in very poor shape – do not attempt to drive it in muddy or snowy conditions.

THE DRIVE
Head back to Hwy 550 and head north. At Bloomfield, turn right onto Hwy 64, then make a pretty quick left onto Hwy 544. It's 75 miles total.

04 AZTEC

Although little Aztec has a handful of interesting turn-of-the-19th-century buildings on the National Register of Historic Places, the town's main draw is the 27-acre **Aztec Ruins National Monument** (nps.gov/azru). This ancient Puebloan settlement features the largest reconstructed kiva in the country, with an internal diameter of almost 50ft, originally built around 1100 CE. Though the site itself isn't as amazing or extensive as Chaco, the Great Kiva is pretty impressive. During summer, rangers give early-afternoon talks about ancient architecture, trade routes and astronomy.

THE DRIVE
Take Hwy 516 to Farmington, which makes a good lunch stop, then Hwy 64 west to the town of Shiprock. Cross the San Juan River and continue straight ahead on Hwy 491 (formerly Hwy 666, nicknamed the Devil's Hwy). At mile marker 85, turn right onto Indian Rte 13. It's about 60 miles total.

05 SHIPROCK

The most striking sight in New Mexico's northwestern corner is Shiprock, a 1700ft volcanic plug that is eerily eroded into what looks like a schooner – at least to white people. The Navajo name for it, Tsé Bit'a'í, means 'rock with wings.' According to one Navajo history, the tribe had been under attack in a place far to the north when the ground beneath them became a giant bird that flew them to safety, delivering them to their homeland; the bird then turned back into earth, but kept its shape. It's also said that for some time Navajos dwelt atop the great rock, coming down to farm and tend sheep, but that one day the trail to the desert floor was destroyed by lightning; those up at the summit couldn't descend and died there. Climbing Shiprock is strictly forbidden (yes, illegal), in part for fear that the spirits of the dead will be disturbed. You can't even hike over to it, but there are some great views about 5 miles west along Indian Rte 13.

THE DRIVE
Head back to Hwy 491 and turn right, heading south. When you reach the gas station at mile marker 61, turn right onto Indian Rte

DON'T MISS:
Ghost Ranch

Hike, ride horseback or take a van tour through the colorful terrain immortalized in the paintings of Georgia O'Keeffe.

Photo opportunity

Capture the perspective of doorways and stonework at Chaco.

Chaco Culture National Historical Park

19 and go about 12 miles. In all, it's 44 miles.

06 TOADLENA

Tucked against the Chuska Mountains, Toadlena and neighboring Two Grey Hills are renowned as the sources of the finest rugs anywhere in Navajo country. Some weavers from this area continue to reject commercially produced wool and synthetic dyes, preferring the wool of their own churro sheep in its natural hues. They card white, brown, gray and black hairs together, blending the colors to the desired effect, then they spin and weave the wool – tightly – into mesmerizing geometric patterns. The **Toadlena Trading Post** (toadlenatradingpost.com), run by textile expert Mark Winter, is the local market where many of these world-class artisans sell their work. Prices range from about $125 to $7000 or more. The Trading Post has a small museum with extraordinarily fine exhibits.

BISTI BADLANDS

One of the weirdest micro-environments in New Mexico is 38 miles south of Farmington, off Hwy 371. The Bisti Badlands, part of the Bisti/De-Na-Zin Wilderness Area, is an undeveloped realm of multicolored hoodoos, sculpted cliffs and balancing rocks. From the parking area, you have to follow the unmaintained path for at least a mile before getting to the heart of the formations, then wander as you will, taking care not to damage the fragile geology or to get lost. The hours just after sunrise and before sunset are most spectacular.

14

NEW MEXICO

Highway 4: Jemez Mountains

BEST FOR RELAXING

Soak up the waters in Jemez Springs.

DURATION	DISTANCE	GREAT FOR
2 days	128 miles / 206km	Outdoors, history and culture

BEST TIME TO GO	May to October, when the weather is best.

Valles Caldera National Preserve

One minute you're in the scientific community where the atomic bomb was built, the next you're exploring ancient cliff dwellings. And by day's end, you're soaking in hot springs. This route takes you across the mesas to Bandelier National Monument, then into the Jemez Mountains (pronounced 'hem-ez'), before you descend through the red-walled Jemez River canyon into the horse pastures of Albuquerque's north valley.

Link your trip

11 High & Low Roads to Taos

While driving the Low Road south from Taos, take Hwy 30 to Hwy 502 to Los Alamos to start your Jemez trip.

13 Georgia O'Keeffe Country

Take Hwy 550 north to join this colorful route near Chaco Canyon.

01 LOS ALAMOS

The top-secret Manhattan Project sprang to life in Los Alamos in 1943, turning a sleepy mesa-top village into a laboratory of secluded geniuses busy developing the first atomic bomb. The project was led by renowned physicist J. Robert Oppenheimer, he of the 2023 Christopher Nolan film *Oppenheimer*. Los Alamos National Laboratory still develops weapons, but it's also been at the cutting edge of other scientific advances, including mapping the human genome and supercomputing. The Lab dominates

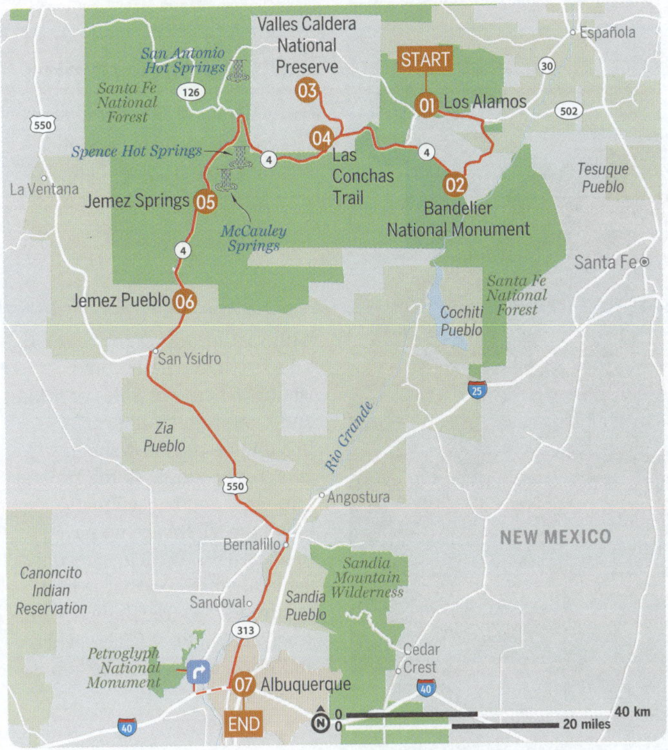

everything here and gives Los Alamos County the highest concentration of PhDs per capita in the US, along with the highest per-capita income in the state. It's set atop a series of mesas and hugged by national forest, much of which unfortunately burned in the 48,000-acre Cerro Grande fire of 2000, leaving the hills behind town eerily barren. More of the surrounding forest was ablaze in 2011, as the fire around Las Conchas scorched over 150,000 acres – the largest ever recorded in New Mexico. Fortunately, it narrowly missed the Lab.

The **Los Alamos Historical Museum** (losalamoshistory.org) has interesting exhibits on what daily life was like in 'the town that didn't exist' during the Manhattan Project era. The **Bradbury Science Museum** (lanl.gov/museum) has compelling displays on the bomb's development and the political context of the time, along with modern research in medical and computer sciences. A short film introduces the history of the Manhattan Project.

THE DRIVE
Drive 12 miles, taking East Jemez Rd to Hwy 4 West, which curves around finger-like mesas. Turn left onto the entrance road for Bandelier.

02 BANDELIER NATIONAL MONUMENT

The sublime, peach-colored cliffs of Frijoles Canyon are pocked with caves and alcoves that were home to Ancestral Puebloans until the mid-1500s. Today, they're the main attraction at **Bandelier National Monument** (nps.gov/band) – a rewarding stop whether you're interested in ancient Southwestern cultures or just want to walk among pines and watch the light glowing off the canyon walls. The **Alcove House**, 140ft above the ground and reached by climbing four ladders, is a highlight (though it's not for those with vertigo). The more adventurous can strike out on rugged trails that traverse 50 sq miles of canyon and mesa wilderness dotted with archaeological sites; backpackers should pick up a free backcountry permit from the visitor center. Kids love it here.

THE DRIVE
Head back out of Bandelier and turn left on Hwy 4, heading west as the road twists its way 16 miles into the heart of the Jemez. Take a right at the sign for Valles Caldera.

03 VALLES CALDERA NATIONAL PRESERVE

Ever wonder what the crater of a dormant supervolcano looks like 1,250,000 years after it first blows? Just check out **Valles Caldera National Preserve** (nps.gov/vall) – the prehistoric explosion here was so massive that chunks were thrown as far away as Kansas. The 89,000-acre bowl – home to New Mexico's largest elk herd – is simply breathtaking,

SUMIKOPHOTO/SHUTTERSTOCK ©

Bandelier National Monument (p111)

Photo opportunity

Climbing a ladder to a cave dwelling in Bandelier National Monument.

with vast meadows from which hills rise like pine-covered islands. There are miles of hiking and mountain-biking trails in summer and snowshoeing and cross-country skiing trails (groomed and backcountry) in winter. There are no paved roads; a 4WD vehicle is recommended when weather is bad. In summer, 35 free daily permits are available for vehicles. There's an information center in Jemez Springs.

THE DRIVE
Back on Hwy 4 west, continue until you come to the trailhead for Las Conchas – about 0.25 miles past the fishing/picnic area of the same name – between mile markers 37 and 36.

04 LAS CONCHAS TRAIL

A perfect spot to get out of the car and stretch your legs, the Las Conchas Trail follows the East Fork of the Jemez River as it meanders through grassy meadows and rocky canyons. For the first couple of miles, it's a blissful, easy hike. Las Conchas is also a popular climbing area, with a number of routes bolted into the volcanic rhyolite. Note that the weather can change quickly here, especially during the summer monsoon season.

THE DRIVE
There's only one main road here, so follow Hwy 4 west then south for 19 miles, as it descends into the tight Jemez River Canyon.

05 JEMEZ SPRINGS

The little village of Jemez Springs was built around a cluster of hot springs, as was the ruined pueblo that's preserved at the **Jemez Historic Site** (nmmonuments.org). Today, most visitors come for the waters, which you can experience yourself at the rustic **Jemez Springs Bath House** (jemezspringsbathhouse.com), which has private tubs, massages and more. There's also the friendly, outdoor **Jemez Hot Springs** (jemezhotsprings.com), rich in scenic atmosphere.

THE DRIVE
Keep heading down canyon on Hwy 4 for 12 miles, between the red rock walls and past popular fishing pullouts. All the locals advise against speeding here – you will get a ticket.

06 JEMEZ PUEBLO

Twelve miles south of Jemez Springs, in a Martian-red landscape, the Walatowa Visitor Center (jemezpueblo.com) at Jemez Pueblo houses the small, sort-of-interesting **Museum of Pueblo Culture**. The gift shop sells the pottery for which the pueblo's artisans are renowned.

THE DRIVE
Follow Hwy 4 to the end, turn left on Hwy 550 south, then right onto Hwy 313. After 8 miles, at the roundabout, take 4th St, then go right on Hwy 528. Turn left on S Rio Grande Blvd, through surprisingly rural North Valley horse country as you head downtown. It's 48 miles total.

07 ALBUQUERQUE

The largest city in the state, Albuquerque offers some unique introductions to Hispanic and American Indian culture. The **Indian Pueblo Cultural Center** (indianpueblo.org) is a must-see even on the shortest of Albuquerque itineraries. The history exhibits are fascinating, and the arts wing features the finest examples of each pueblo's work. The IPCC also houses a large gift shop and retail gallery. Along with serving Pueblo-style cuisine, the on-site **Pueblo Harvest Cafe** holds weekend art demonstrations, bread-baking demos and dances.

South of downtown, the **National Hispanic Cultural Center** (nhccnm.org) for visual, performing and literary arts has three galleries and the nation's premier Hispanic genealogy library. The work in the permanent collection is exciting and provocative, with many pieces by Albuquerque-based artists. Each June the center hosts the **Festival Flamenco**. The Old Town Plaza is a good spot to go for a stroll.

DETOUR
Petroglyph National Monument
Start: 07 Albuquerque

Along the edge of an ancient lava field on Albuquerque's west side are more than 20,000 petroglyphs on basalt slabs at **Petroglyph National Monument** (nps.gov/petr). It's easy to spot the rock art in the park's three viewing areas: **Rinconada Canyon** has the longest trail (2.2 miles round trip) and is best if you want some solitude; **Boca Negra Canyon** features three short trails; **Piedras Marcadas** has 300 petroglyphs along a 1.5-mile trail. For powerful views but no rock art, hit the **Volcanoes Trail**, where you'll hike among cinder cones. Note: smash-and-grab thefts have been reported at some trailhead parking lots, so don't leave valuables in your vehicle.

The visitor center, on Western Trail at Unser Blvd, is 7.5 miles north of Old Town; head west on I-40 across the Rio Grande and take exit 154 north.

MORE HOT SPRINGS

Along Hwy 4 just north of Jemez Springs, there are a number of natural hot springs that you can hike into. One of the most accessible is **Spence Hot Springs**, between miles 25 and 24. The temperature's only about 95°F (35°C), but it's a gorgeous setting and the inevitable weird naked guy adds authenticity to the experience. The nearby **McCauley Springs**, with a trailhead at Battleship Rock Picnic Area, is also lukewarm. For something more ambitious, seek out **San Antonio Hot Springs** – it's a 5-mile hike in to the pools – but worth it! From Hwy 4, take Hwy 126 and watch for signs for Forest Rd 376 and the trailhead.

15

NEW MEXICO

Enchanted Circle & Eastern Sangres

BEST FOR SEANCES

Cimarron's St James Hotel.

Taos Pueblo

DURATION	DISTANCE	GREAT FOR
2 days	297 miles / 479km	Outdoors

BEST TIME TO GO	August to October: after monsoon season, before winter.

Hike the Rio Grande Gorge, stay at a haunted hotel, hit some hot springs, spot pronghorns and feed alpacas on this scenic trip up and over the Sangre de Cristos. You'll catch views of 13,107ft Wheeler Peak and pass through gorgeous valleys with classic New Mexican villages. You'll probably see plenty of wildlife – from elk and antelope to bighorn sheep. And if you're into meditating, we've got the spot for you!

Link your trip

11 High & Low Roads to Taos
Join these two loops at Taos to cover both sides of the Sangre de Cristos.

12 El Camino Real & Turquoise Trail
From Las Vegas, continue south on I-25 to hop on these historic routes in Santa Fe.

01 TAOS

For over 100 years, Taos has been a magnet for artists, writers and creative thinkers of all types. Painters were entranced by the light here in 1898 and established an art colony; DH Lawrence hoped to build a utopia outside of town; Carl Jung was deeply affected by visiting Taos Pueblo, the place that also inspired Aldous Huxley's *Brave New World;* Georgia O'Keeffe and Ansel Adams were here; Dennis Hopper shot key scenes from *Easy Rider* around Taos, then moved here himself. It's easy to see why.

KTAO: SOLAR-POWERED RADIO

When in Taos, disconnect your device and turn on the radio. Set the dial to 101.9 KTAO, which claims to be the 'world's largest solar-powered radio station.' The real live DJs play whatever they feel like playing and daily features include horoscope readings (at 10am and 6pm) by local psychic Elissa Heyman. Weekly shows include 'Moccasin Wire' (7pm to 10pm Monday), devoted to American Indian music.

Attached to the station is the **KTAO Solar Center** (ktao.com), one of the best places in town to see concerts or just have a drink and a meal in the bar-restaurant. It's family-friendly, with a playground on the lawn for kids.

Innovators today include architect Michael Reynolds, designer of Earthships – self-sustaining, environmentally savvy houses built with recycled materials such as used automobile tires and cans. Earthships heat and cool themselves, make their own electricity and catch their own water. You can visit one Earthship community by heading west 1.5 miles past the **Rio Grande Gorge Bridge** – itself well worth seeing – on Hwy 64. Granted, the Earthship **self-guided tour** (earthship.com) is a little disappointing – you basically watch a short DVD and check out the visitor center. Actually staying in an **Earthship Rental** (earthship.com) overnight is way better.

To see some choice works of the original Taos Society of Artists, visit the **Blumenschein Home & Museum** (taoshistoricmuseums.org).

THE DRIVE
Take Hwy 522 north just past Questa, then turn left onto Hwy 378. It's 40 miles in total.

02 WILD RIVERS

One of the most impressive stretches of the Rio Grande Gorge is where it meets the Red River. At **Wild Rivers Recreation Area** some trails plunge 800ft down into the canyon while others meander along the mesa. If you don't feel like a hike, drive the scenic 13-mile Wild Rivers Backcountry Byway loop and stop at La Junta, the perfect spot for a picnic overlooking the twin gorges. The waters are popular with anglers fishing for trout.

THE DRIVE
A total of 27 miles; backtrack to Questa, then take Hwy 38 east.

03 RED RIVER

A blend of Bavaria and the Old West, Red River brings people in with festivals and events year-round – except mid-March to mid-May, when the town is dead. In summer, kids love **Frye's Old Town Shootout**, a Wild West drama.

THE DRIVE
A 40-mile drive, continue east on Hwy 38, over Bobcat Pass (9820ft) and down through the little lakeside village of Eagle Nest. Drive Hwy 64 east through curvaceous Cimarron Canyon, where there's good fishing, camping and rock climbing.

04 CIMARRON

Cimarron has a wild past. It once served as a stop on the Santa Fe Trail, and a hangout for gunslingers, train robbers, desperadoes, lawmen and other Wild West figures including Kit Carson, Buffalo Bill Cody, Annie Oakley, Wyatt Earp, Jesse James and Doc Holliday. The old **St James Hotel** alone saw the deaths of 26 men within its walls. Today, the restored hotel is said to be so haunted that one of its rooms is never rented out. It's really the main reason for stopping in Cimarron, either for the night or a bite to eat.

THE DRIVE
Head 5 miles south on Hwy 21. You might see herds of Boy Scout burros here!

DETOUR
Capulin Volcano National Monument
Start: 04 Cimarron

Rising 1300ft above the surrounding plains, Capulin is the most accessible of several volcanoes in the area. From the visitor center at **Capulin Volcano National Monument** (nps.gov/cavo), a 2-mile road spirals up the mountain to a parking lot at the crater rim (8182ft), where trails lead around and into the crater. From Cimarron, take Hwy 64 north, hop on I-25 for 5 miles, take exit 451, and head east on Hwy 87/64. The park entrance is 3 miles north of Capulin village, off Hwy 325. The visitor center, on Western Trail at Unser Blvd, is 7.5 miles north of Old Town; head west on I-40 across the Rio Grande and take exit 154 north.

05 PHILMONT SCOUT RANCH

The largest Boy Scout camp in the country, Philmont Scout Ranch covers 137,000 acres along the breathtaking eastern slope of the Sangre de Cristos. While you need to be a Scout to trek the trails, anyone can drop into the **Philmont Museum** (philmontscoutranch.org) or tour **Villa Philmonte**, a Spanish Mediterranean mansion built in 1927 by Waite Phillips, the oil baron who was Philmont's original benefactor. Pick up high-quality outdoor gear and all sorts of Philmont-related souvenirs at **Tooth of Time Traders**.

THE DRIVE
Continue south, then east, on Hwy 21. Look out for antelope! At Springer, pick up I-25 south. Before long, you'll see why Wagon Mound is so-named. Get off the interstate at exit 345. It's a 98-mile drive.

DON'T MISS:
Pueblos

Find some of the oldest continuously inhabited places in North America, rich in culture including dances and crafts.

06 LAS VEGAS

Once a major stop along the Santa Fe Trail and later the Santa Fe Railroad, 19th-century Las Vegas was one of the biggest, baddest boomtowns in the West. Billy the Kid held court here with his pal Vicente Silva (leader of the Society of Bandits – the roughest, toughest gang in New Mexico) and Doc Holliday owned a saloon (although ultimately his business failed because he kept shooting at the customers).

Today, aside from strolling around the plaza, the best reasons to visit Las Vegas are 5 miles northwest of town on Hwy 65, near Montezuma Castle (you'll know it when you see it), which is part of the United World College of the West. Along the road in front of the castle, you can soak in a series of natural **hot spring pools**. Bring a swimsuit and test the water – some are scalding hot! And don't miss the **Dwan Light Sanctuary** on the school campus, a meditation chamber where prisms in the walls cast rainbows inside.

THE DRIVE
Head north on Hwy 518; at mile marker 12, turn left onto Hwy 94, which will take you 30 miles all the way to Mora – but pay attention, as a couple of turns are required. Between mile markers 4 and 5, look south for great views of Hermit Peak.

07 MORA VALLEY

This scenic agricultural valley, whose hub is the town of Mora, is known throughout northern New Mexico as an enclave where traditional Hispanic ways still remain strong.

Photo opportunity

Capture the confluence of the Red River and the Rio Grande from above.

In 2013, Mora County became the first in the nation to ban fracking, though the ordinance has since been overturned by a federal judge.

Two miles west of Mora is the **Cleveland Roller Mill Historical Museum** (clevelandrollermillmuseum.org), housed in a functional 19th-century adobe-and-stone flour mill, with gears and cogs and pulleys inside.

THE DRIVE
Take Hwy 434 north, through Guadalupita and the ski-resort town of Angel Fire. Turn left on Hwy 64 west, which will take you back into Taos. Watch for elk – sometimes in the middle of the road! This last leg is about 60 miles.

RICHARD SUSANTO/SHUTTERSTOCK ©

Rio Grande Gorge

16

NEW MEXICO

Las Cruces to Carlsbad Caverns

DURATION	DISTANCE	GREAT FOR
2–3 days	215 miles / 346km	Outdoors, family

BEST TIME TO GO	September till November offers the best weather.

BEST NATURAL SIGHT

Carlsbad Caverns is like nothing else in the Southwest.

Carlsbad Caverns (p120)

Crossing the southern swath of the state, you can visit White Sands, which means two things in these parts: the national monument where you can frolic in dunes that look like giant snowdrifts, and the missile range surrounding it that's the largest military installation in the US. From this sandy basin, the route climbs into pine-clad forests and descends 755ft underground into the subterranean world of Carlsbad Caverns.

Link your trip

12 El Camino Real & Turquoise Trail

From Las Cruces, head north up the Rio Grande Valley along the 400-year-old route that linked Mexico City to Santa Fe.

20 Billy the Kid Trail

From Artesia, drive 30 miles north on US 285 to Roswell, for a trip that covers UFOs and outlaws.

01 LAS CRUCES

Though this city at the southern crossroads of I-25 and I-10 doesn't have a wealth of attractions, it does have one museum you won't want to miss. The **New Mexico Farm & Ranch Heritage Museum** (nmfarmandranchmuseum.org) has more than just engaging displays about the agricultural history of the state – it's got livestock! There are daily milking demonstrations and an occasional 'parade of breeds' of cattle, along with stalls of horses, donkeys, sheep and goats. Other demonstrations include blacksmithing (Friday to

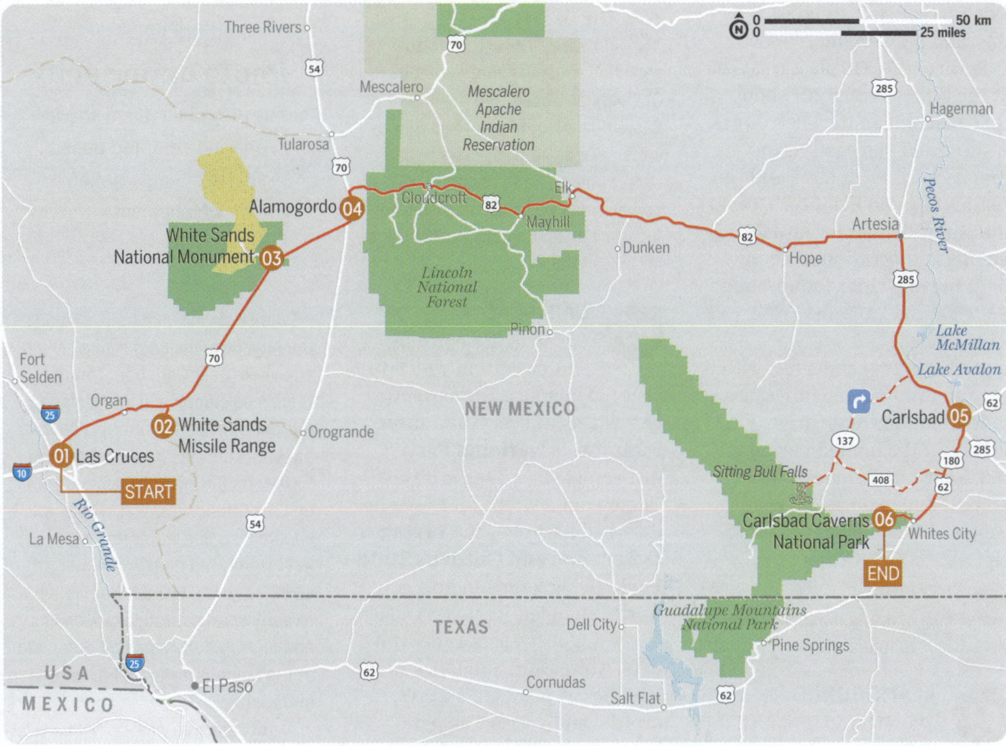

Sunday), spinning and weaving (Wednesday), and heritage cooking (call for times). You'll understand much more about New Mexican life and culture after a visit here.

THE DRIVE
Take I-25 north to Hwy 70. Drive east through a notch in the Organ Mountains and drop into the Tularosa Valley. Between mile markers 169 and 170, exit at White Sands Missile Range; it's 26 miles in total.

02 WHITE SANDS MISSILE RANGE

If it flies, explodes and was made in America, there's a good chance it was tested here. (Occasionally, Hwy 70 even closes to prevent 'collateral damage' during launches.) The **White Sands Missile Test Center Museum** (wsmrmuseum.com) features an outdoor missile garden, a real V-2 rocket and exhibits with lots of defense-related artifacts. Park outside the Test Center gate and check-in at the office before walking to the museum.

THE DRIVE
Continue northeast on Hwy 70 for 34 miles. Be prepared to stop along the way at a Border Patrol checkpoint, which are sometimes manned with drug-sniffing dogs.

03 WHITE SANDS NATIONAL MONUMENT

Undulating through the Tularosa Basin like something straight out of a dream, the ethereal dunes at **White Sands National Monument** (nps.gov/whsa) are a highlight of any trip to New Mexico and a must on every landscape photographer's itinerary. Try to time a visit to White Sands with sunrise or sunset (or both), when it's at its most magical. From the visitor center drive the 16-mile scenic loop into the heart of the dazzlingly white sea of sand that is the world's largest gypsum dune field, covering 275 sq miles. Along the way, get out of the car and romp around a bit. Hike the **Alkali Flat**, a 4.5-mile (round-trip) backcountry trail through the heart of the dunes, or the simple 1-mile loop nature trail.

Don't forget your sunglasses – the sand is as bright as snow!

Spring for a $15 plastic saucer at the visitor center gift shop then **sled** one of the back dunes. It's fun, and you can sell the disc back for $5 at day's end (no rentals to avoid liability). Check the park calendar for **sunset strolls** and occasional moonlight **bicycle rides** (adult/child $5/2.50), the latter best reserved in advance.

Backcountry campsites, with no water or toilet facilities, are a mile from the scenic drive. Pick up one of the limited permits ($3, issued first-come, first-served) in person at the visitor center at least one hour before sunset.

THE DRIVE
Keep heading northeast on Hwy 70 for 16 miles.

04 ALAMOGORDO

Alamogordo (Spanish for 'fat cottonwood') might not be laden with charm, but it's super convenient to White Sands.

The main attraction is the four-story **New Mexico Museum of Space History** (nmspacemuseum.org). Nicknamed the 'golden cube,' it looms over town and has excellent exhibits on space research and flight. Its **theater and planetarium** shows films on everything from the Grand Canyon to the dark side of the moon, as well as laser shows and multimedia presentations on a huge wraparound screen.

Railroad buffs and kids flock to the **Toy Train Depot**, an 1898 railway depot with five rooms of train memorabilia and toy trains, and a 2.5-mile narrow-gauge mini-train you can ride through Alameda Park.

THE DRIVE
Take Hwy 82 east, and you'll soon find yourself rising from the Chihuahuan Desert into the forested Sacramento Mountains. Pass Cloudcroft – maybe stop to grab a bite or stay overnight – and continue on, downhill and across open plains. At Artesia, turn south onto Hwy 285. It's 147 miles total.

05 CARLSBAD

Carlsbad is a convenient base from which to visit the famous caverns south of town, as well as **Guadalupe Mountains National Park** just across state lines in Texas. There's not a whole lot to see in Carlsbad itself, but the **Living Desert Zoo and Gardens State Park** (livingdesertnm.org) is worth a gander. It's a great place to see and learn about roadrunners, wolves and antelopes, along with desert plants like agave, ocotillo and yucca. The park has a good 1.3-mile trail that showcases different habitats of the Chihuahuan Desert, plus a reptile house.

THE DRIVE
Take Hwy 62/180 south for 20 miles to White's City, then Hwy 7 into Carlsbad Caverns National Park.

DETOUR
Sitting Bull Falls
Start: 05 Carlsbad

An oasis in the desert, **Sitting Bull Falls** is tucked among the burly canyons of the Guadalupe Mountains, 42 miles southwest of Carlsbad. A spring-fed creek pours 150ft over a limestone cliff, with natural pools below and above the falls that are big enough to splash around in. There are a series of caves behind the waterfalls, which can be explored with a ranger.

Twenty-six miles of trails around the falls offer the best hiking anywhere near Carlsbad. Though there's no camping in the designated recreation area right around the falls, backpackers may hike in and camp further up Sitting Bull Canyon, or up Last Chance Canyon, where you should also find water flowing. It can get brutally hot here in summer, so hiking is generally best from late fall to early spring. Arrange cave walks and pick up trail maps and other info at the **Lincoln National Forest office** in Carlsbad.

To get here, turn west on NM 137 (also called the 'Queen Hwy') from US 285 just north of Carlsbad, or turn west on County Rd 408 (the Dark Canyon Rd) from US 180/62 just south of Carlsbad, and follow the signs to Sitting Bull Falls.

Photo opportunity

The play of light and shadow on wind-sculpted dunes at White Sands National Monument.

06 CARLSBAD CAVERNS NATIONAL PARK

Huge caves hide under the hills at **Carlsbad Caverns National Park** (nps.gov/cave), where you can walk through a weird subterranean wonderland that's covered in stalactites, stalagmites and other fantastical geological features. You can ride an elevator from the visitor center (descending the length of the Empire State Building in under a minute) to the Big Room – an underground chamber about 8.2 acres in

White Sands National Monument (p119)

size and over 800ft below the surface – but it's more enjoyable to hike in 1.25 miles from the cave mouth. Wear a sweatshirt: the temperature is 56°F (13°C) year-round.

The cave's other claim to fame is the 300,000-plus Mexican free-tailed bat colony that roosts here from mid-May to mid-October. Be here by sunset, when they cyclone out for an all-evening insect feast.

Guided tours of **additional caves** (recreation.gov) are available, and should be reserved well in advance.

Wilderness backpacking – above ground, in the desert – requires a permit (free); the visitor center sells topographical maps of the hiking trails. November to March is the best time for backpacking (no rattlesnakes, better temperatures). To get an up-close glimpse of the desert in air-conditioned comfort, consider the 9-mile gravel **Walnut Canyon Desert Drive**.

This road was damaged in floods in 2022 – at the time of writing, repairs were proposed for 2024, so make sure you check nps.gov for the latest information before going.

17

NEW MEXICO

BEST FOR VIEWS

Emory Pass: gape at the Rio Grande Basin panorama and beyond.

Gila Cliff Dwellings National Monument

Geronimo Trail

DURATION	DISTANCE	GREAT FOR
2–3 days	190 miles / 306km	History and culture

BEST TIME TO GO	May to October, for warm days that linger into evening.

Follow the trail of this legendary Apache chief, through old mining towns, over serpentine passes and into the box canyon where he ultimately surrendered. From the former boomtown of Silver City, you'll snake your way over Emory Pass and out to the Rio Grande Valley. You can soak in the mineral springs at Truth or Consequences before heading for the Gila's Black Range and north to the Plains of San Agustin.

Link your trip

18 Into the Gila
Check out the west side of the range on this trip, which connects at Silver City.

20 Billy the Kid Trail
From the Very Large Array, take Hwy 60 east, I-25 south, then Hwy 380 east to link up with this outlaw's route at Valley of Fires.

01 SILVER CITY

Way back in the day, the site of Silver City was settled by Apache people. When the Spanish came to the area to mine copper, they opted to set up residence outside this little valley. Less tactful were the American prospectors who arrived in the late 1860s, and flooded in following the silver strike in 1870. They established the town and conflict with the Apache people erupted. Silver City's founder, John Bullard, was killed in 1871. Since then, the fortunes of the town have risen and fallen a few times. Today, the economy is

largely based on copper mining from the nearby Santa Rita mine.

These days, Silver City is a pretty lively place. The town attracts adventure addicts, who come to work and play in the nearby mountains and rivers. It's also home to a healthy student population – Western New Mexico University is based here. The **University Museum** (wnmu.edu/univ/museum.shtml) boasts the world's largest collection of Mimbres pottery and was completely renovated in 2017.

THE DRIVE
Take Hwy 180 east, then at Santa Clara turn left onto Hwy 152. After about 5.5 miles, look for the Chino Mine Observation Point on your right.

DETOUR
Gila Cliff Dwellings
Start: 01 Silver City

It's easy to imagine how the mysterious, relatively isolated **Gila Cliff Dwellings National Monument** (nps.gov/gicl) might have looked in the 13th century. Here, the influence of the Ancestral Puebloans on the Mogollon culture is writ large. Take the 1-mile round-trip self-guided trail that climbs 180ft to the dwellings, overlooking a lovely forested canyon. Parts of the trail are steep and involve ladders. The trail begins at the end of Hwy 15, 2 miles beyond the visitor center.

To get here, take twisting Hwy 15 north from Silver City (figure on a two-hour drive). Heading back from the cliff dwellings, take Hwy 35 down the pleasant Mimbres Valley for a change of scenery, or to skip onwards to stop 3 on this trip.

02 SANTA RITA CHINO OPEN PIT COPPER MINE OBSERVATION POINT

Worked by American Indians and Spanish and Anglo settlers, this is the oldest active mine in the Southwest. From the observation point along Hwy 152, you can get an eyeful of it. A staggering 1.5 miles wide, the open pit is 1800ft deep, and produces 300 million pounds of copper annually.

THE DRIVE
Continue east on Hwy 152 for 26 miles. After San Lorenzo, the road becomes increasingly serpentine as you climb over the Black Range. There are a number of Forest Service campgrounds along this section.

03 EMORY PASS

Your journey over the Black Range tops out at the 8228ft Emory Pass. The lookout point offers expansive views of the Rio Grande basin to the east and the rows of craggy peaks that jut from it like sharp teeth. There's a hiking trailhead here that leads north along the spine of the Black Range.

THE DRIVE
You're not done with the curves yet – you've still got to go 16.5 miles down the other side of the pass!

04 HILLSBORO

Precious ore, including gold, silver and copper, was discovered around Hillsboro in the mid-1800s, but the boom didn't last long. When the silver market crashed in 1893 so did most of the towns. Today, Hillsboro is one of the largest ones left, with a population of around 300. It's best known for its Apple Festival on the Labor Day weekend (early September), featuring everything apple, including freshly baked pies and delicious cider. See some historical miscellany at the **Black Range Museum** (hillsborohistoricalsociety.com); if it's closed, go around back and yell for Jim and he'll likely open up.

KINGSTON

A blink-and-you'll-miss-it community of just 30 people (compared to 7000 in its heyday), Kingston is a small clutch of wooden buildings about a quarter mile off Hwy 152, between Emory Pass and Hillsboro. It's hard to believe this was one of the baddest cities in New Mexico, boasting 28 bars catering to everyone from Chinese fortune seekers to Billy the Kid, Butch Cassidy and Mark Twain. The only building that looks almost like it did during the 19th century is the beautifully restored Percha Bank, c 1884. Complete with an enormous working vault, the bank building is now a museum and art gallery. If no one's there, ask over at the Black Range Lodge (blackrangelodge.com), a comfortably rustic B&B that was once a casino and saloon.

THE DRIVE
Continue east, out of the foothills and into the Rio Grande Valley. Take I-25 north. It's 31 miles total.

05 TRUTH OR CONSEQUENCES

According to local lore, Geronimo himself came to this place to partake of the healing hot waters – and you should too. Long said to have therapeutic properties, the waters range in temperature from 98°F to 115°F (36°C to 46°C) and have a pH of 7 (neutral). Our favorite spot to soak is **Riverbend Hot Springs** (riverbendhotsprings.com), which has shared and private tubs overlooking a – wait for it – bend in the river. For something more spa-tastic, and way more expensive, hit the **Sierra Grande lodge and spa** (tedturnerreserves.com/sierra-grande), with posh private pools and a full menu of massages, facials, scrubs and even private yoga classes.

To engage your brain as well as your body, stop by the **Geronimo Springs Museum** (sierracountynewmexico.info), an engaging mishmash of minerals, local art and historical artifacts ranging from prehistoric Mimbres pots to beautifully worked cowboy saddles.

THE DRIVE
After filling up with gas, head north out of Truth or Consequences on Hwy 181, then turn left onto Hwy 52, bearing west, toward the Black Range. The road winds around Cuchillo Mountain, into the little town of Winston. At the T intersection, turn left and follow signs for 2.7 miles to Chloride. In total, it's 40 miles.

06 CHLORIDE

In the foothills of the Black Range, tiny Chloride (population eight) was abustle in the 19th century with enough silver miners to support eight saloons. By the end of the 20th century, the town was on the verge of disintegration. Fortunately, the historic buildings are being restored by Don and Dona Edmund, who began renovating the old **Pioneer Store** (pioneerstoremuseum.com) in 1994. Today, this general store from 1880 is a museum with a rich collection of miscellany from Chloride's heyday, including wooden dynamite detonators, farm implements, children's coffins, saddles and explosion-proof telephones used in mines. You can see the Hanging Tree to which rowdy drunks were tied until they sobered up, the Monte Cristo Saloon (now an artist co-op and gift shop) and a few other buildings in various stages of rehabilitation.

THE DRIVE
Backtrack to Winston and keep going north on Hwy 52. After 9 miles, continue straight onto the dirt road, toward Dusty. After 9 more miles, turn right onto Forest Rd 140/CRE 14. Drive to the parking/turnaround area just before the track crosses the stream.

07 MONTICELLO BOX

This steep-walled canyon that rises abruptly along Alamosa Creek was frequented by Geronimo and his renegade Chiricahua Apache band during the mid-1870s, in part because of a sacred warm spring inside the gorge. Outside, not far from the junction of Hwy 52 and Forest Rd 140, sat

Photo opportunity

Frame an antique at Chloride's Pioneer Store.

Pioneer Store, Chloride

the headquarters of the Warm Springs Apache reservation. It was here, in April 1877, that Geronimo arrived for what he believed would be a peaceful meeting with 'Indian agent' John Clum; instead, Geronimo was captured, shackled and interned at the San Carlos reservation in Arizona (from which he would later escape).

Note that the land surrounding the canyon is private and access has become the subject of fierce debate over the past several years. At the time of writing, Monticello Box was closed to the public.

THE DRIVE

Heading north on Hwy 52 for about 40 miles, you'll traverse some of New Mexico's most subtly stunning terrain, up intermittent Alamosa Creek and out onto the undulating Plains of San Agustin. Bonus points if you can manage to time this around sunset. You'll hit the Very Large Array just before reaching Hwy 60.

08 VERY LARGE ARRAY RADIO TELESCOPE

If you make it to this literally otherworldly looking spread of massive antenna dishes before dark, check out the museum and take a walking tour of the facility (p127). If you arrive too late, it's still worth the trip just to see the silhouettes against the twilight sky. For the museum, turn left on Hwy 166.

18

NEW MEXICO

BEST FOR DESSERTS

Pie Town – c'mon, the town is named for its pie.

Into the Gila

DURATION	DISTANCE	GREAT FOR
2 days	299 miles / 481km	Outdoors, family

BEST TIME TO GO	May to October, when it's warm enough to enjoy.

Pie Town

From the otherworldly to the earthy, take a trip into New Mexico's wild southwest. With its huge dish antennas spread across a swath of the Plains of San Agustin and pointing at the sky, the Very Large Array launches this trip to an out-of-this-world beginning. Hwys 12 and 180 curve around the Gila massif, bringing you to the Catwalk, the San Francisco Hot Springs and on into the historic Wild West town of Silver City.

Link your trip

17 Geronimo Trail
At Silver City, just keep on going to follow the path of this Apache legend.

19 Highway 53 to Acoma
Take the scenic back roads north of Pie Town to check out lava flows, pueblos and more.

01 SOCORRO

Named in 1598 by conquistador Don Juan de Oñate after local Piro Indians gave him and his men corn, Socorro (which means 'aid' or 'help') has a pleasant plaza, with a couple of good places to grab a bite nearby – but that's about it. The main sight in town is the **San Miguel Mission** (sdc.org/~smiguel), sections of which date to the 1600s. Socorro is also close to the Bosque del Apache National Wildlife Refuge (p102).

THE DRIVE Head west on Hwy 60 for 45 miles, then turn left onto Hwy 52; go 2.3 miles and turn right on Hwy 166 to the Very Large Array Radio Telescope. Don't expect to have mobile phone service for most of this drive.

02 VERY LARGE ARRAY RADIO TELESCOPE

Twenty-seven huge antenna dishes (each weighing 230 tons) together comprise a single superpowered telescope – the **Very Large Array Radio Telescope** (VLA; nrao.edu), run by the National Radio Astronomy Observatory. The dishes move along railroad tracks that crisscross the open plains, their layout reconfigured as needed to study the outer limits of the known universe. To match the resolving power of the VLA, a regular telescope would have to be 22 miles wide!

The VLA has increased our understanding of black holes, space gases and radio emissions, among other celestial phenomena. And it's had starring and cameo roles in Hollywood films, including *Contact*, *Armageddon* and *Independence Day*. If none of that's enough to interest you, well, they're just unbelievably cool. There's a small museum at the visitor center, where you can take a free, self-guided tour with a window peek into the control building.

THE DRIVE Back on Hwy 60 head west for 35 miles; when you see the striking crags of the Sawtooth Mountains to the north, you're getting close. Hope you're hungry.

03 PIE TOWN

Yes, seriously, a town named after pie. And for good reason. They say you can find the best pies in the universe here (which makes you wonder what they've really been doing at the VLA). The **Pie-O-Neer Café** (pieoneerhomestead.com) just might prove their case. The pies are dee-lish, the soups and

Hate to Backtrack?

If you're in Pie Town, you don't need to retrace your route to Datil to pick up Hwy 12. Instead, from Hwy 60, head south on the dirt road that's directly across from the junction with Hwy 603 North. Go straight on this for 6.2 miles, then take the left fork onto Green Gap Rd/A56. At the next fork 8.8 miles later, continue straight toward Horse Springs. Then 2 miles later, go left at an unsigned fork, down a hill (there's a mailbox at the fork). Stay on that for 28 miles, until you hit Hwy 12 at Horse Springs. (If you're trying to do this route backwards, there's no sign on Hwy 12 at Horse Springs, so look for the dirt road heading north at the windmill between mile markers 48 and 49.) In dry weather, two-wheel-drive vehicles should be OK; in wet weather, you'd definitely want a 4WD, if you attempt it at all.

stews are homemade, and you'll be hard pressed to find another host as welcoming as Kathy Knapp – who advises you to call in advance to make sure they won't run out of pie before you get here, and just to check that it's even open.

On the second Saturday of September, Pie Town holds its annual **Pie Festival** (pietownrisingstars.org), with baking and eating contests, the crowning of the Pie Queen, Wild West gunfight reenactments and horned toad races.

THE DRIVE
Backtrack 20 miles to Datil, then turn south on Hwy 12. Curve into the Gila, past Reserve, which is a good lunch stop, and head south on Hwy 180. Turn left at Hwy 159 and follow it for nine vertiginous, slow-going miles on a route that's often impassable in winter. It's 130 miles total – let the carsick-prone ride shotgun!

DETOUR
Lightning Field
Start: 03 Pie Town

Heading on toward the Arizona border on Hwy 60, out in the high desert plains around Quemado, gleams the **Lightning Field** (diaart.org/sites/main/lightningfield), an art installation created by Walter de Maria in 1977. Four hundred polished stainless-steel poles stand in a giant grid, with each pole about 20ft high – but the actual lengths vary so the tips are all level with each other. During summer monsoons, the poles seem to draw lightning out of hovering thunderheads. The effect is truly electrifying! You can only visit if you stay overnight in the simple on-site cabin, with only six visitors allowed per night. Advance reservations are required. Check out the website for more details.

04 MOGOLLON

Once an important mining town, Mogollon is now a semi-ghost town with only a few antique and knick-knack shops and, as is typical for middle-of-nowhere New Mexico, one proud little restaurant. This one is called the **Purple Onion**, and it's as good as you'd hope after making the trip. You can poke around in spring and fall, but things here are mostly only open on summer weekends.

THE DRIVE
Wind your way back to Hwy 180 and continue south for 3 miles, then turn left on Hwy 174 and follow signs for the Catwalk.

05 THE CATWALK

Sixty-five miles north-west of Silver City, the Catwalk trail follows a suspended metal walkway through narrow Whitewater Canyon, where you can see the creek rushing beneath your feet. The Catwalk is wheelchair-accessible and great for kids. While some will find it disappointingly short, it offers a painless way to experience a bit of the Gila.

THE DRIVE
Back on Hwy 180, head south for about 7 miles to the turn off for San Francisco Hot Springs (between mile markers 59 and 58) and continue to the parking lot.

06 SAN FRANCISCO HOT SPRINGS

Down in the bottom of a cottonwood-shaded oasis, right along the gently flowing San Francisco River, are a couple of hot-spring pools. To reach them you've got to hike about 2 miles, gradually descending until you reach the canyon's edge, when

Very Large Array Radio Telescope (p127)

Photo opportunity

Focus on the telescope that's the Very Large Array.

The Gila

FOTOLUMINATE LLC/SHUTTERSTOCK ©

THE GILA

The 3.3 million acres of the Gila (hee-lah) cover eight mountain ranges, including the Mogollon, Tularosa, Blue and Black. This rugged country is just right for black bears, mountain lions and the reintroduced Mexican gray wolves (despite what the billboards around Reserve may say), plus four species of endangered fish including Gila trout. Really, it's no surprise that it was here that legendary conservationist Aldo Leopold spearheaded a movement to establish the world's first designated wilderness area, resulting in the creation of the Gila Wilderness in 1924; in 1980, the adjacent terrain to the east was also designated as wilderness and named after Leopold.

the trail becomes steeper – but from there it's only a hundred feet or so down to the bottom. You've got to wade across the river to reach the springs, but poke around a bit and you'll find them. In summer it can be extremely hot at midday – and afternoon skies can suddenly brew with thunderstorms – so be sure to take drinking water and watch the weather.

THE DRIVE
Continue on Hwy 180 south for 57 miles, all the way into Silver City.

07 SILVER CITY

The granddaddy of New Mexico's boom-bust-boom town success stories, Silver City's streets are dressed with a lovely mishmash of old brick and cast-iron Victorians and thick-walled red adobe buildings. The place still emits a Wild West air. Billy the Kid spent some of his childhood here, and a few of his haunts can still be found mixed in with the new coffee shops, quirky galleries and Italian ice-cream parlors gracing the historic downtown. Ensconced in an elegant house from 1881, the **Silver City Museum** (silvercitymuseum.org) features mining and household artifacts from Silver City's Victorian heyday, as well as stunning photographs of the aftermaths of some of the flash floods that ripped through town.

19

NEW MEXICO

Highway 53 to Acoma

BEST FOR CULTURE

Dances at Zuni Pueblo.

DURATION	DISTANCE	GREAT FOR
2 days	200 miles / 322km	Outdoors, history and culture

BEST TIME TO GO	May to October, after the winds and before the snows

Powwow, New Mexico

Take the back road from Gallup to Acoma Pueblo, where you can meet wolves, explore lava caves and check out old-school graffiti. Your GPS may tell you that the best route is I-40, but humans are still (sometimes) smarter. Prove it by taking this road, first to Zuni Pueblo, then across rippling hills and alongside a lava field set. Before hitting mesa-top Acoma Pueblo, you'll spend some time on the interstate – but not much.

Link your trip

13 Georgia O'Keeffe Country
Head north from Gallup along Hwy 491 for Navajo culture and ancient ruins.

18 Into the Gila
Take small roads south from Hwy 53 to Hwy 60, for rugged mountains, high-tech telescopes – and pie!

01 GALLUP

The mother town on New Mexico's Mother Road seems stuck in time. Settled in 1881, when the railroad came through, Gallup had her heyday during the road-tripping 1950s, and many of the dilapidated old hotels, pawn shops and billboards, mixed in with today's galleries and trading posts, seem like they haven't changed much since the Eisenhower administration.

Modern-day Gallup is an interesting mix of Anglos and American Indians; it's not unusual to hear people speaking Navajo on their cell phones

while buying groceries at the local Walmart. Tourism is limited mostly to Route 66 road-trippers and those in search of American Indian history and handicrafts: Route 66 runs straight through downtown Gallup's historic district and is lined with pretty, renovated light-red sandstone buildings housing dozens of kitschy souvenir shops as well as high-quality American Indian art.

Downtown, stretch your legs and check out the murals – some from the 1930s – painted on numerous buildings. Then stop into the **Ellis Tanner Trading Company** (etanner.com). The shop doubles as a sort of social gathering place for local Navajos and still operates a functional trade counter. If you don't have anything to swap, your dollar is good in the huge pawn room. Dig around for one of the unique pieces of turquoise jewelry tucked away behind a collection of vintage sheep-wool rugs.

THE DRIVE
Take Hwy 602 south, then fork right onto Indian Rte 4. Turn right on Hwy 53, toward Zuni. This leg is 38 miles.

02 ZUNI PUEBLO

Zuni is the name given by the Spanish to the pueblo known to the tribe that dwells there as Halona-weh, meaning 'red ant hill' – which symbolizes the center of the universe. Its artisans are famed for their jewelry and fetishes, and you can buy beautiful pieces at little shops throughout the town. For a good selection in one place, go to **Turquoise Village** (turquoisevillage.com).

The **A:shiwi A:wan Museum & Heritage Center** (ashiwi-museum.org) traces Zuni history with tribal artifacts and early photos. Nearby, the massive **Our Lady of Guadalupe Mission** features impressive locally painted murals of about 30 life-size kachinas (ancestral spirits). The church dates from 1629, although it has been rebuilt twice

Photo opportunity

A howling wolf at Wild Spirit Wolf Sanctuary.

Gray wolf

since then. The **Zuni Tourism Office** (zunitourism.com) is a good place to start your visit.

The most famous ceremony at Zuni is the all-night **Shalak'o ceremonial dance**, held on the first weekend in December and continuing for the next several days. The **Zuni Tribal Fair** (late August) features a powwow, local food and arts-and-crafts stalls. To observe any ceremony in Zuni, you must attend an orientation; call the tourist office for more information.

THE DRIVE

Take Hwy 53 east 8 miles past Ramah, which makes a good lunch stop, turn right onto Indian Rte 125, then go 7.8 miles and hang a right on Indian Rte 120. Your next stop is 4 miles up, on your left.

03 WILD SPIRIT WOLF SANCTUARY

Animal-lovers won't want to miss the **Wild Spirit Wolf Sanctuary** (wildspiritwolfsanctuary.org). Home to rescued captive-born wolves and wolf-dog mixes, the sanctuary offers four interactive walking tours per day, where you walk with the wolves – and get closer than you imagined – that roam the sanctuary's large natural-habitat enclosures. On the quarter-mile walk you'll learn everything you ever wanted to know about wolves, from behavior to what they like to eat to why they make terrible watchdogs. For a special 'photo tour' ($50 per person per hour) – when you can actually get inside the pens –

make reservations two weeks in advance. Primitive camping is available for $15 per night, with all the wolf howling you ever wanted to hear included. There's also a guest cabin with two bedrooms, a big loft and full kitchen.

THE DRIVE
Having got your wolf fix, get back on Hwy 53 and head east for 3 miles.

04 EL MORRO NATIONAL MONUMENT

Also called Inscription Rock, **El Morro National Monument** (nps.gov/elmo) has been autographed by passers-by since 1250, when the first pueblo petroglyphs were etched near the top of this 200ft hunk of sandstone rising above a permanent pool of water. Spanish conquistadors, Anglo pioneers and railway surveyors all paused to fill their canteens at the 200,000-gallon waterhole, and when they stopped many couldn't help leaving a record of their visit behind. It's quite a sight – more than 2000 messages were carved into the soft rock before President Teddy Roosevelt turned El Morro into America's second national monument. Of the two trails that leave the visitor center, the paved, half-mile loop to **Inscription Rock** is wheelchair accessible. The unpaved, 2-mile **Mesa Top loop trail** requires a steep climb to the pueblos. Trail access ends one hour before closing.

THE DRIVE
Continue east for about 19 miles on Hwy 53, past the Cimarron Rose.

05 EL MALPAIS

The rugged **El Malpais National Monument** (nps.gov/elma), pronounced el-mahl-pie-ees and meaning 'bad land' in Spanish, consists of almost 200 sq miles of lava flows bounded by Hwy 53 to the north and Hwy 117 to the east. Five major flows have been identified, the most recent pegged at only 2000 to 3000 years old. Prehistoric American Indians may have witnessed the final eruptions: local legends refer to 'rivers of fire.'

There are numerous trails here, though expect very strenuous, exposed hikes (bring a compass). Stop by the **Information Center** to pick up permits to explore nearby lava tubes – some of which are ice caves – or get the lowdown on possible hikes. Alternatively, stop by the **Northwest New Mexico Visitor Center** in Grants.

THE DRIVE
Continue on Hwy 53 and then join I-40 and head east to exit 96. Turn right on Hwy 124, then left on Indian Rte 27. Go left again on Indian Rte 30 (Pueblo Rd), then right on Indian Rte 38 (Haaku Rd), and keep going for about 6 miles. The total distance is 54 miles.

DETOUR
Chain of Craters Backcountry Byway
Start: 05 El Malpais

For a real backcountry adventure, follow the rugged Chain of Craters Backcountry Byway (aka County Rd 42) across the western and southern quadrants of the Malpais. The road connects with Hwy 53 a few miles west of El Malpais Information Center and bounces along for 33 miles until it hits Hwy 117, about 15 miles south of La Ventana arch. Along the way, it passes several craters, caves and lava tubes (reached by signed trails). Unless you paid for full coverage on your rental car, a high-clearance vehicle is highly recommended, but 4WD isn't (usually) necessary; in wet or snowy weather, the road might be impassable.

For further exploration, follow Hwy 117 north. Possible hikes here include the recommended Narrows Trail (8 miles), with views of La Ventana arch, and the Lava Falls Loop (1 mile), which traverses the now-frozen ripples, fissures, vents and craters of a lava flow.

06 ACOMA PUEBLO

Journeying to the top of Sky City is like climbing into another world. There are few more dramatic mesa-top locations – the village sits 7000ft above sea level and 367ft above the surrounding plateau. It's one of the oldest continuously inhabited settlements in North America; people have lived at Acoma since the 11th century. In addition to a singular history and a dramatic location, it's also justly famous for its pottery, which is sold by individual artists on the mesa. There is a distinction between 'traditional' pottery (made with clay dug on the reservation) and 'ceramic' pottery (made elsewhere with inferior clay and simply painted by the artist), so ask the vendor.

Visitors can only go to Sky City on **guided tours** (acomaskycity.org), which leave from the visitor center at the bottom of the mesa. Check the website or phone to confirm that it'll be open. Note that between July 10 and July 13 and either the first or second weekend in October, the pueblo is closed to visitors. Though you must ride the shuttle to the top of the mesa, you can choose to walk down the rock path to the visitor center on your own.

20

NEW MEXICO

Billy the Kid Trail

DURATION	DISTANCE	GREAT FOR
2 days	128 miles / 206km	History and culture, family

BEST TIME TO GO	July to October, for the UFO Festival, hot summer days and fall foliage.

BEST FOR HISTORY

The legendary Wild West town, Lincoln.

Smokey Bear (p139)

Walk in the bootprints of Billy the Kid, the pawprints of Smokey Bear and the ET-prints (just roll with it...) of the Roswell aliens. Crisscross classic outlaw country in a section of New Mexico that's rife with mystery. Did aliens crash near Roswell? Did Pat Garrett kill Billy the Kid? Here, the Rio Hondo carves a canyon through the foothills of the Capitan Mountains and Sierra Blanca Peak towers over the Tularosa Basin.

Link your trip

12 El Camino Real & Turquoise Trail

From Valley of Fires, continue west on 380 to hop on this historic route at Bosque del Apache National Wildlife Refuge.

16 Las Cruces to Carlsbad Caverns

Connect Roswell and Carlsbad to see the caverns, White Sands and more.

01 ROSWELL

Whether or not you're a true believer, a visit to Roswell is worthwhile to experience one of America's most enduring, eclectic and fanatical pop-culture phenomena. Sure it's about as cheesy as it gets for some, but conspiracy theorists and X-Files fanatics descend from other worlds into Roswell in real seriousness. Oddly famous as both the country's largest producer of wool and its UFO capital, Roswell has built a tourist industry around the alleged July 1947 UFO crash, after which the military quickly closed the area and allowed no

more information to filter out for several decades. Was it a flying saucer? The local convention and visitors bureau suggests that Roswell's special blend of climate and culture attracted touring space aliens who wanted a closer look. Decide for yourself at the **International UFO Museum & Research Center** (roswellufomuseum.com), where original photographs and witness statements form the 1947 Roswell Incident Timeline and explain the 'great cover-up.' The library claims to have the most comprehensive UFO-related materials in the world, and we have no reason to be skeptical.

THE DRIVE
Take Hwy 70/380 west for almost 50 miles, across the plains and into the scenic Hondo Valley. At the fork where Hwys 70 and 380 split, go left onto Hwy 70 and travel about 4 miles.

DETOUR
Billy's Grave
Start: 01 Roswell

If you're driving this route as a pilgrimage to Billy, then you might want to make the 84-mile trek north from Roswell to **Fort Sumner**, where Sheriff Pat Garret shot and killed Billy the Kid on July 14, 1881, when the outlaw was just 21 years old. Billy's grave is next to the poignant **Bosque Redondo Memorial** (bosqueredondomemorial.com). His tombstone is protected by an iron cage to keep 'souvenir hunters' from stealing it. Again.

02 SAN PATRICIO

San Patricio, a tranquil country village along the Rio Ruidoso, boasts the kind of golden glow and gentle scenery that's been drawing artists to New Mexico for more than a century. Stop in at the **Hurd-La Rinconada Gallery** (wyethartists.com), set on a huge spread with an orchard and a polo field, to see (and purchase) the work of classic New Mexican artist Peter Hurd and his son Michael, plus that of their relatives,

the Wyeths. You can also stay overnight here in one of five lovely **casitas**.

THE DRIVE
Backtrack to Hwy 380 and turn left at the fork, heading west for 13 miles.

03 LINCOLN

More of a museum than a town, Lincoln is where the gun battle that turned Billy the Kid into a legend took place. Favoring authenticity over Hollywood stereotypes, Lincoln is about as close to 19th-century reality as it gets. Some say it's the best preserved Wild West town in America. Modern influences, such as souvenir stands, are not allowed, and the main street has been designated the **Lincoln Historic Site** (nmhistoricsites.org/lincoln). It's a pretty cool place to get away from this century for an afternoon. Start at the **Anderson-Freeman Visitors Center**, where exhibits on the Buffalo soldiers, Apaches and the Lincoln County War explain the town's history. Then stroll the main street to the **Tunstall Store** (with a remarkable display of late 19th-century merchandise), the courthouse where the Kid famously shot his way to freedom, and **Dr Wood's house**, an intact turn-of-the-century doctor's home and office.

THE DRIVE
Continue west for 12 miles on Hwy 380.

04 CAPITAN

You've seen his likeness in state and national forests everywhere around the region. But did you know that Smokey Bear was also a real black bear? Once upon a time (back in 1950), a little cub was found clinging to a tree, paws charred from a 17,000-acre forest fire in the Capitan Mountains. What better name to give him than that of the famous cartoon bear that had been the symbol of fire prevention since 1944? Nursed back to health, Smokey spent the rest of his days in the National Zoo in Washington, DC, and became a living mascot. At the 3-acre **Smokey Bear Historical Park**, in the village of Capitan, 12 miles west of Lincoln, you can see the bear's grave and learn all about forest fires. Every 4th of July, a **Smokey the Bear Stampede** features a parade, a rodeo, cookouts and other festivities. **Smokey Bear Days**, celebrated the first weekend in May, includes a street dance, a wood-carving contest, and craft and antique-car shows.

THE DRIVE
Head uphill on Hwy 48 south for 17 miles, which skirts the eastern edge of the million-acre Lincoln National Forest – this is the part of the drive that really rocks in fall when the leaves put on a spectacular color show. The Sacramento Mountain range to the west of the highway adds to the scenic allure.

DON'T MISS:
Lincoln

The entire town is a historical monument, including the courthouse from which Billy the Kid shot his way to freedom.

05 RUIDOSO

You want lively in these parts? You want Ruidoso. Downright bustling in the summer and big with punters at the racetrack, resortlike Ruidoso has an utterly pleasant climate thanks to its lofty and forested perch near the Sierra Blanca (11,981ft). Neighboring Texans and local New Mexicans escaping the summer heat of Alamogordo and Roswell are happy campers here (or more precisely, happy cabiners). The lovely Rio Ruidoso, a small creek with good fishing, runs through town. Summertime hiking and wintertime skiing at Ski Apache keep folks busy, as do a number of galleries.

Ruidoso Downs (raceruidoso.com) has weekend horse racing, including Labor Day's All American Futurity, the world's richest quarter-horse race, with a purse of $3 million.

THE DRIVE
Take Hwy 48 north, then turn left onto Hwy 37. At Hwy 380, hang a left, then another left once you reach Hwy 54/Central Ave in Carrizozo. In total, it's around 30 miles.

06 CARRIZOZO

Sitting where the Sacramento Mountains hit the Tularosa Basin, Carrizozo is worth a quick stop to peruse historic 12th St, once the town's main axis. Take a look into **Gallery 408** (gallery408.com). In addition to the work

Ruidoso Downs race

BEST VISTAS

The best views for many miles are at the summit of **Sierra Blanca Peak** (11,981ft); to claim them, you'll have to leave the car and set out on foot for a day. Park in the smaller lot at Ski Apache, and set out on Trail 15. Follow signs west and south along Trails 25 and 78 to the top of Lookout Mountain (11,580ft). From there, an obvious beaten path continues due south for 1.25 miles up Sierra Blanca. On the way up you'll gain about 2000ft of elevation; the round-trip hike is just over 9 miles long. It's best done from June to October. The **ranger station** (fs.usda.gov/lincoln) in Ruidoso has more information.

of a number of regional artists, you can see what remains of the herd of Painted Burros – a local public sculpture project similar to the Cow Parades of Chicago and New York, but on a slightly smaller scale. Some have pun-tastic names, like the Asstronomer, its body decorated with the night sky. Proceeds from donkey sales benefit the local animal shelter, Miracles Paws for Pets.

THE DRIVE

Backtrack to Hwy 380 then head west a few miles to the sprawling slab of basalt. You can't miss it.

07 VALLEY OF FIRES

Four miles west of Carrizozo, explore the rocky blackness of a 125-sq-mile lava flow that's 160ft deep in the middle. A 0.6-mile nature trail at **Valley of Fires Recreation Area** is well paved, easy for kids and marked with informative signs describing the geology of the volcanic remains. You're also allowed to hike off-trail, simply cutting cross-country over the flow as you like to create your own adventure. There are campsites and shaded picnic tables near the visitor center.

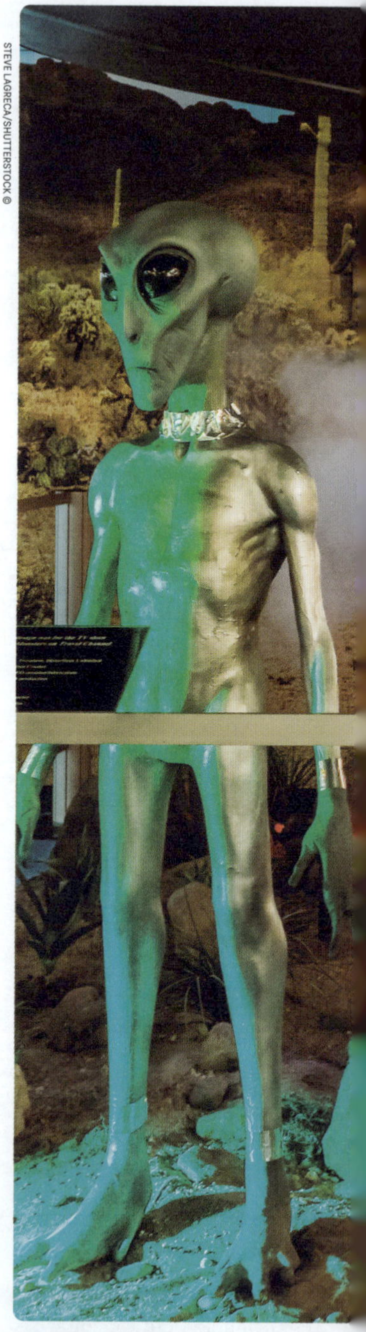

STEVE LAGRECA/SHUTTERSTOCK ©

International UFO Museum & Research Center (p137)

Photo opportunity

Pose with aliens in Roswell.

OKLAHOMA
ARKANSAS
NEW MEXICO
TEXAS
USA
LOUISIANA
MEXICO
Gulf of Mexico
Springdale
Tulsa
Oklahoma City
Conway
Little Rock
Hot Springs
Pine Bluff
Ouachita National Forest
Lawton
Durant
Red River
Wichita Falls
Sherman
Paris
Texarkana
Denton
Fort Worth
Dallas
Longview
Shreveport
Monroe
Tyler
Corsicana
Waco
Nacogdoches
Toledo Bend Reservoir
Lufkin
Alexandria
Sam Rayburn Reservoir
Lake Livingston
Huntsville
Sam Houston National Forest
Bryan
Austin
Brazos River
Beaumont
Lake Charles
Lafayette
Houston
Galveston
Gonzales
New Braunfels
San Antonio
Victoria
Corpus Christi
Kingsville
Padre Island National Seashore
Rio Grande City
Harlingen
Port Isabel
Laredo
Rio Grande
Eagle Pass
Del Rio
Kerrville
Fredericksburg
Buchanan Lake
Brownwood
Abilene
San Angelo
Sonora
Big Spring
Midland
Odessa
Fort Stockton
Alpine
Marfa
Presidio
Big Bend National Park
El Paso
Rio Grande (Rio Bravo)
Perryton
Lake Meredith
Amarillo
Lubbock
Brownfield
Texico
Santa Fe
Las Vegas
Albuquerque
Tucumcari
San Antonio
Sierra Blanca Peak
Roswell
Alamogordo
Deming
Las Cruces
Lincoln National Forest
21
22
23
24
0
500 km

SEAN PAVONE/SHUTTERSTOCK ©

El Paso (p154)

Texas

Explore

Texas

The Lone Star State is vast, diverse and welcoming: from big-city lights to small-town simplicity, white-sand beaches to high-country hikes. The only way to truly appreciate its size is to hit the road and discover what's out there beneath those endless horizons.

What's your pleasure? Fields of wildflowers and rolling hills in the land of Lyndon Johnson? Beaches and seafood in coastal towns along the Gulf? An epic journey from the US–Mexico border to the Texas panhandle? Or intriguing desert landscapes and an enormous national park? Whatever route you choose, saddle up for adventure on a grand scale.

San Antonio

Much the most attractive of Texas' major cities – and much the oldest, too, having celebrated its 300th birthday in 2018 – San Antonio is a rather pleasurable Texas base. It has the legendary Alamo, symbol of Texan independence, at the very heart of the city, while the River Walk, a glorious network of waterside pathways tucked below street level and lined with bars and restaurants, offers leisurely strolling through downtown and beyond. Start your Hill Country excursion here, but you'll long to return at journey's end.

El Paso

Big-city El Paso is very much a city on the up, and a central part of its charm is its appropriation of its border location to celebrate the country's diversity. The city has also had a facelift in recent years, and it can now boast some excellent museums, a fistful of new hotels, a restored streetcar line, the Chihuahuas baseball team and even its very own crop of microbreweries. It's a fun, proudly multicultural place with a culinary scene that draws inspiration from its Mexican near-neighbors just across the border.

Austin

If you thought that Texas was big oil and conservative politics, Austin will change your mind. The state's capital may be dwarfed by Dallas, Houston and the other big and brash cities of old Texas, but Austin has a real buzz about it, with a small-town heart that survives in the great live music, an exciting culinary scene and, surrounding it, an

WHEN TO GO

Deciding when to drive Texas is very often a question of avoiding the state's brain-frying heat. For milder temperatures, try spring or fall: February to April and September to November are ideal. In the Hill Country and parts of the state's heartland, March and April are when you'll drive amid glorious fields of wildflowers.

extensive patchwork of parks, lakes and seemingly endless trails for exploring the great outdoors by bike or on foot.

Houston

Houston is where laid-back, boot-scooting, pickup truck town meets high-powered, high-cultured and high-heeled metropolis. Texas' largest city, and the fourth largest in the US, is the energy capital of the world. While it can be a pricey place to eat and stay, the choice is as broad as any city in the US, the nightlife is legendary, and the city has some of the best museums anywhere in the Southwest, and on no account miss NASA's Space Center Houston, just outside town. If think laterally and explore the diverse residential neighborhoods, you'll find enclaves, each with their own personality, of restaurants and luxurious shops spread far and wide. Just be sure you don't underestimate Houston's sauna-like summer months.

TRANSPORT

The sheer size of Texas means most people fly into the state. The airports with the best connections are in Houston, Austin, Dallas and San Antonio; El Paso is another option out west. If you're driving, the transcontinental interstate for the southern USA is I-10; it cuts through Texas en route between Florida and California.

WHAT'S ON

South by Southwest

The US music industry's major annual gathering in Austin in March.

Houston Art Car Parade

Wacky, arted-out vehicles hit the streets en masse in April.

Historic Homes Tour

Galveston's finest privately owned old houses are on display in May.

Fiesta San Antonio

There are river and street parades and more in a mammoth, citywide party over 10 days in late April.

WHERE TO STAY

Texas has every possible accommodations possibility, from ubiquitous chain hotels and motels to family-run B&Bs brimful of warmth and charm. Austin and Houston have the largest numbers of hostels, but historic hotels occupy even some of the smaller towns and you'll find delightfully positioned resorts in places like the Hill Country. Beyond the town limits, head to the Bandera area for guest or dude ranches that include horseback rides and fun cowboy activities in your stay, and to any of the national and state parks for campgrounds in scenic locations; a handful of national parks also have lodges.

Resources

Travel Texas (traveltexas.com) State tourism website; request the huge *Texas Travel Guide*.

Texas Monthly (texasmonthly.com) Great writing about Texas, dining and shopping guides.

Texas Highways (texashighways.com) Travel magazine with extensive festival and event listings.

Texas Parks & Wildlife (tpwd.texas.gov) A complete guide to Texas' outdoor recreation and environment.

21

TEXAS

BEST FOR CULTURE

Two-stepping at Texas' oldest dance hall in Gruene.

Hill Country

DURATION	DISTANCE	GREAT FOR
2–5 days	229 miles / 369km	Outdoors, family, history and culture

BEST TIME TO GO	In March and April for wildflower season

The Alamo

Gently rolling hills are blanketed with wildflowers and dotted with vineyards. Friendly locals enjoy an easy way of life, with dance halls, lazy rivers and local art adding to the fun. In March and early April, this is one of the prettiest drives in all of Texas – perfect for a day trip or a meandering and low-stress vacation. Along this route, you can rummage through antique stores, listen to live music and dig in to a plate of barbecue.

Link your trip

23 Texas Gulf Coast
From San Antonio, drive 143 miles south along Hwy 37 to reach the coastal town of Corpus Christi.

24 Heart of Texas
From Kerrville, travel 149 miles northwest to San Angelo.

01 SAN ANTONIO

While sprawling San Antonio isn't part of the Hill Country, it's a great launching point for your trip. Don't miss the lovely, European-style **River Walk**, a paved canal that winds its way through downtown and is lined with colorful cafes, hotel gardens and stone footbridges. It stretches north to the museum district and south to the missions, adding pretty mileage for walking and cycling. For the best overview, hop on a Rio San Antonio cruise.

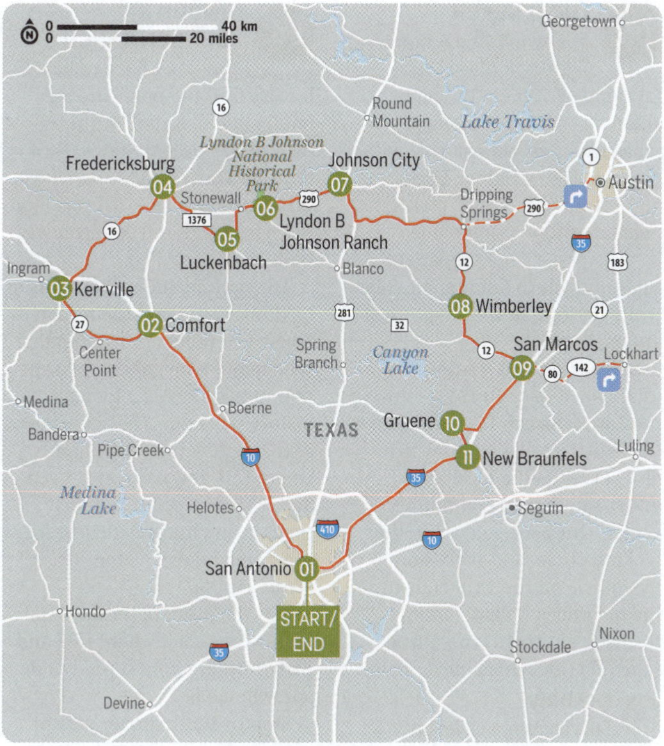

WHY I LOVE THIS TRIP

Amy Balfour, writer

An easy drive from Austin and San Antonio, the Hill Country will lure you in with its natural beauty and easygoing but festive spirit. You can drive this entire loop in under five hours, but what's the rush? The small towns here hide historic treasures and culinary finds, plus there's a new gorgeous view around every bend. You'll be glad if you decide to linger.

Whatever you do, pay your respects at the **Alamo**, the beloved historical site where revolutionaries fought for Texas' independence from Mexico.

THE DRIVE

Ready to get out of town? Head northwest on I-10 to get to Comfort, less than an hour from downtown San Antonio. When the wildflowers are blooming, detouring north on Waring Welfare Rd then back on TX 473 makes a nice scenic drive.

02 COMFORT

Remarkably under the tourist radar, Comfort is a 19th-century German settlement and perhaps the most idyllic of the Hill Country bunch, with rough-hewn limestone homes from the late 1800s and a beautifully restored historic center in the area around High and 8th Sts.

Shopping for antiques is the number-one activity, but you'll also find a few good restaurants, a winery and, as the town's name suggests, an easy way of life. Start at the **Comfort Antique Mall** (visitcomfortantiquemall.com), where you can pick up a map of antique stores, or go to the Comfort chamber of commerce website (comfort-texas.com) to discover your options.

THE DRIVE

The interstate is a straight shot, but we prefer the back road of TX 27 west to Kerrville that takes you through serene farmland.

03 KERRVILLE

The Hill Country can feel a bit fussy at times, but not Kerrville. What it lacks in historic charm, it makes up for in size, offering plenty of services for travelers, as well as easy access to kayaking, canoeing and swimming on the Guadalupe River. Stretch your legs on the new **River Trail** (kerrvilletx.gov), which runs alongside the Guadalupe River for several miles. The best place to hop in the water is **Kerrville-Schreiner Park** (kerrvilletx.gov).

Check out an eye-catching collection of cowboy art at the **Museum of Western Art** (museumofwesternart.com). The building itself is beautiful, with hand-made mesquite parquet floors and unique vaulted domes overhead.

THE DRIVE
Take TX 16 northeast of town for half an hour to get to Fredericksburg.

04 FREDERICKSBURG

The unofficial capital of the Hill Country, Fredericksburg is a 19th-century German settlement that specializes in 'quaint.' The town packs a lot of charm into a relatively small amount of space, with a boggling array of welcoming inns and B&Bs and a main street lined with historic buildings housing German restaurants, biergartens, antique stores and shops. The informative **National Museum of the Pacific War** (pacificwarmuseum.org) spotlights the Pacific Theater in WWII. Admiral Chester Nimitz, Commander of the US fleet there during the war, grew up in Fredericksburg.

Many of the shops are typical tourist-town offerings, but there are enough interesting stores to make it fun to wander. Plus, the town is a great base for checking out the surrounding peach orchards and vineyards. A few miles east of town, **Wildseed Farms** (wildseedfarms.com) has cultivated fields of wildflowers and sells seed packets along with wildflower-related gifts.

THE DRIVE
Five miles southeast of town on Hwy 290, turn right on RR 1376 and follow it 4.5 miles into Luckenbach. There are only a handful of buildings here, so don't worry that the actual town is somewhere else.

05 LUCKENBACH

You won't find a more laid-back place than Luckenbach, where the main activity is sitting at a picnic table under an old oak tree with a cold bottle of Shiner Bock and listening to guitar pickers (who are often accompanied by roosters). Come prepared to relax and get to know some folks while basking in the small-town atmosphere.

Start at the old trading post established back in 1849 – now the **Luckenbach General Store** (luckenbachtexas.com), which also serves as the local post office, saloon and community center. Out back you'll find the picking circle, and there's often live music on the weekends in the old dance hall; go online to check out the town's music schedule (luckenbachtexas.com).

THE DRIVE
Take Luckenbach Rd back north to Hwy 290. The LBJ Ranch is just 7 miles down and the entrance is right off the highway.

DON'T MISS:

Waring Welfare Drive

When the wildflowers are in bloom, take this short but worthwhile detour on the way to Comfort, TX.

06 LYNDON B JOHNSON RANCH

You don't have to be a history buff to appreciate the family home of the 36th president of the United States. Now the **LBJ Ranch** (nps.gov/lyjo), this beautiful piece of Texas land is where Lyndon B Johnson was born, lived and died.

The park includes the Johnson birthplace, the one-room schoolhouse where he briefly attended school and a neighboring farm that now serves as a living history museum. The centerpiece of the park is the ranch house where LBJ and Lady Bird lived and where he spent so much time during his presidency that it became known as the 'Texas White House.'

You can also see the Johnson family cemetery, where LBJ and Lady Bird are both buried under sprawling oak trees.

Stop by the visitor center to get your free park permit and a map.

THE DRIVE
LBJ's childhood home is just 15 minutes east on Hwy 290.

07 JOHNSON CITY

You might assume Johnson City was named after President Johnson, but the bragging rights go to James Polk Johnson, a town settler back in the late 1800s. The fact that James Johnson's grandson went on to become president of the United States was just pure luck.

Here you'll find **Lyndon B Johnson's Boyhood Home** (nps.gov/lyjo), which Johnson himself had restored for personal posterity. Park rangers from the visitor center (nps.gov/lyjo) – where you can also find local information

Luckenbach General Store

U. S. POST-OFFICE
1850 LUCKENBACH, TX. 1971
OPEN
No Smokin'
OPEN 9 AM
LIVE MUSIC DAILY
830·997·3224
www.luckenbachtexas.com

Photo opportunity

Bluebonnets – pose your kids or yourself in a field full of wildflowers.

Bluebonnets, Texas

DEAN FIKAR/SHUTTERSTOCK ©

and exhibits on the president and first lady – offer free guided tours every half-hour that meet on the front porch. On the surface, it's just an old Texas house, but it's fascinating when you think about the boy who grew up there.

THE DRIVE
Follow Hwy 290 south toward Blanco then east toward Dripping Springs. At Dripping Springs, turn right on RR 12 to Wimberley.

DETOUR
Austin
Start: 07 Johnson City

Since this trip is all about winding your way through the Hill Country, we didn't list Austin as a stop. After all, it warrants its own whole trip, which we hope your central Texas itinerary already includes.

However, we'd be remiss if we didn't mention that when you get to Dripping Springs, you're only half an hour from the Texas state capital. While you're there, do some exploring and stretch your legs with a walking tour.

08 WIMBERLEY

A popular weekend spot for Austinites, this artists community gets absolutely bonkers during summer weekends – especially on the first Saturday of each month from March to December, when local art galleries, shops and craftspeople set up booths for **Wimberley Market Days**, a bustling collection of live music, food and more than 475 vendors at Lion's Field on RR 2325. Keep an eye out for the 50 painted cowboy boots scattered around town (bootifulwimberley.com).

For excellent scenic views of the surrounding limestone hills, take a drive on FM 32, otherwise known as the Devil's Backbone. From Wimberley, head south on RR 12 to FM 32, then turn right toward Canyon Lake. The road gets steeper, then winds out onto a craggy ridge – the 'backbone' – with a 360-degree vista.

Afterwards, cool off at Wimberley's famous **Blue Hole** (cityofwimberley.com), one of the Hill Country's best swimming holes. It's a privately owned spot in the calm, shady and crystal-clear waters of Cypress Creek.

THE DRIVE
Keep going south on RR 12; San Marcos is about 15 minutes southeast through some more (mostly) undeveloped countryside.

09 SAN MARCOS

Around central Texas, 'San Marcos' is practically synonymous with 'outlet

SCENIC DRIVE: WILDFLOWER TRAILS

You know spring has arrived in Texas when you see cars pulling up roadside and families climbing out to take the requisite picture of their kids surrounded by bluebonnets, Texas' state flower. From March to April in Hill Country, Indian paintbrushes, winecups and bluebonnets are at their peak.

Check the **Wildflower Hotline** to find out what's blooming where. Taking Rte 16 and FM 1323, north from Fredericksburg and east to Willow City, is usually a good route.

malls.' Bargain shoppers can make a full day of it at two side-by-side shopping meccas. It's not exactly in keeping with the spirit of the Hill Country, but it's a popular enough activity that we had to point it out.

The fashion-oriented **San Marcos Premium Outlets** (premiumoutlets.com) is enormous – and enormously popular – with 140 name-brand outlets. Across the street, **Tanger Outlets** (tangeroutlet.com/sanmarcos) has more modest offerings, with brands that aren't that expensive to start with, but it's still fun to hunt for deals.

THE DRIVE
Shoot 12 miles down I-35 to the turnoff for Canyon Lake. Gruene is just a couple of miles off the highway.

DETOUR
Lockhart
Start: 09 San Marcos

People travel from all over the state to dig into brisket, sausage and ribs in Lockhart, officially designated in 1999 as the Barbecue Capital of Texas. Lucky for you, you only have to detour 18 miles to experience the smoky goodness. You can eat very well for under $15 at the following places.

Black's Barbecue (blacksbbq.com) is a longtime Lockhart favorite since 1932, with sausage so good Lyndon Johnson had them cater a party at the nation's capital.

Kreuz Market (kreuzmarket.com) has been serving Lockhart since 1900. The barn-like Kreuz Market uses a dry rub, which means you shouldn't insult them by asking for barbecue sauce – they don't serve it, and the meat doesn't need it.

The blackened pit room and homely dining room of **Smitty's Market** (smittysmarket.com) are all original (knives used to be chained to the tables). Ask them to trim off the fat on the brisket if you're particular about that.

RICHARD A MCMILLIN/SHUTTERSTOCK ©

Guadalupe River

10 GRUENE

Get a true taste of Texas at **Gruene Hall** (gruenehall.com), a dance hall where folks have been congregating since 1878, making it Texas' oldest. It opens early, so you can stop by anytime to toss back a longneck, two-step on the well-worn wooden dance floor or play horseshoes out in the yard. There's only a cover charge on weekend nights and when big acts are playing, so at least stroll through and soak up the vibe.

The town is loaded with antique stores and shops selling housewares, gifts and souvenirs, and **Old Gruene Market Days** are held the third weekend of the month, February through November, and the first weekend of December.

DON'T MISS:

Beer Drinking

Grab an ice-cold Shiner Bock and join the locals at Gruene Hall or on the Terlingua Porch.

THE DRIVE You don't even have to get back on the interstate; New Braunfels is just 3 miles south.

11 NEW BRAUNFELS

The historic town of New Braunfels was the first German settlement in Texas. In summer, visitors flock here to float down the Guadalupe River in an inner tube – a Texas summer tradition. There are lots of outfitters in town, like **Rockin' R River Rides** (rockinr.com). Their rental prices include shuttle service, and for an additional fee they can also hook you up with an ice chest to keep your drinks cold and a tube to float it on.

THE DRIVE From New Braunfels it's 32 miles on I-35 back to San Antonio.

22

TEXAS

Big Bend Scenic Loop

BEST FOR OUTDOORS

McDonald Observatory's nighttime star parties.

DURATION	DISTANCE	GREAT FOR
5–7 days	690 miles / 1110km	Outdoors

BEST TIME TO GO	Best between February and April – before the heat sets in

McDonald Observatory

Although it's known for wide-open spaces, west Texas is packed with surprising experiences that makes this a well-rounded drive. Getting to visit Big Bend National Park is reason enough to make this trip. But you'll also have plenty of fun along the way, exploring the quirky towns that are prime road-trip material. Unforgettable experiences in west Texas include art installations, astronomy parties and thriving ghost towns.

Link your trip

21 Hill Country

From Kent (the turnoff for Fort Davis) continue east on I-10 for 334 miles to join this loop at Kerrville.

24 Heart of Texas

From Marathon, go 243 miles east on Hwy 90 to catch up with this trip at Uvalde.

01 EL PASO

Start your trip in El Paso, a border city that's wedged into a remote corner of west Texas. While here, take advantage of the great Mexican food you can find all over the city – it's right across the river from Mexico – and enjoy El Paso's many free museums. Downtown, the **El Paso Museum of Art** (elpasoartmuseum.org) has a terrific Southwestern collection.

And don't miss the **El Paso Holocaust Museum** (elpasoholocaustmuseum.org), which hosts amazingly thoughtful and moving exhibits that

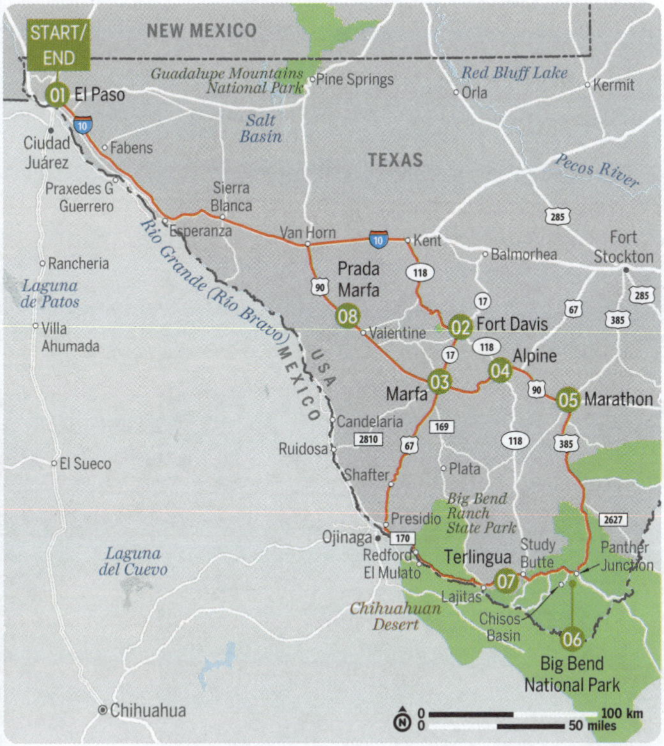

MARFA LIGHTS VIEWING AREA

The Marfa Lights that flicker beneath the Chinati Mountains have captured the imagination of many a traveler over the decades, with accounts of mysterious lights that appear and disappear on the horizon that go all the way back to the 1800s. Numerous studies have been conducted to explain the phenomenon, but the only thing scientists all agree on is that they have no idea what causes the apparition.

Catch the show at the Marfa Lights Viewing Area, on the south side of the road between Marfa and Alpine. From the platform, look south and find the red blinking light (that one's real). Just to the right is where you will (or won't) see the Marfa Lights doing their ghostly thing.

are imaginatively presented for maximum impact.

To the west, you'll find several good restaurants and watering holes in the new and developing Montecillo commercial and residential district.

THE DRIVE

Head east on I-10 for two hours, then turn onto TX 118 toward Fort Davis. The area is part of both the Chihuahuan Desert and the Davis Mountains, giving it a unique setting where the endless horizons are suddenly interrupted by rock formations springing from the earth.

02 FORT DAVIS

Here's why you'll want to plan on being in Fort Davis on either a Tuesday, Friday or Saturday: to go to an evening star party at **McDonald Observatory** (mcdonaldobservatory.org). The observatory has some of the clearest and darkest skies in North America, not to mention some of the most powerful telescopes.

Besides that, nature lovers will enjoy **Davis Mountains State Park** (tpwd.state.tx.us), and history buffs can immerse themselves at the 1854 **Fort Davis National Historic Site** (nps.gov/foda), a well-preserved frontier military post that's impressively situated at the foot of Sleeping Lion Mountain.

THE DRIVE

Marfa is just 20 minutes south on TX 17, a two-lane country road where tumbleweeds bounce slowly by and congregate around the barbed-wire fences.

03 MARFA

Marfa got its first taste of fame when Rock Hudson, Elizabeth Taylor and James Dean came to town to film *Giant* (1956).

But these days, this tiny town with one stoplight draws visitors from around the world for a different reason: its art scene. Donald Judd single-handedly put Marfa on the art-world map in the 1980s when he used a bunch

DON'T MISS:

Prada Marfa

This roadside art installation is dramatically set against the backdrop of dusty west Texas.

Santa Elena Canyon

of abandoned military buildings to create one of the world's largest permanent installations of minimalist art at the **Chinati Foundation** (chinati.org).

Art galleries are sprinkled around town, exploring everything from photography to sculpture to modern art. **Ballroom Marfa** (ballroommarfa.org) is a great gallery to catch the vibe. Try not to visit on a Monday or Tuesday, when many businesses are closed.

THE DRIVE
Alpine is about 30 minutes east of Marfa on Hwy 90/67.

04 ALPINE

The biggest little town in the area, Alpine is the county seat, a college town (Sul Ross University is here) and the best place to stock up on whatever you need before you head down into the Chihuahuan Desert.

Stop by the **Museum of the Big Bend** (museumofthebigbend.com) to brush up on the history of the Big Bend region. But don't expect it to be dry and dusty. The multimedia exhibits are big and eye-catching, and display-reading is kept to a minimum. Most impressive? The enormous replica wing bone of the Texas pterosaur found in Big Bend – the largest flying creature ever found, with an estimated wing span of more than 50ft.

THE DRIVE
Keep heading east. In 15 miles, look south for the guerilla art installation Target Marathon, a fun nod to Prada Marfa. In another 15 miles you'll reach the seriously tiny town of Marathon (mar-a-thun). The views aren't much during this stretch of the drive, but Big Bend will make up for all that.

05 MARATHON

This tiny railroad town has two claims to fame.

BILL KENNEDY/SHUTTERSTOCK ©

It's the closest town to Big Bend's north entrance – providing a last chance to fill up your car and your stomach – and it's got the **Gage Hotel** (gagehotel.com), a true Texas treasure that's worth a peek, if not an overnight stay.

THE DRIVE Heading south on Hwy 385, it's 40 miles to the northern edge of Big Bend, and 40 more to get to the Chisos Basin, the heart of the park. The flat road affords miles and miles of views for most of the drive.

06 BIG BEND NATIONAL PARK

At 1252 sq miles, this national park is almost the size of Rhode Island. Some people duck in for an afternoon, hike a quick trail and leave, but we recommend staying at least two nights to hit the highlights.

Seventeen miles south of the Persimmon Gap Visitor Center, pull over for the **Fossil Discovery Exhibit** (nps.gov/bibe), which spotlights the dinosaurs and other creatures that inhabited this region beginning 130 million years ago.

With more than 200 miles of trails to explore, it's no wonder hiking is one of the most popular activities, with many of the best hikes leaving from the Chisos Basin. Hit the short, paved **Window View Trail** at sunset, then hike the 4.4-mile **Window Trail** the next morning before it gets too hot. Spend the afternoon hiking the shady 4.8-mile **Lost Mine Trail**, or take a scenic drive to see the eerily abandoned **Sam Nail Ranch** or the scenic **Santa Elena Canyon**.

THE DRIVE From the west park entrance, turn left after 3 miles then follow the signs for Terlingua Ghost Town, just past Terlingua proper. It's about a 45-minute drive from the middle of the park.

Photo opportunity

Prada Marfa, a quirky roadside art installation.

07 TERLINGUA

Quirky Terlingua is a unique combination: it's both a ghost town and a social hub. When the local cinnabar mines closed down in the 1940s, the town dried up and blew away like a tumbleweed, leaving buildings that fell into ruins.

But the area has slowly repopulated, businesses have been built on top of the ruins, and locals gather here for two daily rituals. In the late afternoon, everyone drinks beer on the porch of **Terlingua Trading Company** (facebook.com/TerlinguaTradingCompany). And after the sun goes down, the party moves next door to **Starlight Theater** (thestarlighttheatre.com), where there's live music every night.

THE DRIVE Continue west on Rte 170, also known as the River Road, for a gorgeous drive along the Rio Grande inside Big Bend Ranch State Park. In 60 miles or so you'll reach Presidio. Head north on Hwy 67 to return to Marfa, then cut west on Hwy 90.

08 PRADA MARFA

So you're driving along a two-lane highway out in the middle of nowhere, when suddenly a small building appears in the distance like a mirage. You glance over and see … a Prada store? Known as the 'Prada Marfa' (although it's really closer to Valentine) this art installation set against the backdrop of dusty west Texas is a tongue-in cheek commentary on consumerism.

THE DRIVE Take Hwy 90 back to I-10 and head west to El Paso.

23

TEXAS

Texas Gulf Coast

DURATION	DISTANCE	GREAT FOR
4 days	470 miles / 756km	Outdoors, food and drink

BEST TIME TO GO	November to March, for cool weather and peak bird-watching

BEST FOR BEACHES

From Port Aransas to South Padre Island are miles and miles of white sand.

Padre Island (p161)

Cruise over 450 miles along the coastline with stops to spot endangered whooping cranes, party in chilled-out beach towns or live a little Texas history. You'll never quite get the sand out of your shorts on this trip – from the Galveston Seawall through the bird-watching trails of Aransas National Wildlife Refuge and South Padre Island beach life. There's good food and good fun all the way down the curve of the Texas coast.

Link your trip

21 Hill Country
Head north on I-37 from Corpus Christi to San Antonio, linking with this trip through the rolling landscapes of the Texas Hill Country.

24 Heart of Texas
It's 180 miles west of Hwy 77 from Harlingen up the Rio Grande Valley to Laredo and the deserts of west Texas.

01 GALVESTON

Miles of sandy beach front Galveston's Gulf Coast seawall, starting from the empty expanses of **East Beach** and stretching on down south. This island is part sunburned beach bum, part genteel Southern lady. Yet the massive spring-break and Mardi Gras party crowds coexist with smitten tourists wandering through the sizable Victorian districts (which date to the city's heyday as a port of entry for immigrants heading west) – maybe it's just that they can all get along over a table at one of the island's many great restaurants.

In the historic Strand district, old-fashioned brick-front buildings are spiffily refurbished, and there are boutiques, ice-cream parlors and general stores. Look into the history of the families that built Galveston at the **Bishop's Palace** (galvestonhistory.org) and **Moody Mansion** (moodymansion.org).

THE DRIVE
From the seawall, head south across the San Luis pass bridge to Follets Island. At Surfside Beach, the end of the road, go 21 miles inland on TX 332/288 via Lake Jackson to TX 35. Head south for 13 miles.

02 WEST COLUMBIA

The lands west of modern Houston were once a hub of frontier life, among the first of Mexican lands settled by Stephen F Austin's 'Old 400' under the empresario migration system. Though sleepy today, the historic **Varner-Hogg Plantation** (thc.texas.gov) and **Old Columbia Cemetery** give a glimpse into the lives of the hardy families that settled this land.

THE DRIVE
Continue along TX 35 for 54 miles.

03 PALACIOS

Once the domain of presidents and railroad barons, the 1903 **Luther Hotel** (facebook.com/lutherhotel) is something of a diamond in the rough, though it is currently closed – however, locals are fighting to preserve and reopen it, and the views out over Tres Palacios Bay certainly haven't lost their charm.

THE DRIVE
Continue on TX 35 for 50 miles through Port Lavaca to just past tiny Tivoli, where you turn southeast on TX 239. Follow the signs for 12 miles through corn farms until you reach Aransas National Wildlife Refuge.

DETOUR
Historic Goliad
Start: 03 Palacios

'Remember the Alamo!' is the modern icon of the Texas revolution, but contemporaries would have also recognized 'Remember Goliad!' where, on Palm Sunday, March 27, 1836, Mexican general Antonio López de Santa Anna ordered 350 Texian prisoners shot, after their surrender on the plains outside of town. The death toll was double that at the Alamo and helped inspire the Texians in their victory over Santa Anna at San Jacinto the following month.

There is a wealth of historic sites in and around the lovely town of Goliad. Start at the 1749 church and fort **Presidio La Bahia** (thc.texas.gov). It's 36 miles each way from Tivoli.

04 ARANSAS NATIONAL WILDLIFE REFUGE

Aransas National Wildlife Refuge (fws.gov/refuge/aransas) is a 115,000-acre wetland park that protects the wintering

RICHARD SEELEY/SHUTTERSTOCK ©

Photo opportunity

A whooping crane in flight at Aransas National Wildlife Refuge.

Whooping cranes, Aransas

ground of 240 or so whooping cranes, of which in the 1940s only 15 remained in a small flock that wintered here. Standing nearly 5ft tall, with a 7ft wingspan, whooping cranes are an impressive sight. Easy hiking trails and observation platforms let you spot the birds from November to March.

To get a ground-level experience and close-up views from out on the water, take a tour with **Rockport Birding & Kayak Adventures** (whoopingcranetours.com). It's not uncommon to spot 60 bird species on a half-day excursion by boat or kayak.

THE DRIVE
Follow FM 774 through a series of turns 16 miles west until it rejoins TX 35. Turn south and go 13.5 miles to Lamar and turn east.

05 GOOSE ISLAND STATE PARK

The main part of **Goose Island State Park** (tpwd.state.tx.us), where admission is charged, is right on Aransas Bay (there are beaches, but no swimming). The busiest times at the park are during the summer and whooping-crane season (November to March), but it's better for fishing than bird-watching.

The oldest tree on the coast is an oak more than 1000 years old, located near the main part of the park off 12th St, in an idyllic spot in a sea of wildflowers. En route back to the highway, follow signs for the 1835 **Stella Maris Chapel**.

THE DRIVE
It's only 5 miles south on TX 35 to the twin coastal towns of Rockport and Fulton.

06 ROCKPORT & FULTON

A pedestrian-friendly waterfront, fishing boats plying their trade (plus fresh-caught seafood at restaurants nearby) and Rockport's small, revamped downtown make the adjoining towns of Rockport and Fulton an enjoyable stop.

The side streets between TX 35 and Aransas Bay are dotted with numerous art galleries, especially in the center of Rockport; the towns claim to be home to the state's highest percentage of artists. Check in with the local creative scene at the **Rockport Center for the Arts** (rockportartcenter.com), just across from the harbor.

THE DRIVE
Head 10 miles south on TX 35 to Aransas Pass, turn east on TX 361

for 6.5 miles of wetland views until you reach the free 24-hour ferries for the 10-minute transfer to Port Aransas. Be prepared for a wait in the busy season.

07 PORT ARANSAS

Port Aransas (ah-ran-ziss), or 'Port A,' is for many the most appealing beach town on the Texas coast. On the northern tip of Mustang Island, it's small enough that you can ride a bike or walk anywhere but large enough to have plenty of activities and nightlife. Days are relaxed, dominated by hanging out on the beach, fishing and doing nothing.

THE DRIVE
Head south 28 miles on what starts as TX 361 to Padre Island National Seashore. It's beaches all the way, and places like Mustang Island State Park make good stops.

08 PADRE ISLAND NATIONAL SEASHORE

If you're looking for solitude, **Padre Island National Seashore** (nps.gov/pais) fits the bill. The tidal flats, shifting dunes and shallow lagoon waters provide plenty of opportunity for hiking, swimming and windsurfing. Most of the 70 miles of this island refuge are only accessible by 4WD along the undeveloped beach. Hike in a mile or two and you'll have the place all to yourself.

THE DRIVE
Drive 15 miles back north to TX 358 and cross the John F Kennedy Causeway. Another 16 miles leads into the heart of downtown Corpus Christi.

09 CORPUS CHRISTI

In addition to a large marina and walkable waterfront, the 'Sparkling City by the Sea' has a small downtown strand and several good museums nearby. Anchored across the bay, in front of beach-bum restaurants and souvenir shops, is the unmissable **USS Lexington Museum** (usslexington.com), a 900ft-long aircraft carrier. Explore what's under the waves next door at the **Texas State Aquarium** (texasstateaquarium.org), whose interactive exhibits are a hit with all ages.

THE DRIVE
Drive 18 miles west to Hwy 77. Turn south and go 35 miles past Kingsville (and the historic King Ranch) to CR 628. It's a bumpy 9 miles east to the coastal hamlet of Loyola Beach.

10 LOYOLA BEACH

The little **King's Inn** (kingsinnriviera.com) is the stuff of legends, with seafood by the pound and plate after plate of avocado salad that draws visitors from up and down the Gulf Coast. Come hungry.

DON'T MISS:

Goliad

Although not as well remembered as the Alamo, this fort has an equally important place in Texas history.

THE DRIVE
Returning to Hwy 77, head 93 miles south to TX 100 and the turnoff for Los Fresnos. It's an easy side trip to the Palo Alto Battlefield, or keep on for 25 miles to Port Isabel.

11 PORT ISABEL

The atmospheric 1852 **lighthouse** (portisabellighthouse.com) sets the small-town vibe in Port Isabel. It has great restaurants and is a delightful place for a waterfront stroll.

THE DRIVE
A mere 3-mile jaunt over the Queen Isabella Causeway and you're on South Padre Island.

12 SOUTH PADRE ISLAND

The town of South Padre Island (SPI) works hard to exploit its sunny climate and beaches. For most of the year mellow beach bars and waterfront restaurants let you lounge away the day. But annually in March, SPI becomes a frenetic madhouse during spring break.

Wave-runner rental and parasailing opportunities abound and there are bird-watching trails. You can learn about the slowest-moving coastal denizens at **Sea Turtle Inc** (seaturtleinc.com), a rescue facility that offers tours and feeding presentations every half-hour. For a drink, try **Coco Beach Club** (cocobeachspi.com), one of the few bars right on the sand on the Gulf side. As you go north up the 34-mile-long island, the beach becomes ever more quiet and remote ... until the road dead-ends and only sand dunes remain.

24

TEXAS

Heart of Texas

DURATION	DISTANCE	GREAT FOR
4 days	709 miles / 1141km	Food and drink, history and culture, outdoors

BEST TIME TO GO	March to June and September to November, to avoid scorching heat but enjoy wildflowers

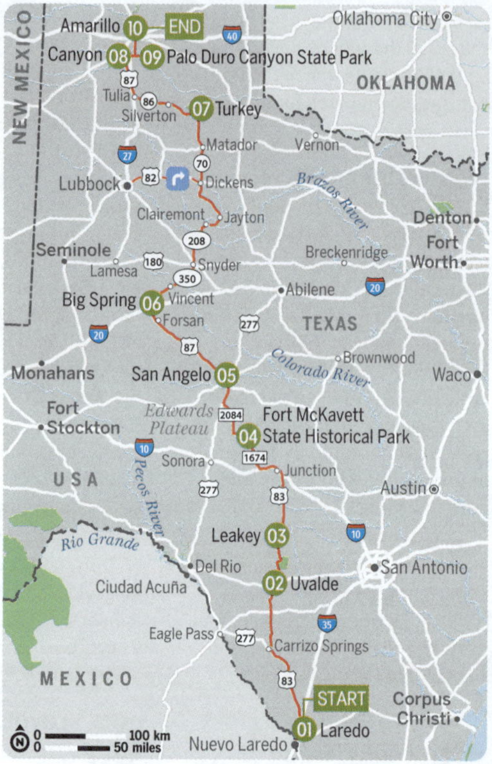

From the Mexico border to the panhandle city of Amarillo you'll cross the rural length and breadth of a timeless Texas. The big-city sprawls of Houston, Dallas or San Antonio seem very far away as you pass through hundreds of miles of open land barely touched by humans. By the time you reach Fort McKavett, you may even wonder what century you're in. At Palo Duro Canyon you'll wonder at timeless geologic wonders.

Link your trip

02 Route 66: The Southwest
The Mother Road passes right through Amarillo.

21 Hill Country
Outside of Junction, head southeast on I-10 to link to Kerrville, 54 miles away.

01 LAREDO

Even more than other Texas border towns, Laredo has always been tightly entwined with its sister city to the south, the fittingly named Nuevo Laredo.

While the border situation remains unsettled, Laredo's historic old downtown is evocative. Start at leafy San Agustín Plaza and stop into the **Republic of the Rio Grande Museum** (republicofthe riogrande.org) and grand **San Agustín Cathedral** (dioceseoflaredo.org). Then be sure to spend time at any of the many excellent local restaurants.

SILVIO LIGUTTI/SHUTTERSTOCK ©

Garner State Park

THE DRIVE
Drive 112 miles north on Hwy 83. The first 60 miles are through minimalist, arid south Texas country; the route then becomes more lush as the road begins following rivers and fertile valleys.

02 UVALDE

A pioneer town founded in 1853, Uvalde is a busy crossroads with a great **main square**, which is crowned by the grand neoclassical 1928 courthouse. Stop and stroll the square, pausing for something cool and refreshing along Main St.

THE DRIVE
Continue 40 miles north on Hwy 83 through scenery that rivals the Hill Country in its oak-tree-dotted beauty.

03 LEAKEY

Since prehistoric times, humans have been enjoying the beauty of the Frio River and its lovely canyon and valley. Tiny Leakey is little more than a crossroads, but what a crossroads! Hwy 83 follows the river north and south, while FM 337 runs east and west through wooded hills and secluded little valleys.

Just 10 miles south of town, **Garner State Park** (tpwd.texas.gov/state-parks/garner) is popular with campers.

THE DRIVE
Go 57 miles north on Hwy 83, then jog west for 18 miles on I-10. Continue north 25 miles on RR 1674 through hilly, uninhabited land textured with shrubs and trees.

04 FORT MCKAVETT STATE HISTORICAL PARK

General William Tecumseh Sherman once called this fort along the San Saba River 'the prettiest post in Texas.' Today, **Fort McKavett State Historical Park** (thc.texas.gov/historic-sites/fort-mckavett-state-historic-site) preserves the striking ruins of a once-important fort; some of the 25 buildings have been restored.

THE DRIVE
Drive east on FM 864, then head west 17 miles on Hwy 190. Turn north onto the wonderfully named Toe Nail Trail/RR 2084 (so dubbed for the toll it took on the feet of the first soldiers to march the route) and drive 27.5 miles north to Hwy 277; from there San Angelo is another 19 miles north.

05 SAN ANGELO

Situated on the fringes of the Hill Country, San Angelo is a purely Western town with an appealing overlay of gentility. The Concho River, which scenically runs through the town, offers walks along its wild, lush banks on the **El Paseo de Santa Angela**.

Fort Concho National Historic Landmark (fortconcho.com), dating to 1867 and the years of westward expansion, may be the best-preserved Western frontier fort in the US.

At the heart of not-to-be-missed downtown, the **Concho Avenue Historic District** is a good place to stroll – be sure to pick up a historic walking tour brochure at the **visitor center** (visitsanangelo.org). The most interesting section, known as Historic Block One, is between Chadbourne and Oakes Sts. Stop into **Miss Hattie's Bordello Museum** (misshatties.com), which recalls the town's wilder days.

At night you'll find great food, beer and music.

THE DRIVE
Follow the green ribbon of the North Concho River 87 miles northwest on US 87, through lands on the edge of oil country.

06 BIG SPRING

West of Big Spring, the land is flat and brown for 40 miles to the Permian Basin, where the cities of Midland and Odessa are at the heart of the energy boom. But here it's quiet and time moves slow. Everywhere, that is, except at the 15-story **Hotel Settles** (hotelsettles.com), a long-closed 1930s luxury hotel (the product of an oil boom) that has opened again after a lavish restoration.

Nearby, 380-acre **Big Spring State Park** (tpwd.texas.gov/state-parks/big-spring) has a fine nature trail. There are few west Texas dance halls more authentic than the **Stampede**, a bare-bones, early-1950s affair 1.5 miles northeast of Big Spring. (The schedules, however, are sporadic.)

THE DRIVE
Drive 190 miles north through some of the most lonesome terrain in Texas via TX 350, TX 208 and finally the scenic gem TX 70. Be sure to keep your tank filled – even some county seats around here don't have gas stations anymore.

DON'T MISS:
Miss Hattie's Bordello Museum

You can tell everyone you visited a notorious Texas brothel at this only slightly risqué stop.

DETOUR
Buddy Holly's Lubbock
Start: 06 Big Spring

The hub for the Western music that is emblematic of the Texas plains, Lubbock is the hometown of one of the genre's greatest legends: Buddy Holly. The town celebrates his legacy at the unmissable **Buddy Holly Center** (buddyhollycenter.org). It's possible to still find the rockabilly sound that Holly made famous in the surrounding **Depot District**, at venues like the legendary **Cactus Theater** (cactustheater.com). Be sure to listen to KDAV 1590AM radio, which stills plays the music of Holly's era.

See how people lived on the plains over the last 200 years at the excellent **National Ranching Heritage Center** (depts.ttu.edu/nrhc), which features dozens of restored old structures in a park-like setting.

From TX 70, Lubbock is 58 miles west on Hwy 82.

07 TURKEY

Tiny Turkey is one of those vanishing back-road towns that seems about to fall off the map and become a mere footnote in a history book. Bob Wills is one of Texas' most important musicians, and his life is recalled at the modest but worthwhile **Bob Wills Museum** (bobwillsday.com).

THE DRIVE
It's 54 miles of flat, Texas two-lane driving west on TX 86. Then turn north, following the train tracks 32 miles north on Hwy 87.

08 CANYON

Small yet cultured, Canyon once had Georgia O'Keeffe teaching art at its West Texas A&M University. Today's campus is home to what many people figure is the best

Photo opportunity

Palo Duro Canyon glowing in a rainbow of colors.

Palo Duro Canyon State Park

history museum in Texas: the **Panhandle-Plains Historical Museum** (panhandleplains.org), where the many highlights include the myriad ways to skin a buffalo.

THE DRIVE
The geologic wonders of Palo Duro Canyon are a straight 15 miles east on TX 217.

09 PALO DURO CANYON STATE PARK

At 120 miles long and about 5 miles wide, Palo Duro Canyon is second in size in the USA only to the Grand Canyon. The cliffs striated in yellows, reds and oranges, the rock towers and other geological oddities are a refreshing surprise among the seemingly endless flatness of the plains, and are worth at least a gander.

Prehistoric American Indians lived in the canyon 12,000 years ago. The more than 26,000 acres that make up the **park** (tpwd.state.tx.us) attract hikers, horseback riders and mountain bikers.

THE DRIVE
Retrace your drive 7 miles west on TX 217 and turn due north for 15 miles on FM 1541 N/S Washington St.

10 AMARILLO

Although Amarillo may seem as featureless as the surrounding landscape, there's plenty here to sate even the most attention-challenged. Beef, the big local industry, is at the heart of Amarillo and features in many of its attractions.

Don't miss the **San Jacinto District** for Amarillo's best shopping, dining and entertainment.

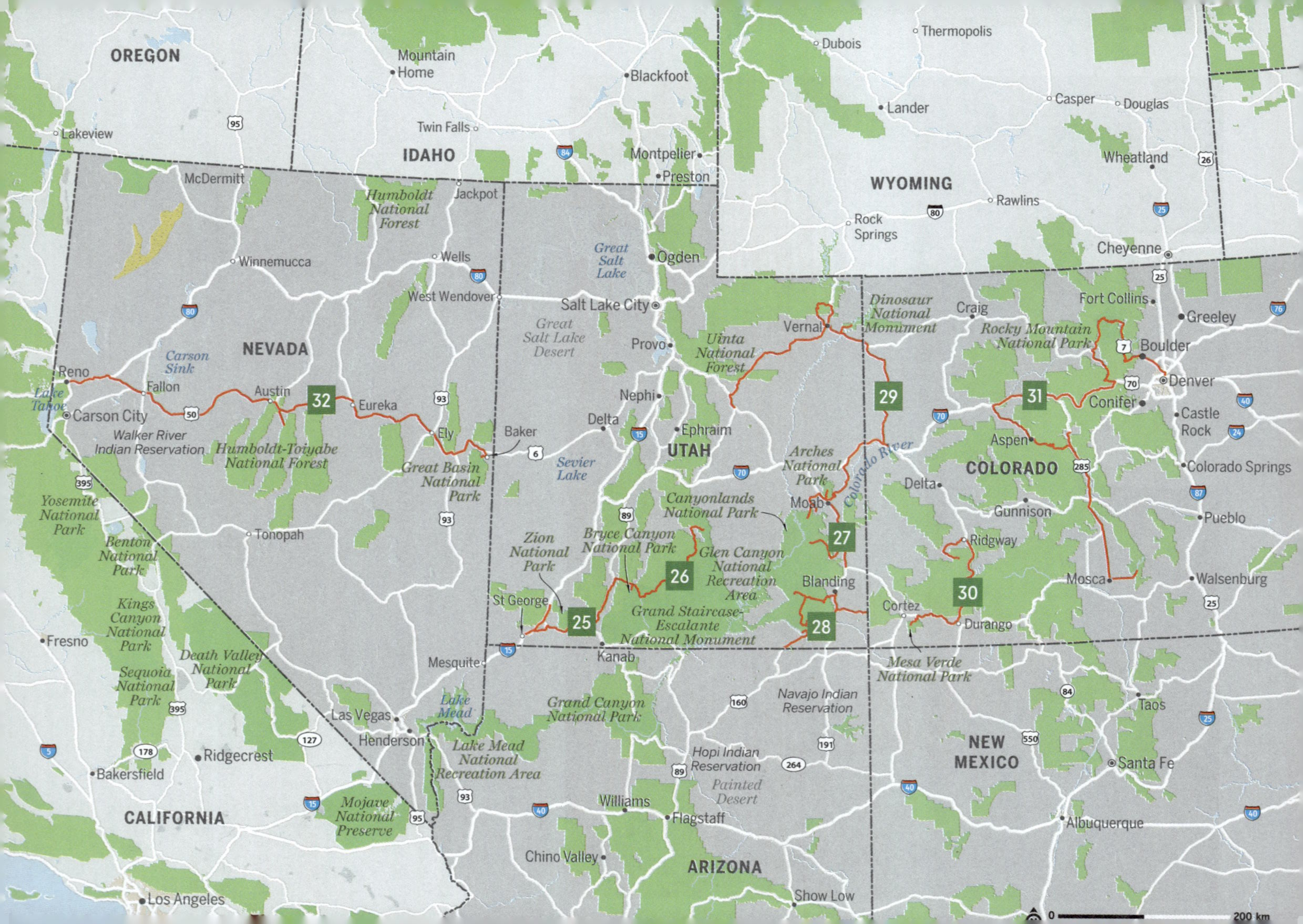

OREGON
IDAHO
WYOMING
NEVADA
UTAH
COLORADO
CALIFORNIA
ARIZONA
NEW MEXICO
Lakeview
Mountain Home
Twin Falls
Blackfoot
Montpelier
Preston
Dubois
Thermopolis
Lander
Casper
Douglas
Wheatland
Rawlins
Rock Springs
Cheyenne
McDermitt
Jackpot
Humboldt National Forest
Winnemucca
Wells
West Wendover
Great Salt Lake
Ogden
Salt Lake City
Great Salt Lake Desert
Provo
Vernal
Dinosaur National Monument
Craig
Fort Collins
Greeley
Rocky Mountain National Park
Boulder
Denver
Uinta National Forest
Carson Sink
Reno
Lake Tahoe
Fallon
Carson City
Austin
Eureka
Ely
Walker River Indian Reservation
Humboldt-Toiyabe National Forest
Great Basin National Park
Baker
Nephi
Delta
Ephraim
Sevier Lake
Arches National Park
Colorado River
Aspen
Conifer
Castle Rock
Colorado Springs
Pueblo
Gunnison
Moab
Canyonlands National Park
Ridgway
Tonopah
Yosemite National Park
Benton National Park
Kings Canyon National Park
Zion National Park
Bryce Canyon National Park
Glen Canyon National Recreation Area
Blanding
Mosca
Walsenburg
St George
Grand Staircase-Escalante National Monument
Cortez
Durango
Fresno
Death Valley National Park
Sequoia National Park
Mesquite
Kanab
Mesa Verde National Park
Lake Mead
Las Vegas
Henderson
Grand Canyon National Park
Navajo Indian Reservation
Taos
Lake Mead National Recreation Area
Hopi Indian Reservation
Santa Fe
Ridgecrest
Bakersfield
Painted Desert
Mojave National Preserve
Williams
Flagstaff
Albuquerque
Chino Valley
Los Angeles
Show Low
25
26
27
28
29
30
31
32
0
200 km

Monument Valley (p186)

Utah, Colorado & Nevada

Explore

Utah, Colorado & Nevada

There's no more beautiful corner of the US than Utah, Colorado and Nevada, with its sculpted red terrain, alpine meadows carpeted in wildflowers and snowcapped Rocky Mountain peaks. This is real road-trip country, at its best when traveling through ghost towns and the quiet back roads of rural US.

Stunning and strange, southern Utah alone has nine national parks and monuments. The region's human story is just as varied, stretching from the Age of Dinosaurs, through Ancestral Puebloan peoples and Old West mining towns, to today's Navajo Nation. Populated or barren, desert or snow-bound, high elevations and low: it's all in this one ripe-for-adventure region.

Denver

One of the fastest-growing cities in the US, Denver combines great energy, beautiful weather and beautiful people. It also has good restaurants, even better bars, great accommodations, and a pretty lively arts and music scene. It's numerous oh-so-cool neighborhoods all have their own personality and the entire city is connected through bike paths and parks. Best of all, within a couple of hours' drive there are vast areas of wilderness, as well as world-class skiing and hiking.

Cedar City

Quiet little Cedar City, in Utah's southwest, has a fabulous collection of B&Bs, as well as a 6000ft-above-sea-level location that offers respite from the heat of the deserts on the plains down below. These would be reason enough to base yourself here. But there are state parks, dramatic landforms and a hearty pizza-and-steak gastronomic sensibility, all before you set out to explore Zion, Bryce and beyond.

Bluff

Bluff is a blink-and-you'll miss it kinda place. This is even more likely because of the jaw-dropping, red-rock scenery that will capture your attention as you approach town. But stay a while and you'll find campgrounds, motels and B&Bs, as well as a handful of restaurants and cafes. Best of all, you're perfectly placed for exploring a whole slew of natural wonders, among them Moki Dugway (30 miles), Hovenweep National Monument (40 miles), Monument Valley (47 miles) and

WHEN TO GO

Summer is usually the best time to visit: the snow is gone, all roads are passable, all attractions are open and many festivals take center stage. The only downside is the heat: scorching temperatures are the norm; temperatures are much milder in spring or fall. Winter skiing is excellent on the Colorado slopes.

Natural Bridges National Monument (61 miles).

Telluride

Towering peaks surround Telluride on three sides – no other town in Colorado feels this close to a Swiss mountain village. As a base, it's a superb place to linger, not least because skiing, hiking and biking are all possible here, and Telluride is known across the nation for its fine summer festivals. There's also an emphasis on quality rather than quantity when it comes to restaurants and nightlife spots. You're also well placed for exploring just about anywhere in the Southwest.

Reno

The starting point of many a Nevada road trip, Reno, in the shadow of the Sierra Nevada, is more than the glitz and bright lights of its many casinos. Beyond the somewhat garish downtown, with its photo-worthy, mid-century modern architecture, cool new bars, top-notch restaurants and vibrant arts spaces, sprawls a city of parks and pretty houses inhabited by a friendly bunch eager to welcome you. Only an hour from Lake Tahoe, the city is also a fun urban basecamp for exploring the lake and the Sierra foothills.

TRANSPORT

The main air gateways are in Denver, Reno, Las Vegas and Utah's Salt Lake City. Many transcontinental bus and rail routes, as well as highways, pass through Utah, Nevada and/or Colorado. The Oakland–Chicago Amtrak service, for example, passes through Salt Lake City. Road routes are similar: I-70 runs east–west across the USA, passing through central Colorado and Utah.

WHAT'S ON

Telluride Bluegrass Festival

This festival in June promises top-notch bluegrass.

Telluride Film Festival

In September, one of the best film festivals in the US, attracting big-name stars.

Great American Beer Festival

More than 500 microbreweries adorn this Denver beer fest in September or October.

Moab Folk Festival

Folk music dominates this fun, sustainable festival in Utah in September.

Resources

Colorado Tourism Board (colorado.com) All things Colorado.

Colorado Trail Explorer (trails.colorado.gov) Info on 39,000 miles of trails.

Nevada Commission on Tourism (travelnevada.com) What to see and do in Nevada.

Utah Office of Tourism (utah.com) Online guide to Utah.

National Park Service (nps.gov) Covers the region's national parks.

WHERE TO STAY

Pitch a tent under a starlit Colorado or Utah sky, learn new cowboy skills at a dude ranch, or stay in a heritage B&B, adobe inn or historic hotel that evokes the glory days of the Old West. Everything's possible out here, including, of course, that great American stalwart, the roadside motel. In general, Colorado has the best places to stay but they can be expensive; Utah's campgrounds in national parks are simply glorious; and Nevada is usually (but not always) about the triumph of quantity over character. Fun fact: Las Vegas has more hotel rooms than any other city in the world (around 150,000).

25

UTAH, COLORADO & NEVADA

Zion & Bryce Canyon National Parks

BEST FOR HIKING

Zion Canyon has easy walks to strenuous, canyon-climbing hikes.

DURATION	DISTANCE	GREAT FOR
6 days	178 miles / 286km	Outdoors

BEST TIME TO GO	
	In April and September you'll likely have warm weather both at low and high elevations.

Snow Canyon State Park

From canyon floor to cliff-top perches, the red-rock country in southwestern Utah will delight your eyes and challenge your muscles. From the sheer wall of Zion to the pastel sentinels of hoodoos that form Bryce Canyon, these are the landscapes that no one traveling in the Southwest should miss. This trip takes in the parks' classic highlights as well as tiny Western towns and off-the-beaten-path nature sanctuaries.

Link your trip

04 Grand Canyon North Rim & Lake Powell

Leaving Zion National Park, detour southeast down Hwy 89 for 115 miles to Page to start exploring northern Arizona.

28 Scenic Byway 12

From outside Bryce Canyon National Park, Scenic Byway 12 heads east through rugged and remote public lands and parks.

01 KOLOB CANYONS

Start your visit at the **Kolob Canyons Visitor Center** (nps.gov/zion), gateway to the less-visited, higher elevation section of Zion National Park off I-15. Even in peak season you'll see relatively few cars on the scenic 5-mile **Kolob Canyons Road**, a high-plateau route where striking canyon and rangeland views alternate. The road terminates at **Kolob Canyons Viewpoint** (6200ft); from there the **Timber Creek Overlook Trail** (1-mile round trip) follows a 100ft ascent to a small

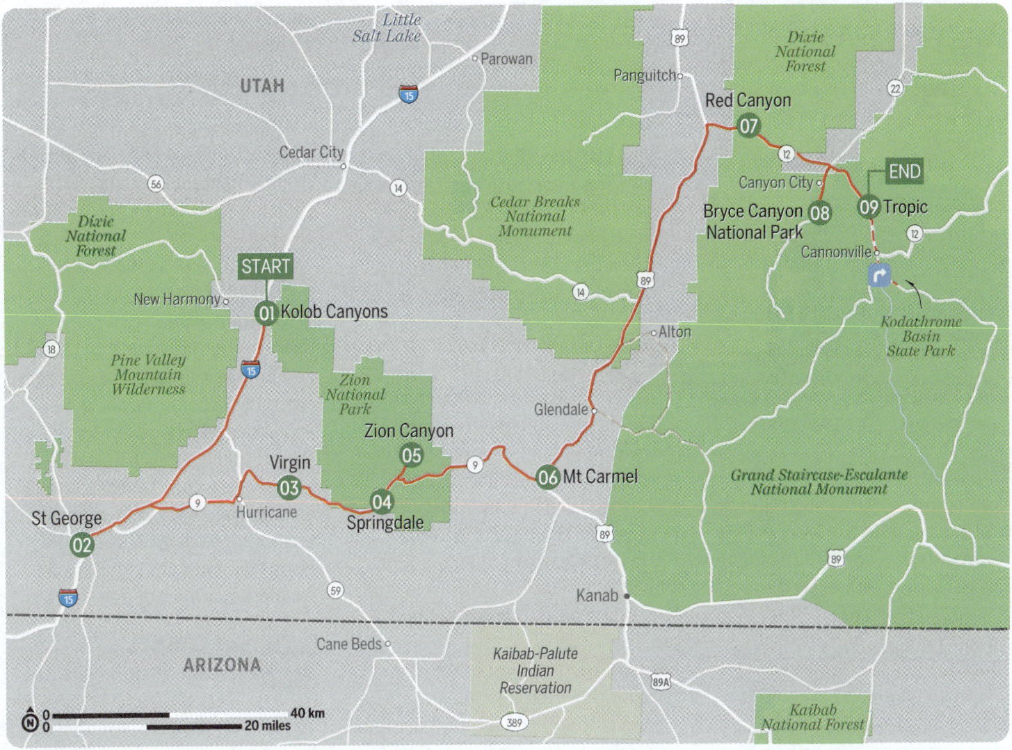

peak with great views of the Pine Valley Mountains beyond. In early summer the trail area is covered with wildflowers. Note that the upper section of the road may be closed due to snow from November through May.

The best longer hike in this section of the park is the **Taylor Creek Trail** (5-mile round trip), which passes pioneer ruins and crisscrosses a creek, with little elevation change.

THE DRIVE
Distant rock formations zoom by as you cruise along at 70-plus mph on I-15. St George is 41 miles south.

02 ST GEORGE

A spacious Mormon town with an eye-catching temple and a few pioneer buildings, St George sits about equidistant between the two halves of Zion. The **Chamber of Commerce** (stgeorgechamber.com) can provide information on the historic downtown. Otherwise, use this time to stock up on food and fuel in this trip's only real city (population 77,000). Eleven miles north of town, **Snow Canyon State Park** (stateparks.utah.gov) is a 7400-acre sampler of southwest Utah's famous land features. Easy trails that are perfect for kids lead to tiny slot canyons, cinder cones, lava tubes and fields of undulating slickrock.

THE DRIVE
Off the interstate, Hwy 9 leads you into canyon country. You'll pass the town of Hurricane before sweeping curves give way to tighter turns (and slower traffic). Virgin is 27 miles east of St George.

03 VIRGIN

The tiny-tot town of Virgin, named after the river (what else?), has an odd claim to fame – in 2000 the city council passed a largely symbolic law requiring every resident (about 600 of them) to own a gun. You can't miss **Fort Zion**, which sells homemade fudge, ice

WHY I LOVE THIS TRIP

Carolyn McCarthy, writer

There's a reason these national parks have seen an enormous uptick in visitors in recent years. Zion and Bryce offer some of the most thrilling scenery out there. Wander among the odd pastel hoodoos of Bryce Canyon or wade the river through Zion's Narrows under sheer cliff walls. Welcome to the cathedrals of the American West.

cream and every Western knick-knack known to the free world. Stop and have your picture taken in the 'Virgin Jail' or 'Wild Ass Saloon' in the replica Old West village here. It's pure, kitschy fun.

THE DRIVE
Springdale is 14 miles further along Hwy 9 (55 minutes from St George).

04 SPRINGDALE

Stunning orangish-red mountains, including the **Watchman** (6555ft), form the backdrop for a perfect little park town. Here eclectic cafes and eateries are big on locally sourced ingredients. Galleries and artisan shops line the long main drag, interspersed with indie motels, lodges and a few B&Bs. Make this your base for three nights exploring Zion Canyon and surrounds. **Outfitters Zion Guru** (utahcanyonoutdoors.com) and **Zion Adventure Company** (zionadventures.com) lead canyoneering, climbing and 4WD trips outside the park; the latter has inner-tube rentals for summer float trips. They both outfit for backcountry hikes through Zion National Park's popular Narrows.

THE DRIVE
The entrance to the Zion Canyon section of Zion National Park is only 2 miles east of Springdale. Note that here you're at about 3900ft, the lowest (and hottest) part of your trip.

05 ZION CANYON

More than 100 miles of trails cut through the surprisingly well-watered, deciduous-tree-covered Virgin River canyon section of Zion National Park. Map out your routes at the **Zion Canyon Visitor Center** (nps.gov/zion). Your first activity should be the 6-mile **Scenic Drive**, which pierces the heart of the park. From April through October, using the free shuttle is mandatory, but you can hop off and on at any of the scenic stops and trailheads along the way.

The paved, 2.2-mile return **Riverside Walk**, at the end of the road, is an easy stroll. When the trail ends, you can continue hiking along in the Virgin River for 5 miles. Alternatively, a half-mile one-way trail leads up to the lower of the **Emerald Pools** where water tumbles from above a steep overhang stained by desert varnish.

The strenuous, 5-mile round-trip **Angels Landing Trail** (four to five hours, 1488ft elevation gain) is a vertigo-inducer with narrow ridges and 2000ft sheer drop-offs. Succeed and the exhilaration is unsurpassed. Canyon views are even more phenomenal from the top of the even higher **Observation Point** (8 miles round trip; 2148ft elevation change).

For the longer trips down through the **Narrows** – spectacular slot canyons of the Virgin River – you need to plan ahead. An outfitter shuttle and gear plus a backcountry permit from the park are required; make advance reservations via the park website.

THE DRIVE
Driving east, Hwy 9 undulates over bridges and up 3.5 miles of tight switchbacks before reaching the impressive gallery-dotted Zion–Mt Carmel Tunnel. From there until the east park entrance, the canyon walls are made of etched, light-colored slickrock, including Checkerboard Mesa. Mt Carmel lies 26 miles (45 minutes) northwest of Zion Canyon.

06 MT CARMEL

Several little towns line Hwy 89 north of the Hwy 9 junction. As you drive, look for little rock shops, art galleries and home-style cafes. Stop into the **Maynard Dixon Living History Museum** (thunderbirdfoundation.com) in Mt Carmel to explore the rustic retreat of this seminal Western artist. The Great Depression–era painter created breathtaking, light-infused landscapes and scenes of social struggle. Guides lead visitors through the log home and studio where solitude fueled the artist's imaginative drive.

THE DRIVE
Hwy 89 is a fairly straight shot through pastoral lands; turn off from there onto Scenic Byway 12 where the red rock meets the road. Red Canyon is 45 miles northeast of Mt Carmel.

Zion Narrows

CHRISTOPHER MOSWITZER/SHUTTERSTOCK ©

Photo opportunity

The amphitheater's color at sunrise on Fairyland Point.

Fairyland, Bryce Canyon National Park

07 RED CANYON

Impossibly red monoliths rise up roadside as you reach **Red Canyon** (fs.usda.gov/recarea/dixie). These parklands provide super-easy access to eerie, intensely colored formations. Check out the excellent geologic displays and pick up maps at the visitor center, where several moderate hiking trails begin. The 0.7-mile one-way **Arches** Trail passes 15 arches as it winds through a canyon. Legend has it that outlaw Butch Cassidy once rode in the area; a tough 8.9-mile hiking route, **Cassidy Trail**, bears his name.

THE DRIVE
Stop to take the requisite photo before you drive through two blasted-rock arches to continue on. Bryce

DON'T MISS: Canyoneering

Rock-climb up then rappel down through narrow slot canyons.

Canyon National Park is only 9 miles down the road.

08 BRYCE CANYON NATIONAL PARK

The pastel-colored, sandcastle-like spires and hoodoos of **Bryce Canyon National Park** (nps.gov/brca) look like something straight out of Dr Seuss' imagination. The 'canyon' is actually an amphitheater of formations eroded from the cliffs. **Rim Road Scenic Drive** (18 miles one way) roughly follows the canyon rim past the visitor center (8000ft), the lodge, incredible overlooks and trailheads, ending at **Rainbow Point** (9115ft). From early May through early October, an optional free shuttle bus (8am until at least 5:30pm) departs from a staging area just north of the park.

The easiest walk would be to follow the **Rim Trail** that outlines Bryce Amphitheater from Fairyland Point to Bryce Point (up to 5.5 miles one way). Several sections are paved and wheelchair accessible, the most level being the half-mile between Sunrise and Sunset Points.

A number of moderate trails descend below the rim to the maze of fragrant juniper and undulating high-mountain desert. The **Navajo Loop** drops 521ft from Sunset Point. To avoid a super-steep ascent, follow the **Queen's Garden Trail** on the desert floor and hike up 320ft to Sunrise Point. From there take the shuttle, or follow the Rim Trail back to your car (2.9-mile round trip).

Note that the high altitude means cooler temperatures here – 80°F (27°C) average in July – than at scorching Zion National Park.

THE DRIVE

Only 11 miles east of Bryce Canyon, the town of Tropic is 2000ft lower in elevation – so expect it to be 10 degrees warmer.

09 TROPIC

A farming community at heart, Tropic does offer a few services for park-goers. There's a grocery store, a couple of restaurants and several motels. Basing yourself here for two nights is definitely less expensive than staying in the park. Note that the town is entirely seasonal: many businesses shut their doors tight from October through March.

EAST MESA TRAIL

It feels deliciously like cheating to wander through open stands of tall ponderosa pines and then descend to Observation Point instead of hiking more than 2100ft uphill from the Zion Canyon floor. On East Mesa Trail (6.4 miles round trip, moderate difficulty) you can do just that, because your vehicle does all the climbing. North Fork Rd is about 2.5 miles beyond the park's east entrance; follow it 5 miles north up Hwy 9 from there. Getting to the trailhead in some seasons requires 4WD; inquire about conditions and maps at the Zion Canyon Visitor Center. Nearby **Zion Ponderosa Ranch Resort** (zionponderosa.com), which also has accommodations and activities, can provide hiker shuttles. Note that at 6500ft, these roads and the trail may be closed due to snow November through May.

DETOUR

Kodachrome Basin State Park

Start: 09 Tropic

Dozens of red, pink and white sandstone chimneys punctuate **Kodachrome Basin State Park** (stateparks.utah.gov), named for its photogenic landscape by the National Geographic Society in 1948. The moderately easy, 3-mile round-trip **Panorama Trail** provides an overview of the otherworldly formations. Be sure to take the side trails to **Indian Cave**, where you can check out the handprints on the wall (cowboys' or Indians'?), and **Secret Passage**, a short spur through a narrow slot canyon. **Red Canyon Trail Rides** (redcanyontrailrides.com) offers horseback riding in Kodachrome.

The park lies 26 miles southeast of Bryce Canyon National Park, off Cottonwood Canyon Rd, south of Cannonville.

26

UTAH, COLORADO & NEVADA

BEST FOR DRIVING

Switchbacks and narrow Hogback Ridge rule the challenging road between Escalante and Boulder.

Scenic Byway 12

DURATION	DISTANCE	GREAT FOR
5 days	124 miles / 200km	Outdoors

BEST TIME TO GO	Summer, when the snow is gone and all attractions are open

Dixie National Forest

Arguably Utah's most stunning drive, Scenic Byway 12 traverses moonscapes of sculpted slickrock, crosses razor-thin ridgebacks and climbs over an 11,000ft-tall mountain. Until 1940, only wagon trails connected Escalante with Boulder and the mail was delivered by mule. Today's Scenic Byway 12 wasn't fully paved until 1985. Few people live here even today. Expect rural tranquility and scenery that stuns at every turn.

Link your trip

25 Zion & Bryce Canyon National Parks

Scenic Byway 12 begins in Bryce, so you can just continue your exploration of Utah's national parks west from there.

27 Moab & Southeastern National Parks

From Capitol Reef, Moab is 145 miles to the northeast.

01 BRYCE CANYON CITY

What would a road trip be without kitschy roadside stops? **Bryce Museum** (brycewildlifeadventure.com), a barnlike natural history exhibit, contains more than 400 taxidermied animals, in addition to American Indian artifacts, from one man's private collection. Out back, paid admission also allows you to visit the herd of exotic deer he raises. **Dixie National Forest** (fs.usda.gov/dixie) surrounds Scenic Byway 12 here, just northeast of Bryce Canyon National Park. The museum and several other roadside stands rent

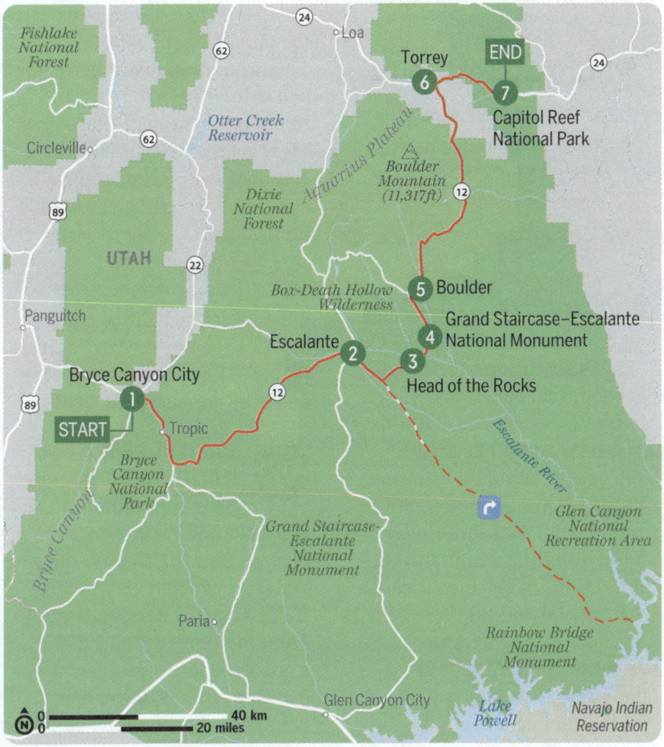

ATVs and bicycles – perfect to take advantage of the nearby **Red Canyon Bicycle Trail**.

THE DRIVE
Past the town of Tropic, Byway 12 enters national monument parklands. A few grandfathered farming communities sit roadside as you wind your way the 41 miles (one hour) from Bryce City to Escalante.

02 ESCALANTE

Though hardly big enough to be called a town, Escalante does cater to visitors heading out into the rugged Grand Staircase–Escalante National Monument. The handful of restaurants and motels make this a good nighttime base for a day of hiking or driving in the monument. **Escalante Interagency Visitor Center** (blm.gov/visit/escalante-interagency-visitor-center) has exhibits on area geography in addition to a gift shop and information.

Escalante Outfitters (escalanteoutfitters.com) is a traveler's oasis. The large bookstore sells maps, guides, camping supplies and liquor; the cafe has breakfasts, pizza and much-coveted wi-fi. Longtime area outfitter **Excursions of Escalante** (excursionsofescalante.com) leads canyoneering, climbing and hiking trips into the monument.

THE DRIVE
Monument country gets even more rough and rugged as you head further east. You'll find yourself driving up through canyons and down switchbacks to the overlook 8 miles away.

DETOUR
Hole-in-the-Rock Road
Start: 02 Escalante

Almost as soon as the saints arrived in Salt Lake Valley, the second Mormon church president Brigham Young encouraged pioneers to settle every inch of the Utah Territory. Looking for a shortcut to more hospitable lands, in 1879 more than 200 pioneering Mormons followed this southeasterly route. When the precipitous walls of Glen Canyon on the Colorado River blocked their path, they blasted and hammered through the cliff, creating a hole wide enough to lower their 80 wagons through by rope – a feat that is honored by the road's name. An open-air memorial just west of Escalante town tells the story in greater detail. Today the 57-mile (one way) road is still dusty and desolate. The last 7 miles require 4WD, and even then it can take almost as long to traverse those as the first 50.

03 HEAD OF THE ROCKS

Don't miss the chance to pull off for one of the most arresting roadside viewpoints in Utah. Here atop the Aquarius Plateau you lord over giant mesas, towering domes, deep canyons and undulating slickrock unfurling in an explosion of color. In the far distance you can see Boulder Mountain to the northwest, the Henry Mountains to the east and Navajo Mountain to the southwest.

Continue 6 miles further east for coffee, a snack and more

canyon views at **Kiva Koffeehouse** (kivakoffeehouse.com), built to resemble a traditional American Indian cliff dwelling.

THE DRIVE
From Kiva Koffeehouse, Lower Calf Creek is a 2-mile, downhill drive away.

04 GRAND STAIRCASE–ESCALANTE NATIONAL MONUMENT

At nearly 1.9 million acres, Grand Staircase–Escalante National Monument (blm.gov) is the largest park in the Southwest. Yet, it's one of the least visited. The harsh desert terrain is intimidating, but there are a few easy access points along Byway 12. The graded-dirt **Hole-in-the-Rock Road** begins 5 miles east of Escalante; 12 miles down it is **Devils Garden**, a giant natural playground where rock fists, orbs, spires and fingers rise to 40ft above the desert floor.

Lower Calf Creek is the most popular recreation area in the park. From the picnic area and campground, a sandy, 3-mile one-way trail follows the creekside canyon to a 126ft **waterfall** – a joy on a hot day.

THE DRIVE
The next 16 miles are slow and winding ones as the road climbs from roughly 5300ft to 6700ft elevation in Boulder. That ridge your car is clinging to is called the 'Hogback.' Be sure to stop at the interpretive signs and the overlook of the valley just before Boulder.

05 BOULDER

Once primarily a ranching community, this frontier outpost has attracted a diverse population of down-to-earth folks that range from artists and ecologists to farmers and cowboys. One of the reasons is **Hell's Backbone Grill** (hellsbackbonegrill.com), at Boulder Mountain Lodge. Zen Buddhists Jen Castle and Blake Spalding have been feeding the community since they opened in 2000, training staff in mindfulness and inviting the whole town to celebrations like a July 4 ice-cream social and talent show.

Be sure to stop at **Anasazi State Park Museum** (stateparks.utah.gov), which protects an ancient site inhabited from 1130 to 1175 CE and excavated in the 1950s. The petite museum is well worth seeing for the re-created six-room pueblo and excellent exhibits on the Ancestral Puebloan (or Anasazi) peoples.

Photo opportunity

Sandstone valley formations and distant mountains at Head of the Rocks.

THE DRIVE
Though Boulder is only 32 miles (50 minutes) south of Torrey, you have to cross over 11,317ft-high Boulder Mountain to get there. Tight switchbacks climb quickly up into the pine-forested treeline. The road is maintained, but do note that you can expect snow at these elevations from November through May.

06 TORREY

Old pioneer homestead buildings line the main street of this quiet town as, in the distance, red-rock cliffs catch the sunset light beautifully. The primary industry here long ago shifted from logging and ranching to outdoor tourism. Most visitors to Capital Reef National Park (11 miles away) sleep and eat here – you should do the same.

THE DRIVE
Torrey sits 1300ft above Capitol Reef, and is usually about 10°F (6°C) cooler. The 11-mile cruise through canyonlands to the valley park is all downhill from there.

07 CAPITOL REEF NATIONAL PARK

Sixty-five million years ago when the earth's surface buckled and fell, the 100-mile Waterpocket Fold was created. Today **Capitol Reef National Park** (nps.gov/care) protects a cross-section of geologic history that is downright painterly: chocolate-red cliffs, yellow sandstone arches, giant cream-colored domes and stark gray monoliths.

Make sure to take the 8.2-mile, one-way **Scenic Drive** along the fold. You first pass through Mormon pioneer fruit and nut orchards, which you can freely pick from in season. The historic **Gifford Homestead** is a small homestead museum, where, if you're lucky, you can buy orchard-fruit-filled mini pies. At the end of the road, **Capitol Gorge Trail** (2.5 miles round trip) leads past ancient petroglyphs. Follow the spur trail to the **Pioneer Register**, where names carved in the rock date back to 1871.

Lower Calf Creek Fall

27

UTAH, COLORADO & NEVADA

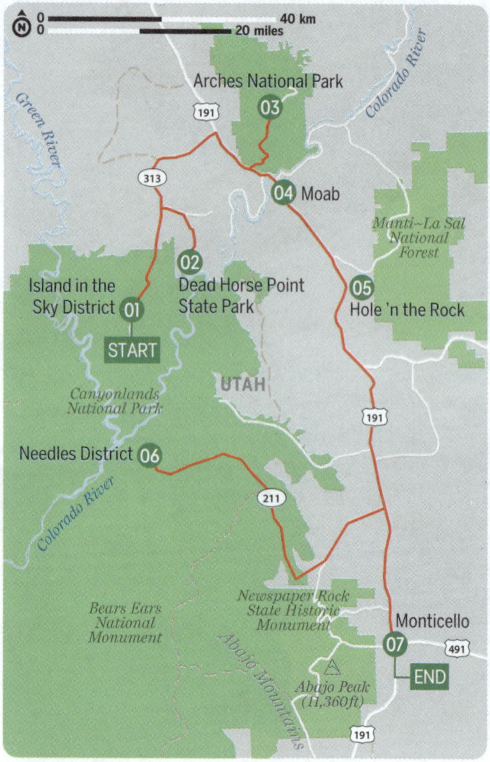

Moab & Southeastern National Parks

DURATION	DISTANCE	GREAT FOR
4 days	196 miles / 315km	Outdoors, family

BEST TIME TO GO	April and October have the most temperate weather and many events

Hiking, biking, rafting, riding (four-wheelers or horses): Moab and the surrounding parks and extensive public lands are activity central. From the graceful forms of Arches National Park to the magnificent depths of Canyonlands, these views provoke stirring emotion. And hiking through Utah's southeastern parks, you get to test your limits and bear witness to the earth's power at its most elemental.

Link your trip

28 Monument Valley & Trail of the Ancients

From Monticello, drive 20 miles south to Blanding to start a trip around the ancient-site-filled far southeastern Utah.

29 Dinosaur Diamond Prehistoric Byway

Start a tour of Jurassic-era formations and fossils in Moab.

01 ISLAND IN THE SKY DISTRICT

Roads and rivers make inroads into the 527-sq-mile desert of **Canyonlands National Park** (nps.gov/cany), but much of it is still untamed wilderness. Vast canyons divide the park into disparate sections. Think of Island in the Sky as the overview: an RVer's special, with paved drives and easy-access lookouts. Here narrow, serpentine valleys tipped with white cliffs loom high over the Colorado and Green Rivers.

BARRY SINGLETON/SHUTTERSTOCK ©

BEST FOR FAMILIES

Both Arches and Canyonlands (Island in the Sky) have short trails and kids' explorer packs.

Canyonlands National Park

A good short hike is the half-mile loop to oft-photographed **Mesa Arch**, a slender, cliff-hugging span framing a picturesque view of **Washer Woman Arch** and **Buck Canyon**. The **Grand View Overlook Trail** (2 miles round trip) follows the canyon's edge and ends at a praise-your-maker precipice atop the mesa.

THE DRIVE
Dead Horse Point State Park is a short detour off slow and scenic Hwy 313, 11 miles northeast of Island in the Sky. Note that though your trip begins at Island, you'll be spending all the nights of this trip 42 miles away in Moab.

02 DEAD HORSE POINT STATE PARK

The views pack a wallop at **Dead Horse Point State Park** (stateparks.utah.gov). At the end of a 4-mile drive you can peer down 2000ft to the Colorado River and 100 miles across a mesmerizing stepped red-rock landscape. (You might remember this epic vista from the final scene in *Thelma & Louise*.) Legend has it that cowboys blockaded the narrow entrance to the mesa to corral wild horses, and that they forgot to release them upon leaving. The stranded equines died within view of the unreachable Colorado River below, hence the park name.

Ranger-led geology talks are presented daily March through October at the point. To escape the small (but sometimes chatty) crowds, take a walk around the mesa rim.

THE DRIVE
Retrace your tracks back to Hwy 313 and then follow Hwy 191 to Arches; it's 26 miles total.

03 ARCHES NATIONAL PARK

More than 2000 red sandstone arches cover the relatively compact **Arches National Park** (nps.gov/arch). Add to that mazelike fins and rock-topped spires and you have one wondrous park.

Arches National Park (p181)

ANDREW REPP/SHUTTERSTOCK ©

There's one main road (19 miles one way) with scenic stops, and two short spurs. In the **Windows section** several arches can be seen from the pavement. Quick walks lead to other named formations, such as **Sand Dune Arch** (0.4-mile round trip). To get to the park's most famous feature, **Delicate Arch**, take the 3-mile round-trip trail near Wolfe Ranch or you can overlook it from the viewing area. At the end of the main road, **Devils Garden** marks the beginning of a 2- to 7.7-mile round-trip hike that passes at least eight arches.

Advance reservations (at least a day or two) are necessary for the free, twice-daily ranger-led hikes into the maze of rock that is the **Fiery Furnace** (nps.gov/arch/planyourvisit/fiery-furnace-hike.htm). Be prepared for fun scrambling up and over boulders, chimneying down between rocks and navigating narrow ledges.

THE DRIVE
Red-rock cliffs surround you on all sides as you drive into the town of Moab.

DON'T MISS:

Ancient Art Appreciation

Ancestral Puebloan cultures left traces as rock art and ruins across the region.

04 MOAB

Southeastern Utah's largest community (population 5100) bills itself as the state's recreation capital – and man, does it deliver. The numerous outfitters here can help you find just about any type of outdoors adventure imaginable. Try **Sheri Griffith Expeditions** (griffithexp.com) for river rafting – family floats to class IV Cataract Canyon rapids. **Poison Spider Bicycles** (poisonspiderbicycles.com) will outfit you for mountain biking on the area's **Slickrock Trail** (discovermoab.com/sandflats.htm). **Dan Mick's Jeep Tours** (danmick.com) specializes in impressive 4WD trips. **Moab Desert Adventures** (moabdesertadventures.com) offers climbing, canyoneering and multisport packages. **Canyonlands Field Institute** (cfimoab.org) leads all-ages interpretive hikes and canoe tours. And **Red Cliffs Lodge** (redcliffslodge.com) has daily horseback trail rides.

The town itself has an outsized offering of restaurants and motels. Look for Southwestern souvenirs around the intersection of Main and Center Sts. On a rainy day, you might peek into the **Museum of Moab** (moabmuseum.org) to learn more about pioneer and American Indian history.

THE DRIVE
Businesses get fewer and further between until Moab ends abruptly in desert nothingness at its southern extent. Hole 'n the Rock is only 15 miles along.

05 HOLE 'N THE ROCK

What didn't Albert and Gladys Christensen do? He was a barber, a painter, an amateur engineer and a taxidermist; she was a cook (their house once contained a restaurant) and lapidary jeweler. But what's really amazing is that they did all this while making their home in a 5000-sq-ft cave. An unabashed tourist trap, **Hole 'n the Rock** (theholeintherock.com) is decorated in knockout 1950s kitsch. The couple lived in the blasted-out home until 1974. Today in addition to the cave, there's a yard full of small wooden buildings with shops, a hodgepodge of metal art and a small exotic animal zoo.

THE DRIVE
Following Hwy 191 south 30 miles the views are in the distance and the road moves fast. The next 42 miles on Hwy 211 cross rugged parkland. Scan the sheer cliffs on the right side as you go along; they're a favorite with rock climbers.

06 NEEDLES DISTRICT

This district is named for the thin sandstone chimneys jutting skyward in the desert. Here on the canyon floor, the jagged terrain is so different from Islands in the Sky, it's hard to believe they're both part of Canyonlands National Park. Keep your receipt, because entry to one is good for the other.

Needles District (nps.gov/cany) receives half as many visitors as other area parks, so it's a great place to get away from it all – especially if you have a 4WD or a mountain bike. Fifty miles of off-road trails (permit required) crisscross the vast landscape.

The 0.6-mile easy to moderate loop of the **Cave Spring Trail** is especially popular with kids. The path leads up ladders and over slickrock to an abandoned cowboy camp. The handprint pictographs on the last cave's walls are haunting. To get among the namesake needle formations **Chesler Park/Joint Trail** is an 11-mile loop hike through desert grasslands, past towering red-and-white-striped pinnacles and between deep, narrow slot canyons.

THE DRIVE
Backtracking along cliffside Hwy 211 to Hwy 191, turn south. The valley opens up then narrows as you gain elevation getting closer to the mountains outside Monticello, 15 miles further along.

07 MONTICELLO

In the foothills of the Abajo (Blue) Mountains, Monticello sits at 7022ft, a good 3000ft higher (and 10°F/6°C cooler) than Moab. If you're hungry after hiking in the Needles, your closest eating options are here. In this tiny town the **Canyon Country Discovery Center** (ccdiscovery.org) has interesting exhibits and educational field trips into the backcountry.

Spring wildflowers and fall tree foliage are a novelty among the arid canyonlands of this region. But here they are just west of the town boundaries in the 1.4-million-acre **Manti–La Sal National Forest** (fs.usda.gov/mantilasal), which rises to 11,360ft at Abajo Peak. **Abajo-Harts Draw**, off N Creek Rd, is the closest recreation area with trails and campgrounds.

Photo opportunity

The quintessential Utah picture: Delicate Arch in Arches National Park.

NEWSPAPER ROCK STATE HISTORIC SITE

This tiny, free recreation area showcases a large sandstone rock panel packed with more than 300 petroglyphs attributed to Ute and Ancestral Puebloan groups during a 2000-year period. The many humanoid and animal figures are etched out of the black, mineralized surface called desert varnish, making for great photos – late-afternoon light is best. Follow the raised boardwalk along the cliffside to see them all. The site lies 12 miles west of Hwy 191 en route to Canyonlands – Needles District.

Manti–La Sal National Forest

28

UTAH, COLORADO & NEVADA

Monument Valley & Trail of the Ancients

BEST FOR ANCIENT SITES

Hire a guide in Bluff or Monument Valley to help you see amazing rock art and ruins.

Bluff Fort

DURATION	DISTANCE	GREAT FOR
5 days	262 miles / 422km	Outdoors, history and culture

BEST TIME TO GO	October through April to avoid scorching desert heat

Extreme desert isolation has preserved rocky natural wonders and numerous Ancestral Puebloan sites in far southeastern Utah and into Arizona. This history courses through the veins of these dusty-hued canyons, pocked with ruins of cliff dwellings and marked with rock art. Photo highlights include the Valley of the Gods and Goosenecks. Much of this area is now protected in the new Bears Ears National Monument.

Link your trip

01 Four Corners Cruise

In Monument Valley pick up this trip to continue exploring the geological wonders and American Indian ancestry of the region.

27 Moab & Southeastern National Parks

One hundred miles north of Bluff, Moab is your base for outdoor activity near Arches and Canyonlands National Parks.

01 MONUMENT VALLEY

Don't worry if you feel like you've seen this place before. Monument Valley's monolithic chocolate-red buttes and colossal, colorful mesas have stared in countless films, TV shows and commercials. The most famous formations are conveniently visible from the 17-mile, rough-dirt scenic drive looping through **Monument Valley Navajo Tribal Park** (navajonationparks.org), down a 4-mile spur road south of **Goulding's Lodge** (gouldings.com), which has a small museum and

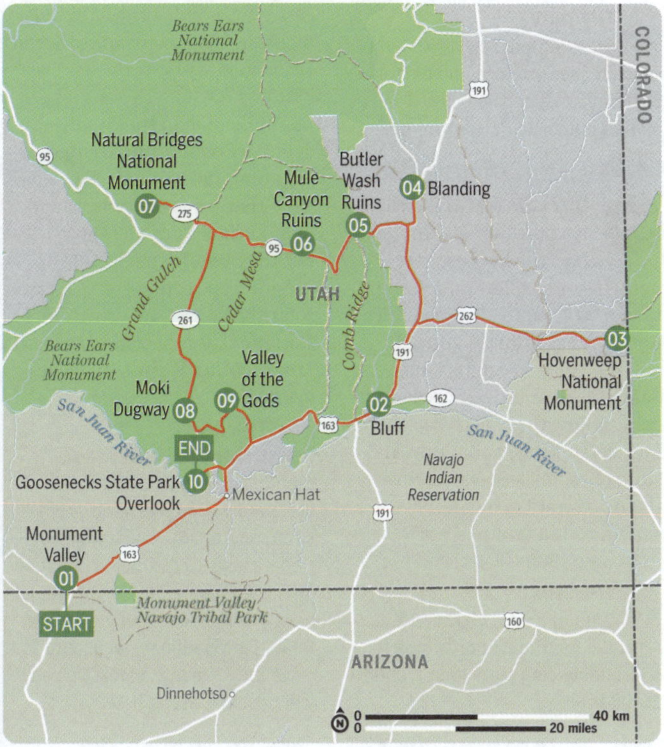

Take Only Pictures

Sadly enough, many invaluable archaeological sites in the area have been vandalized by thieves. Even casual visitors do irreparable damage by climbing on old dwelling walls or picking up 'just one' little pot shard. The old maxim 'take only pictures' bears repeating. Do not touch, move or remove any artifacts; it's against the law. The best way to explore ancient backcountry sites is with a well-informed, responsible guide.

also offers tours. Note that the park and scenery straddle the Utah–Arizona line.

The only way to get into the backcountry to see rock art, natural arches and coves is by taking a Navajo-led tour on foot, on horseback or by vehicle. Easygoing guides have booths set up in the parking lot at the visitor center. Tours are peppered with details about Diné culture, life on the reservation, movie trivia and whatever else comes to mind.

THE DRIVE
The monument's mesas diminish then disappear in your rearview mirror as you head north, crossing the San Juan River and continuing along its valley the 45 total miles to Bluff, UT.

02 BLUFF

Tiny tot Bluff (population 320) isn't much, but a few good motels and a handful of restaurants – surrounded by stunning red rock – make it a cool little base for exploring. We've set up the trip for two nights in Monument Valley, two here in Bluff and one in Mexican Hat or back in the Valley. But distances are short enough that you could spend every night in Bluff and take daily forays to area sights.

Descendants of the town's pioneers re-created a tourable log cabin settlement called **Bluff Fort** (blufffort.org). Three miles west of town on public lands, the accessible **Sand Island Petroglyphs** (bluffutah.org/sand-island-petroglyphs) were created between 800 and 2500 years ago.

A few outfitters in town lead backcountry excursions that access rock art and ruins. **Wild Rivers Expeditions** (riversandruins.com), a history- and geology-minded outfit, rafts along the San Juan. And **Buckhorn Llama** (llamapack.com) leads five- and six-day, llama-supported treks – really, llamas.

THE DRIVE
The best route to Hovenweep is the paved Hwy 262 (past Hatch Trading Post, turn off onto Hwy 191 and follow the signs). From Bluff to the main entrance is a slow, 42-mile drive (1¼ hours).

03 HOVENWEEP NATIONAL MONUMENT

Meaning 'deserted valley' in the Ute language, the archaeological sites of **Hovenweep National Monument** (nps.gov/hove) exist in splendid isolation. Most of the eight towers and unit houses you'll see in the **Square Towers Group**, accessed near the visitor center, were built from 1230 to 1275 CE. Imagine stacking each clay-formed block to create such tall structures on tiny ledges. You could easily spend a half day or more hiking around the gorge's ruins. Other sites, which lie across the border in Colorado, require long hikes.

THE DRIVE
Bluff is the only base in the area, so you'll have to drive both to Hovenweep and back in one day. Moving on to Blanding, 28 miles north of Bluff, Hwy 191 is a rural road unimpeded by too many twists or turns.

04 BLANDING

A special museum elevates small, agriculturally oriented Blanding a little above its totally drab name. The **Edge of the Cedars State Park Museum** (stateparks.utah.gov) is where you can learn more about the area's ancients, with its trove of archaeological treasures that have been gathered from across southeastern Utah. Outside, climb down the rickety ladder into a dark, earthy-smelling ceremonial kiva (an Ancestral Puebloan ceremonial structure) from c 1100 CE. Can you feel a power to the place? (Just ignore the encroaching subdivision noise.)

THE DRIVE
Heading west on Hwy 95, the scenery gets up close and personal. Butler Wash is only 14 miles along on free public lands; look for the signs.

05 BUTLER WASH RUINS

No need to hike for days into the backcountry here: it's only a half-mile tramp to views of the freely accessible Butler Wash Ruins, a 20-room cliff dwelling on public lands. Scramble over the slickrock boulders (follow the cairns) to see the sacred kivas, habitation and storage rooms associated with the Ancestral Puebloan (or Anasazi) Kayenta group of northern Arizona c 1300 CE.

THE DRIVE
Continue west on Hwy 95. After the road veers north, look for a sign announcing more ruins – about 25 miles along.

06 MULE CANYON RUINS

Though not particularly well preserved or evocative, the base of the tower, kiva and 12-room Mule Canyon Ruins sit almost roadside. Pottery found here links the population (c 1000 to 1150 CE) to the Mesa Verde group in southern Colorado.

THE DRIVE
Continue along through the cliffs and canyons of Hwy 95 until you branch off onto the even smaller Hwy 275. The monument is 26 miles west of Mule Canyon.

07 NATURAL BRIDGES NATIONAL MONUMENT

The views at **Natural Bridges** (nps.gov/nabr) are of a white sandstone canyon (it's not red!). All three impressive and easily accessible bridges are visible from a 9-mile winding Scenic Drive loop with overlooks. The oldest is also the closest: take a half-mile hike to the beautifully delicate **Owachomo Bridge**, spanning 180ft at only 9ft thick. Note that trails to Kachina and Siapu bridges are not long, but they require navigating super-steep sections or ladders. Near the end of the drive, don't skip the 0.3-mile trail to the **Horsecollar Ruin** cliff dwelling overlook.

THE DRIVE
Ocher-yellow to reddish-orange sandstone canyons surround you as you wend your way south on Rte 261. To your right is Cedar Mesa–Grand Gulch primitive area, a seriously challenging wilderness environment now part of the Bears Ears National Monument. To drive the 36 miles to Moki Dugway will take at least an hour.

08 MOKI DUGWAY

Along a roughly paved, hairpin-turn-filled section of road, Moki Dugway descends 1100ft in just 3 miles. Miners 'dug out' the extreme switchbacks in the 1950s to transport uranium ore. Note that the road is far from wide by today's standards, but there are places to pull out. You can't always see what's around the next bend, but you can see down the sheer drop-offs. Those afraid of heights (or in trailers over 24ft long), steer clear.

THE DRIVE
At the bottom of the dugway, prepare yourself for another wild ride. The turnoff for Valley of the Gods is less than 5 miles ahead on your left.

Photo opportunity

Monument Valley's monolithic buttes at sunrise or sunset.

Monument Valley (p186)

09 VALLEY OF THE GODS

Think of the gravel road through the freely accessible **Valley of the Gods** (blm.gov) as a do-it-yourself roller coaster, with sharp, steep hills and quick turns around some amazing scenery. Locals call it 'mini-Monument Valley.' Download the public lands office pamphlet to identify the strangely shaped sandstone monoliths and pinnacles (such as Seven Sailors, Lady on a Tub and Rooster Butte). Allow an hour-plus for the 17 miles between Hwys 261 and 163. Do not attempt it without a 4WD if it's rained recently.

THE DRIVE

Once you emerge from the valley, follow Hwy 163 back west and take the little jog up Hwy 261 to the Goosenecks State Park spur, a total of 8 miles away.

10 GOOSENECKS STATE PARK OVERLOOK

Following the 4-mile spur to **Goosenecks State Park** (stateparks.utah.gov) brings you to a mesmerizing view. From 1000ft above you can see how the San Juan River's path carved tight turns through sediment, leaving gooseneck-shaped spits of land untouched. The dusty park itself doesn't have much to speak of besides pit toilets and picnic tables.

29

UTAH, COLORADO & NEVADA

Dinosaur Diamond Prehistoric Byway

DURATION	DISTANCE	GREAT FOR
6 days	408 miles / 656km	Family, outdoors

BEST TIME TO GO May and September have temperate weather, but activities for kiddos happen June to August

BEST FOR FAMILIES

Digging to find 'dinosaur bones' at the Dinosaur Journey museum.

Mill Canyon Dinosaur Trail

Cruise through this incredibly fossil-rich landscape, then dig into the many museums and quarries to learn more. Driving the diamond you'll conquer high plateaus, traverse scenic canyons and cross tall mountains. Though arid now, in the late Jurassic period (154 to 147 million years ago) this was a lush, subtropical forest, and 80 different vertebrates have been found within this one region.

Link your trip

27 Moab & Southeastern National Parks

Before your dinosaur odyssey, spend a few activity-filled days exploring the national parks around Moab.

30 San Juan Skyway & Million Dollar Highway

For incredible vistas and old mining towns, detour 105 miles southwest on Hwy 50 to start this trip in Ouray, CO.

01 MOAB

Situated between two national parks and surrounded by even more public land, Moab makes a good base for outdoor adventure. If you want to track area dinosaurs, pick up the topical pamphlets from the **Moab Information Center** (discovermoab.com). The half-mile **Mill Canyon Dinosaur Trail**, 15 miles north of town, follows a Jurassic-era stream bed where fossils and petrified wood are to be seen. Plus there's a detour to a track site. **Comb Ridge Sauropod Trackway**, 23 miles

north, contains four different sets of fossilized footprints.

Numerous outdoor operators lead excursions into the region. **Adrift Adventures** (adrift.net) offers 4WD trips that focus on prehistoric sites – both dinosaur bones and ancient rock art. With **Canyonlands by Night & Day** (canyonlandsbynight.com), an evening dinner cruise down the Colorado comes complete with a sound-and-light show.

THE DRIVE
Two miles north of Moab, follow the long and winding River Rd (Hwy 128) through the Colorado River gorge for 44 miles (1¼ hours) before exiting at Cisco, which is a further 42 speedy, interstate miles from Fruita.

02 FRUITA

Two miles inside the Colorado state line, stop at the **Trail Through Time** (blm.gov), the best of four interpretive dinosaur trails around town. On the 1.5-mile loop you can learn loads about the prehistoric landscape from interpretive panels, touch in-situ bones and, in summer, check out the active **Mygatt-Moore Quarry**.

Maybe it's the desolation of the dry, rumbling country; maybe it's the lack of anything human-made in your view. Whatever the reason, it seems entirely possible to imagine dinosaurs roaming **Fruita Paleontological Area** (blm.gov). A half-mile loop trail leads past helpful signs illustrating the environment and the six dinosaurs found here during 100 years of off-and-on excavation.

Dinosaur Journey (museumofwesternco.com) is a fantastic little family-friendly museum where kiddos can make their own dinosaur tracks, dig for bones and be surprised by a spitting and spurting, animatronic dilophosaurus. Unlike many big-city museums, the fossils here are actually from the region.

THE DRIVE
Backtracking 4 miles west on I-70, take exit 15 north to CO 139. You start out in Loma, but soon enough the gray cliffs emerge and the road rises to wind its way up and over Douglas Pass (8268ft). Driving the 71 miles to Rangely will take 1½ hours.

DETOUR
Colorado National Monument
Start: 02 Fruita

The **Colorado National Monument** (nps.gov/colm) is the crown jewel of the Western Slope, a place where the setting sun seems to set fire to otherworldly red-rock formations and hikers test themselves against a starkly beautiful environment. Rising 2000ft above the river valley, these colorful canyons expose the geologic history of the area. Learn more about the different sedimentary layers at the visitor center, then step out to overlook the stratification in real life.

The monument contains a variety of hiking trails starting on the 23-mile **Rim Rock Drive**, most of them relatively short, such as the half-mile hike starting from the **Coke Ovens Trailhead** or a quarter-mile stroll starting at the **Devils Kitchen Trailhead**. The park's highest, **Black Ridge Trail** (5.5 miles one way) traipses

Photo opportunity

A lower leg bone big as your body at Dinosaur National Monument.

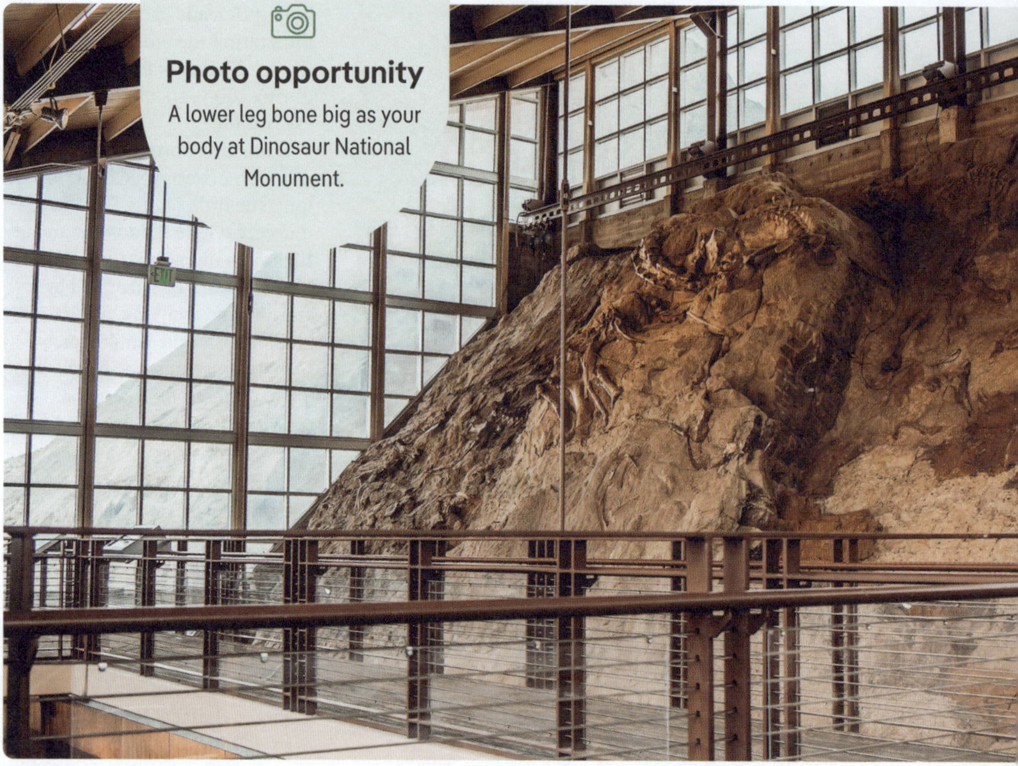

Dinosaur National Monument

up and down through the Morrison Formation of Jurassic dinosaur fame. The west entrance to this 32-sq-mile scenic wonder is 2 miles south of Fruita, off I-70.

03 RANGELY

South of Rangely, **Canyon Pintado National Historic District** (blm.gov) protects the ancient archaeology of the area's Freemont and Ute cultures. Seven rock-art sites are easily accessible off CO 139. Stop at the South Orientation Center sign (Mile 52.8) for information or pick up an interpretive brochure at the **Rangely Chamber of Commerce** (rangelychamber.com). The latter also has a list of other rock-art sites scattered along area back roads.

An oil-service town, Rangely itself isn't much to look at, but its handful of motels and restaurants make it a good stop en route to Dinosaur National Monument.

THE DRIVE
Follow CO 64 out of Rangely, through a stark landscape; after 18 miles be sure to turn east (right) on Hwy 40 to get to the Colorado section of the monument.

04 DINOSAUR NATIONAL MONUMENT

Straddling the Utah–Colorado state line, **Dinosaur National Monument** (nps.gov/dino) protects one of North America's largest dinosaur fossil beds, discovered here in 1909. Though each state's section is beautiful, Utah has the bones.

Start at the **Canyon Area Visitor Center** in Colorado where you can pick up an interpretive brochure for the **Harpers Corner Scenic Drive** (31 miles one way), which cruises from 5921ft to 7625ft with several overlooks along the way.

Visitors need to backtrack to Hwy 40 to access the Utah section, 30 miles west. Absolutely do not miss the **Quarry Exhibit**, which is an enclosed,

SINGLE ACTION PHOTO/SHUTTERSTOCK ©

partially excavated rock wall with more than 1600 actual bones sticking out – an amazing, almost unbelievable sight to see. (The area was once a stream bed where remains collected.) Follow the **Fossil Discovery Trail** (2.2 miles round trip) to touch a few more rock-bound giant femurs and such.

THE DRIVE
From the Utah side of the national monument, Vernal is 15 miles away via UT 149 and Hwy 40.

05 VERNAL

The only town of any size around, Vernal, UT, serves as the gateway for the national monument. Not that you'd notice with a giant pink sauropod statue welcoming you or anything.

The informative film at the **Utah Field House of Natural History State Park Museum** (stateparks.utah.gov) provides a great all-round overview of the region's paleontological history. Interactive exhibits, expert interview videos and, of course, giant mounted fossils further tell the story.

Before you go, stop at the **Dinosaurland Tourist Board** (dinoland.com) for pamphlets on the Red Cloud Loop and other regional driving tours.

THE DRIVE
Following the detailed directions you picked up in Vernal, drive the Red Cloud Loop, keeping your eyes peeled for deer and elk. Note that a substantial portion of this drive is on unpaved roads and you should check on road conditions before you depart.

06 RED CLOUD LOOP

Take a slowly scenic, 74-mile drive on the Red Cloud Loop backway to explore the ancient environs. Check out hundreds of fossilized dinosaur tracks at **Red Fleet State Park** (stateparks.utah.gov). The 200ft of **McConkie Ranch Petroglyphs** are also fascinating. Generous ranch owners built a little self-serve info shack with posted messages and a map, but be advised that the 800-year-old Fremont Indian art here requires some rock-scrambling to see. Being on private land has really helped; these alien-looking anthropomorphs are in much better shape than the many that have been desecrated by vandals on public lands.

THE DRIVE
Red Cloud Loop ends where you started, in Vernal. From there follow Hwy 191 south. The next 110 miles (around two hours) snake through canyons and over ridges to reach Price. For Cleveland-Lloyd quarry, take CO 10 south to the Elmo-Cleveland turnoff and follow signs 15 miles southeast on dirt roads.

07 PRICE

Though limited in scope, the **College of Eastern Utah Prehistoric Museum** (usueastern.edu/museum) has worked to make its fossil displays a bit more dynamic. Get directions there for the remote **Cleveland-Lloyd Dinosaur Quarry** (blm.gov), 32 miles south of Price. More than 12,000 bones have been taken from the ground there, the largest concentration of which belonged to meat-eating allosaurs. Excellent exhibits examine why so many of one species was found in one place. Salt Lake City is 110 miles northeast.

DON'T MISS:

Digging Dinosaurs

Visit three different working quarries and touch actual dinosaur bones in situ at several places.

30

UTAH, COLORADO & NEVADA

San Juan Skyway & Million Dollar Highway

BEST FOR FOODIES

The farm-to-table options in Mancos and Durango.

DURATION	DISTANCE	GREAT FOR
6–8 days	157 miles / 253km	History and culture, outdoors, family

BEST TIME TO GO	Visit from June to October for clear roads and summer fun

Durango farmers market

Encompassing the vertiginous Million Dollar Hwy, the San Juan Skyway loops southern Colorado, traveling magnificent passes to alluring Old West towns. This is the West at its most rugged: a landscape of twisting mountain passes and ancient ruins, with burly peaks and gusty high desert plateaus. And there is the lingering mystery of the region's earliest inhabitants whose cliff dwellings make up Mesa Verde National Park.

Link your trip

27 Moab & Southeastern National Parks

It's a three-hour drive from Telluride. Take CO 145 north to CO 90 west, which becomes UT 26 west.

31 Colorado's High Country Byways

From Durango it's a four-hour drive on the CO 160 to Alamosa; from here take CO 285 north to Great Sand Dunes National Park.

01 MESA VERDE

More than 700 years after Ancestral Puebloans left, the mystery behind their last known home remains. Amateur anthropologists love it; the incredible cultural heritage makes it unique among American national parks. Ancestral Puebloan sites are scattered throughout the canyons and mesas, perched on a high plateau south of Mancos, though many remain off-limits to visitors.

If you only have a few hours, stop at **Mesa Verde Visitor & Research Center** (nps.gov/meve) and drive around **Chapin Mesa** where you can take

WHY I LOVE THIS TRIP

Carolyn McCarthy, writer

This trip is Colorado at its most breathtaking, with winding country roads and spunky mining towns backed by the chiseled San Juan Mountains. Want to feel the Wild West? Try making small talk with the barkeeps and hotel hosts in Ouray, Silverton and Telluride. In these parts, every 19th-century saloon or historic hotel has a ghost story to share. Check out the bullet holes in Telluride's New Sheridan Bar.

a ranger-led tour to **Balcony House** (recreation.gov), climbing to a well-preserved, hidden cliff dwelling via an exposed ladder. Purchase your ticket a day in advance at the visitor center.

If you have a day or more, buy tickets in advance for popular ranger-led tours of Cliff Palace and Balcony House. These active visits involve climbing rung ladders and scooting through ancient passages. The heat in summer is brutal – go early if you want to hike or cool off at the informative **Chapin Mesa Museum** (nps.gov/meve) near Spruce Tree House.

THE DRIVE
Entering Mesa Verde, go immediately left for the visitor center. Return to the main access road. It takes 45 minutes to reach the main attractions on Wetherill Mesa and the road is steep and narrow in places. Leaving the park, head east on Hwy 160 for Mancos, exit right for Main St and follow to the intersection with Grand Ave.

02 MANCOS

Blink and you'll miss this hamlet embracing the offbeat, earthy and slightly strange (witness the puppets dangling through the roof of the local coffee shop). With a vibrant arts community and love for locavore food, Mancos is the perfect rest stop. You will find most points of interest in a three-block radius. These include galleries and good cooking. During the last Friday of each month, the Arts Walk fires up what locals deem 'downtown.'

The area's oddest accommodations is **Jersey Jim Lookout Tower**, a watch tower standing 55ft high with panoramic views. This sought-after lodging is 14 miles north of Mancos at 9800ft. It comes with an Osborne Fire Finder and topographic map.

THE DRIVE
Drive east on Hwy 160. Reaching Durango turn left onto Camino del Rio and right onto W 11th St in half a mile. Main Ave is your second right.

03 DURANGO

A regional darling, Durango's style straddles its ragtime past and a cool, cutting-edge future where townie bikes, caffeine and farmers markets rule. Outdoor enthusiasts get ready to be smitten. The **Animas River** floats right through town; float it or fly-fish it, while hundreds of mountain-bike rides range from scenic dirt roads to steep singletrack. When you've gotten your kicks, you can join the summer crowds strolling **Main Avenue**, stopping at bookstores, boutiques and breweries.

Leave town heading north on the **San Juan Skyway** (Hwy 550), which passes farms and stables as it starts the scenic climb toward Silverton. Bring your hunger to the family-run **James Ranch** just 10 miles out of Durango. The outstanding farmstand grill features the farm's own organic grass-fed beef, cheese and fresh produce market. Steak sandwiches and focaccia cheese melts with caramelized onions simply rock. Kids dig the goats. Take a self-guided tour and check out the live music program.

THE DRIVE Take Main Ave heading north. Leaving Durango it becomes Hwy 550, also part of the San Juan Skyway. James Ranch is 10 miles in on the right side. A band of 14,000ft peaks becomes visible to the right and frequent pullouts offer scenic views. Before Silverton the road climbs both Coal Banks Pass (10,640ft) and Molas Pass (10,910ft).

DETOUR
Narrow Gauge Railroad
Start: 03 Durango

Climb aboard the steam-driven **Durango & Silverton Narrow Gauge Railroad** (durangotrain.com) for the train ride of the summer. The train, running between Durango and Silverton, has been in continuous operation since 1882, and the scenic 45-mile journey north to Silverton, a National Historic Landmark, takes 3½ hours one way. Most locals recommend taking it one way and returning from Silverton via bus; it's faster. It's most glorious in late September and early October when the Aspens go golden.

04 SILVERTON

Ringed by snowy peaks and proudly steeped in tawdry mining-town lore, Silverton would seem more at home in Alaska than the lower 48. At 9318ft the air is thin, but that discourages no one from hitting the bar stool.

Explore it all and don't shy away from the mere 500 locals – they're happy to see a fresh face. It's a two-street town, but only respectable Greene St, now home to restaurants and trinket shops, is paved. One block over, notorious Blair St was a silver-rush hub of brothels and boozing establishments, banished to the back street where real ladies didn't stroll.

Stop at the **Silverton Museum** (sanjuancounty historicalsociety.org), housed in the old San Juan County Jail, to see the original cells. It tells the Silverton story from terrible mining accidents to prostitution, drinking, gambling and robbery, showing the many ways to meet a grisly end in the West.

Most visitors use Silverton as a hub for Jeep tours – sketchy mining roads climbing in all directions offer unreal views. In winter, **Silverton Mountain** (silvertonmountain.com) offers experts the best in untamed, ungroomed terrain.

THE DRIVE Leaving Silverton head north on Hwy 550, the Million Dollar Hwy. It starts with a gentle climb but becomes steeper. Hairpin turns slow traffic at Molas Pass to 25mph. The most hair-raising sections follow, with 15mph speed limits in places. The road lacks guardrails and drops are huge, so stay attentive. Pullouts provide relief between mile markers 91 and 93.

05 MILLION DOLLAR HIGHWAY

The origin of the name of this 24-mile stretch between Silverton and Ouray is disputed – some say it took a million dollars

COLORADO'S HAUTE ROUTE

An exceptional way to enjoy hundreds of miles of singletrack in summer or virgin powder slopes in winter, **San Juan Hut System** (sanjuanhuts.com) continues the European tradition of hut-to-hut adventures with five backcountry mountain huts. Bring just your food, flashlight and sleeping bag – amenities include padded bunks, propane stoves, wood stoves for heating and firewood.

Mountain-biking routes go from Durango or Telluride to Moab, winding through high alpine and desert regions. Or pick one hut as your base. There's terrain for all levels, though skiers should have knowledge of snow and avalanche conditions or go with a guide. The website has helpful tips and information on rental skis, bikes and (optional) guides based in Ridgway or Ouray.

Mesa Verde (p194)

Photo opportunity

Snap Mesa Verde's dramatic cliff dwellings.

a mile to build it in the 1920s; others purport the roadbed contains valuable ore.

Among America's most memorable drives, this breathtaking stretch passes old mine head frames and larger-than-life alpine scenery. Though paved, its blind corners, tunnels and narrow turns would put the Roadrunner on edge. It's often closed in winter, when it's said to have more avalanches than the entire state of Colorado. Snowfall usually starts in October.

Leaving Silverton, the road ascends Mineral Creek Valley, passing the Longfellow mine ruins 1 mile before **Red Mountain Pass** (11,018ft), with sheer drops and hairpin turns slowing traffic to 25mph.

Descending toward Ouray, visit **Bear Creek Falls**, a large turnout with a daring viewing platform over the crashing several-hundred-foot falls. A difficult 8-mile trail here switchbacks to even greater views – not for vertigo sufferers.

Stop at the **lookout** over Ouray at mile marker 92. Turn right for the lovely **Amphitheater Campground** (recreation.gov).

THE DRIVE
The Million Dollar Hwy makes a steep descent into Ouray and becomes Main St.

06 OURAY

A well-preserved mining village snug beneath imposing peaks, Ouray breeds enchantment. It's named after the legendary Ute chief who kept the peace between the white settlers and the crush of miners invading the San Juan Mountains in the early 1870s, by relinquishing the Ute tribal lands. The area is rife

Ouray Ice Festival

with hot springs. One cool cave spring, now located underneath the **Wiesbaden Hotel** (wiesbadenhotsprings.com), was favored by Chief Ouray. Now you can soak there by the hour.

The annual **Ouray Ice Festival** (ourayicepark.com/ouray-ice-festival) draws elite climbers for a four-day competition. But the town also lends thrills to hikers and 4WD fans. If you're skittish about driving yourself, **San Juan Scenic Jeep Tours** (sanjuanjeeptours.com) takes open-air Jeeps into the high country, offering special wildflower or ghost-town trips. It's worth hiking up to **Box Canyon Falls** from the west end of 3rd Ave. A suspension bridge leads you into the belly of this 285ft waterfall. The surrounding area is rich in birdlife – look for the protected black swift, which nests in the rock face.

THE DRIVE
Leave Ouray heading north via Main St, which becomes Hwy 550 N. It's a flat 10-mile drive to Ridgway's only traffic light. Turn left onto Sherman St. The center of town is spread over the next half-mile.

07 RIDGWAY

Wide open meadows backed by snow-covered San Juans and the stellar Mt Sneffels, Ridgway is an inviting blip of a burg. The backdrop of John Wayne's 1969 cowboy classic *True Grit*, today it sports a sort of neo-Western charm.

Sunny rock pools at **Orvis Hot Springs** (orvishotsprings.com) make this clothing-optional hot spring hard to resist. Though it gets its fair share of exhibitionists, a variety of soaking areas (100°F to 114°F/37°C to 45°C) mean you can probably scout out the perfect quiet spot. Less appealing are the private indoor pools lacking fresh air. It's 9 miles north of Ouray, outside Ridgway.

THE DRIVE
Leaving town heading west, Sherman St becomes CO 62. Take this easy drive 23 miles. At the crossroads go left onto CO 145 S for Telluride. Approaching town there's a traffic circle; take the second exit onto W Colorado Ave. The center of Telluride is in half a mile.

08 TELLURIDE

Surrounded on three sides by mastodon peaks, exclusive Telluride was once a rough mining town. Today it's dirtbag-meets-diva – where glitterati mix with ski bums, and renowned music and film festivals create a frolicking summer atmosphere.

The very renovated center still has palpable old-time charm. Stop into the plush **New Sheridan Bar** (newsheridan.com) to find out the story of those old bullet holes in the wall and the plucky survival of the bar itself, even as the adjoining hotel sold off chandeliers to pay the heating bills during waning mining fortunes.

Touring downtown, check out the free box where you can swap unwanted items; the tradition is a point of civic pride. Then take a free 15-minute **gondola** ride up to the Telluride Mountain Village, where you can rent a mountain bike, dine or just bask in the panoramas.

If you are planning on attending a festival, book your tickets and lodging months in advance.

Telluride Festivals

Telluride is mountain magic in the summer when bluebird skies converge with stellar festival opportunities. For more information, see visittelluride.com.

Mountainfilm (late May) A four-day screening of high-caliber outdoor adventure and environmental films.

Telluride Bluegrass Festival (late Jun) Thousands enjoy a weekend of top-notch rollicking alfresco bluegrass going well into the night.

Telluride Film Festival (early Sep) National and international films are premiered throughout town, and the event attracts big-name stars.

31

UTAH, COLORADO & NEVADA

Colorado's High Country Byways

DURATION	DISTANCE	GREAT FOR
5–7 days	552 miles / 888km	Outdoors, family

BEST TIME TO GO	June to September for clear roads, wildflowers, aspens and great views

This breathtaking trip takes you from the front range to the high-country byways that connect the Rocky Mountains with the continental divide and scudding mountains of the south. The trip takes you through hairpin turns, lost alpine lakes, exhilarating landscapes, broken-down mining towns and some of the state's most tanned and toned towns. You'll climb to 12,096ft, then end up in a vast sand-dune wonderworld of surreal landscapes.

Link your trip

15 Enchanted Circle & Eastern Sangres

Head 100 miles directly south on bumpy back roads to Taos, joining the New Mexico crimson-hued Enchanted Circle.

30 San Juan Skyway & Million Dollar Highway

From the Great Sand Dunes National Park, head up to Hwy 50 and past the mysterious Black Canyon of the Gunnison to Ouray.

01 DENVER

Spirited and urbane, Denver is the West's cosmopolitan capital, and well worth a day of exploration. This city is blessed with great museums, tons of sunshine and spectacular parks and bike trails.

THE DRIVE
Take I-25 N on this 30-mile drive, veering west onto Hwy 36 W, which will take you past the worthwhile Butterfly Pavilion on your way to crunched-out Boulder.

Rocky Mountain National Park

BEST FOR WILDLIFE

Capture Colorado's signature peaks in all their alpenglow glory.

02 BOULDER

Tucked up against its soaring signature Flatirons, this idyllic college town has a sweet location and a palpable eco-sophistication.

If you only have a couple of hours, head straight to **Chautauqua Park** (chautauqua.com) for some of the best hikes and views on the Front Range. Then it's down past the University of Colorado at Boulder campus to the **Boulder Creek Bike Path** and its riverfront parks. The pedestrian-only **Pearl Street Mall** is lively and perfect for strolling.

THE DRIVE
From downtown, head west on Canyon Blvd (Hwy 119) winding your way up Boulder Canyon, past towering rock formations and the Barker Reservoir to the hippie mountain enclave of Nederland. From there, it's north on the stunning Peak-to-Peak Hwy 72, past Long's Peak to Estes Park, the eastern entrance to Rocky Mountain National Park. It'll take over an hour (45 miles).

03 ROCKY MOUNTAIN NATIONAL PARK

With one foot on either side of the continental divide and behemoths of granite in every direction, **Rocky Mountain National Park** (nps.gov/romo) takes you to the wild-tufted top of the United States.

Estes Park, with its bumper-to-bumper main drag and plethora of kitsch shopping, is a necessary gateway into the park. From there, head into the park to the **Moraine Park Museum**, before deciding on your route and a day hike.

THE DRIVE
On this day-long drive (165 miles) from downtown Estes, head up Trail Ridge Rd (generally open late May to October, depending on snow). From there, it's down past the resort towns

of Grand Lake and Winter Park, over Berthoud Pass, up I-70, over Vail Pass, and down into Vail.

DETOUR
Steamboat Springs
Start: 03 Rocky Mountain National Park

You can easily extend your trip by heading west from Granby for 80 miles on Hwy 40, to the ski resort and peaced-out mountain village of Steamboat Springs. When you're in town, don't miss hikes and bikes in the nearby wilderness, followed by a soak in **Strawberry Park Hot Springs** (strawberryhotsprings.com).

04 VAIL

If you have a day, hop on the **Vail to Breckenridge Bike Path** (summitbiking.org) and ride it for as far as your lungs will take you. You can also grab one of the gondolas to a cool mountain-top summit and **Epic Discovery** (epicdiscovery.com) for family fun, take a ride at the **Stables** (vailstables.com), or a soar with **Vail Valley Paragliding** (vailvalleyparagliding.com) or **Zip Adventures** (zipadventures.com).

THE DRIVE
From Vail, it's a straight 60-mile shot west along I-70 to Glenwood Springs. Along the way, you pass through the amazing Glenwood Canyon – marvel at the hanging bridge construction and fractured canyon walls.

05 GLENWOOD SPRINGS

Perched at the confluence of the Colorado and Roaring Fork Rivers at the end of Glenwood Canyon, **Glenwood Hot Springs** (hotspringspool.com) have been a travel destination for centuries. The Ute Indians meditated in steamy **thermal caves** (yampahspa.com) here, then called Yampah (Great Medicine). Before or after your hot springs or thermal caves treatment, you can rent a bike with **Canyon Bikes** (canyonbikes.com) or charge class III and IV rapids with **Colorado Whitewater Rafting** (coloradowhitewaterrafting.com) through Glenwood Canyon.

THE DRIVE
From Glenwood, cruise south through the Roaring Fork Valley on CO 82 for about 40 miles to Aspen. The further up the valley you go, the bigger the homes. Stop in old mining towns such as Carbondale and Basalt, to ground yourself before hitting glitzed-out Aspen.

06 ASPEN

Aspen is a singular town unique to the world. Rich, famous, beautiful and brainy, yet somehow down-to-earth and welcoming to all. Flash your best smile and you'll fit right in.

In summer, winter, spring or fall, the four mountains of **Aspen Snowmass Ski Resort** (aspensnowmass.com) offer world-class skiing and mountain adventures. Hikers won't want to miss a day trip to the **Maroon Bells** – quite simply one of the most beautiful summits in the world. Downtown Aspen has some of the Southwest's best restaurants, plenty of galleries and the noteworthy **Aspen Center for Environmental Studies** (aspennature.org).

THE DRIVE
During the summer, it'll only take a few hours to go over Independence Pass (CO 82) to Leadville. Wintertime, you'll need to backtrack clear to Vail to get here on the slow road (130 miles). No matter which route you take, this is spectacular country.

07 LEADVILLE

Leadville was once the second-biggest city in Colorado. But unlike other historic towns with mining roots, Leadville never made the switch to resort status.

Dive into town history at the **National Mining Hall of Fame** (mininghalloffame.org) or bike the **Mineral Belt Trail** (mineralbelttrail.com) before a wilderness outing to nearby **Mt Massive** (14ers.com), Twin Lakes, **Ski Cooper** (skicooper.com) or the **Matchless Mine**.

THE DRIVE
It's only 35 miles south from Leadville to Buena Vista, although you could spend a few days exploring here. First, you pass the headwaters of the Arkansas as you descend into the Arkansas River Valley. The Collegiate Peaks tower to your right, while Buffalo Peaks Wilderness is well worth a stop on your left.

DON'T MISS:
Independence Pass

Quaking aspens surround you as you navigate hairpin turns and experience craggy-rocked mountain-pass bliss.

Photo opportunity

The distinctive peaks of Maroon Bells.

Maroon Bells

08 BUENA VISTA

With the 14,197ft **Mt Princeton** (14ers.com) and the rest of the **Collegiate Peaks** providing a dramatic backdrop to the west, and the icy Arkansas River rushing by the boulder-filled hills east of town, Buena Vista certainly lives up to its name. Whether you're after hiking, biking, paddling through Browns Canyon National Monument, achy-bones-soaking at **Mt Princeton Hot Springs Resort** (mtprinceton.com) or simply stupendous landscapes, this is a town that has adventure playground written all over it.

THE DRIVE
It gets pretty flat for a while, but don't worry, as you head down more than 100 miles south to the Great Sand Dunes, things start to get more interesting at every mile marker. Salida is a fun town worth a stop along the way.

09 GREAT SAND DUNES NATIONAL PARK

For all of Colorado's striking natural sights, this sea of sand is a place where nature's magic is on full display.

At the center of the **park** (nps.gov/grsa) is a 55-sq-mile dune of sand surrounded by rigid mountain peaks on one side and glassy wetlands on the other. After long drives on the straight highways of high plains or twisting byways through the Rocky Mountains, it's a bit unnerving to find yourself so suddenly standing amid the landscape of the Sahara. While you're here, take a while to head out for a hike or mountain bike, or continue north to the spectacular Crestone Needle.

32

UTAH, COLORADO & NEVADA

BEST FOR HISTORY

Old Pony Express stations link visitors to the past.

Highway 50: The Loneliest Road

DURATION	DISTANCE	GREAT FOR
3 days	390 miles / 628km	History and culture, outdoors
BEST TIME TO GO	Spring for snowcapped mountains, fall for colorful leaves	

Reno

Wanted: intrepid travelers unafraid of vast, empty, isolated spaces. If you thought central Nevada was flat to the horizon, this road trip will dispel that misconception, as majestic peaks appear from nowhere to defy the desert. Look for reminders of earlier wayfarers. Prehistoric tribes left rock carvings. The Pony Express abandoned its stone stations. And chunks of the Lincoln Hwy, the nation's first transcontinental road, bake in the sun.

Link your trip

01 Four Corners Cruise

To loop through the Four Corners region, drop south on Hwy 93 to Las Vegas.

25 Zion & Bryce Canyon National Parks

Trade mountain peaks for fiery spires by driving I-50 east to I-15 south in Utah.

01 RENO

Nicknamed 'The Biggest Little City in the World,' Reno is the best place to rest up, load up and blow some cash before entering the sandy wilds of the Great Basin, a series of bowl-shaped depressions between the Sierra Nevada Mountains and the Rockies. Downtown, try your luck at the mining-themed **Silver Legacy** (silverlegacyreno.com), one of several casinos on Virginia St, then walk south to the Riverwalk District (renoriver.org) to watch kayakers run class

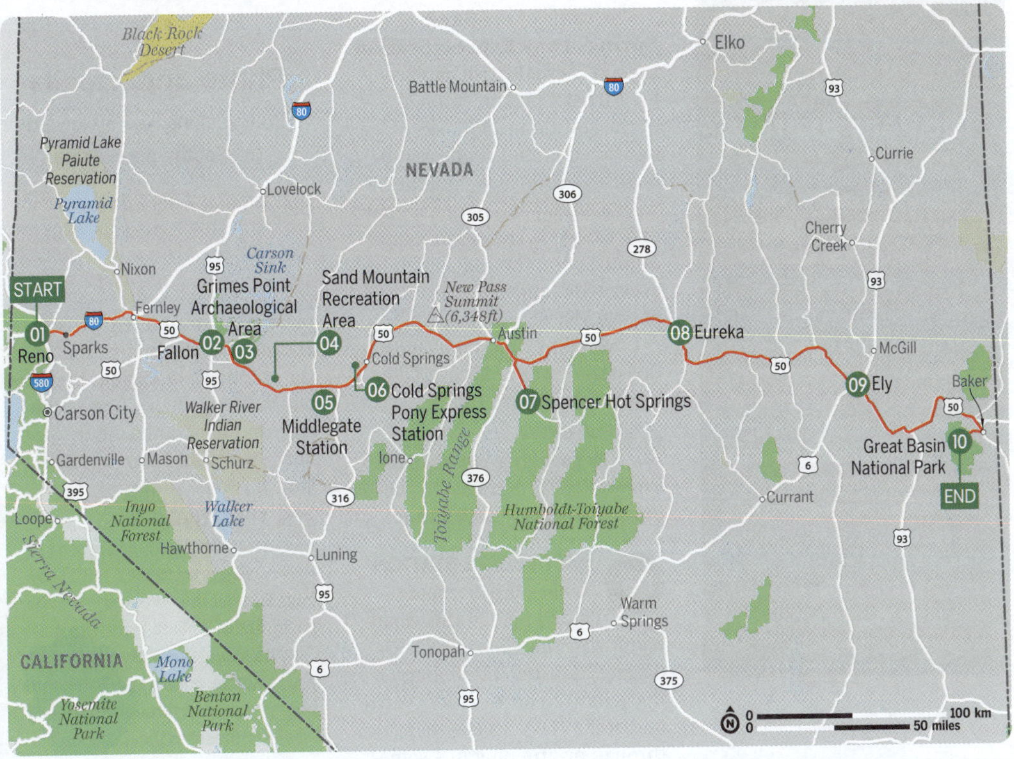

II and III rapids at the 1.5-mile **Truckee River Whitewater Park** (reno.gov). Enjoy the river view while you can; rivers don't flow to the sea in the Great Basin. They meander into lakes, marshes and squishy sinks.

THE DRIVE
Hop on I-80 east. In Sparks, just east of Reno, fuel up on gas and Elvis kitsch at Sierra Sid's Casino (200 N McCarran Blvd, off I-80), which exhibits guns and jewelry owned by Elvis. From I-80, pick up Hwy 50A east in Fernley.

02 FALLON

Look up and you might spot an F-16 flying over Fallon, home of the US Navy's Top Gun fighter-pilot school. On the ground, dragsters compete at the **Top Gun Raceway** (topgunraceway.com) between March and November. The **Churchill County Museum** (ccmuseum.org) is a bit like Fallon's attic. Here you can see a Paiute hut and a Model T Ford, learn about the hardships of pioneers and flip through an impressive collection of historic photographs. You can also reserve tickets for tours of Hidden Cave here.

THE DRIVE
Head east on Hwy 50 for 7 miles. You'll pass cattle, barbed-wire fences and a methamphetamine warning sign or two.

03 GRIMES POINT ARCHAEOLOGICAL AREA

A 0.75-mile interpretive trail at this **archaeological site** (blm.gov/nevada) loops past 200 or so petroglyphs, or rock carvings, some of them dating back 9000 years. For another archaeologically significant site, follow the entrance road back to **Hidden Cave**, a possible cache site in prehistoric times. A short but steep interpretive trail leads to the cave (closed without a guide), or you can join a free, docent-guided cave tour on the second and fourth Saturdays of the month. They begin at 9:30am at the Churchill County Museum.

The Pony Express

Wanted: young, skinny, wiry fellows not over 18. Must be expert riders willing to risk death daily. Orphans preferred.

The Pony Express (1860–61) was the FedEx of its day, using a fleet of young riders and swift horses to carry mail between Missouri and California in an astounding 10 days. Each horseman rode full-bore for almost six hours – changing horses every 10 miles – before passing the mail to the next rider. The Pony Express lasted only 18 months, made obsolete by the telegraph.

THE DRIVE
Continue east about 16 miles. In the spring, the pavement ahead might shimmer in the heat while snowy mountains beckon in the distance.

04 SAND MOUNTAIN RECREATION AREA

That 600ft-high yellow monolith? That's **Sand Mountain** (blm.gov/nevada), a sand dune measuring 1.5 miles by 2 miles. And if you think it might be a peaceful place to ponder nature, roll down your window. Yep, that's the sound of swarming ATVers revving their dune buggies. They're a mesmerizing sight as they zip up and down the dune.

The ruins of the **Sand Springs Pony Express Station** are also here. British explorer Sir Richard Burton stopped at the station in 1860. He described it as '...roofless and chairless, filthy and squalid, with a smoky fire in one corner and a table in the centre of an impure floor, the walls open to every wind and the interior full of dust.' Nice!

Covered by sand for a century, the station was rediscovered by archaeologists in 1976.

THE DRIVE
Continue 21 miles east. The Pony Express Re-Ride re-creates the full run every June (xphomestation.com).

05 MIDDLEGATE STATION

What's the marquee menu item at this wood-plank watering hole? The Middlegate Monster, a 1⅓lb burger that's hard to finish unless you're one of the Navy Seals passing through or dropping in – sometimes they arrive by helicopter. A former stage stop, and later a Pony Express station, Middlegate is a fine place to loiter. Add your dollar bill to the collection on the ceiling.

THE DRIVE
Continue on Hwy 50 and drive east for 15 miles. Watch for ghostly spirits out in the sagebrush: this stretch has seen a lot of untimely death.

06 COLD SPRINGS PONY EXPRESS STATION

A 2-mile trail leads to the stone ruins of this spooky Pony Express station, close to where Jose Zowgaltz was wounded in an ambush. He made it to the station...then perished. On another occasion, the station master was murdered. Cross Hwy 50 for the foundations of the second Cold Springs Station, which doubled as a stagecoach stop and telegraph station. Stop at the new **Cold Springs Station** if you're hungry.

Photo opportunity
Rolling along Hwy 50 toward the South Snake Range.

THE DRIVE
From Cold Springs Station, Hwy 50 twists up to the 6348ft New Pass Summit then drops into another basin. Another climb leads into the Toiyabe Mountains. Fifty miles takes you to Austin, once a mid-19th-century boomtown; blow through and head 20 miles southeast to the next stop.

07 SPENCER HOT SPRINGS

Twenty miles southeast of Austin (the latter half down a dirt track) lies this pool of sulfuric mineral water that will cure whatever ails you. Enterprising locals have shaped the muddy spring into a stone tub. But locals and weary travelers looking to soak the tired out of their bones aren't the only ones who love these springs; if it's been raining, mosquitoes swarm around here, too. Bring DEET-based repellent and a Nevada-size sense of humor.

THE DRIVE
Rejuvenated from your soak, get back on Hwy 50 and roll over basin and range for 58 miles to Eureka, a blink-and-you'll-miss-it old mining town that now relies on tourists. Like you!

Eureka county courthouse (p209)

1879
COURT

'I Survived Hwy 50' Certificate

For travelers who like a challenge, the Nevada Tourism Commission has issued a Hwy 50 Survival Guide (travelnevada.com/travel-guides). The guide includes a basic map, details about Hwy 50 towns and a postcard. Your goal? To get the postcard stamped in five communities along the route. Return the completed card, and you'll receive a personalized 'I Survived Hwy 50' certificate along with a pin. Pre-order a survival guide at ponyexpressnevada.com or pick one up at chambers of commerce, hotels, motels and gas stations along the route.

Great Basin National Park

MALGORZATA LITKOWSKA/ALAMY STOCK PHOTO ©

COLD SPRINGS PONY EXPRESS STATION

The Bureau of Land Management calls the vault toilet at the Cold Springs Pony Express Station 'The Loneliest Rest Stop on the Loneliest Road.' But we hear it gets a lot of use.

08 EUREKA

In the late 19th century, $40 million worth of silver was extracted from the hills around Eureka. Pride of place goes to the **county courthouse**, with its handsome pressed-tin ceilings and walk-in vaults, and the beautifully restored **opera house**, also dating from 1880, which hosts an art gallery and concerts. The **Eureka Sentinel Museum** displays yesteryear newspaper technology and colorful examples of period reportage.

THE DRIVE
Continue east over rolling scrubby hills and watch for deer. It's 77 miles to Ely.

09 ELY

The biggest town for miles around, Ely was established as a mining town in the 1860s. Its old downtown has beautiful regional history murals and awesome vintage neon signs. Downtown, kitsch lovers will dig the **Hotel Nevada**; its funky casino and eclectically Western lobby are worth a look even if you don't spend the night. The bar defines the term 'local color.' You can also buy 'I Survived the Loneliest Road' T-shirts here.

The **Ely Renaissance Village** is a collection of 1908 period homes built by settlers from France, Slovakia, China, Italy and Greece.

THE DRIVE
Continue east on Hwy 50.

10 GREAT BASIN NATIONAL PARK

Near the Nevada–Utah border, this uncrowded **national park** (nps.gov/grba) encompasses 13,063ft Wheeler Peak, rising abruptly from the desert and creating an awesome but compact range of life zones and landscapes. A seasonal 12-mile scenic drive twists up to the summit.

Hiking trails near the summit take in superb country made up of glacial lakes, groves of ancient bristlecone pines (some more than 5000 years old) and even a permanent ice field. June through August, stick around for the astronomy programs (Wednesday, Thursday and Saturday nights). The guided full-moon hikes are also popular.

The **Lehman Caves Visitor Center** (nps.gov/grba) organizes guided tours of the caves, which are brimming with limestone formations. Reservations are recommended. Next to the visitor center, a simple cafe stays open from April through October.

Arriving

If the Southwest is your first point of arrival in the US, expect it to be hassle-free, provided you have all of your documentation (visa or ESTA visa waiver) in order. Queues can, however, be long. Upon arrival, all international visitors must have their fingerprints scanned and a digital photo taken to register with the Department of Homeland Security's Office of Biometric Identity Management program.

Car Rental at Airports

Car rental is a competitive business in the USA. Most rental companies require that you have a major credit card, are at least 25 years old and have a valid driver's license. Some major companies may rent to drivers aged between 21 and 24 for an additional charge. Some rental companies may rent to those 18 and over in Arizona, Utah and possibly Nevada. Elsewhere, those under age 21 are not permitted to rent at all.

Prices vary wildly, so shop around; you'll rarely get the best deal by showing up at an airport car-rental desk, apart from the fact that they may not have much choice.

Most national agencies make 'unlimited mileage' standard, but independents might charge extra for this.

A small car may be less comfortable and not the safest option, while 'trucks' can be real gas guzzlers; a midsized car or SUV should offer the best of both worlds.

Airport to City Center

	Denver	Las Vegas	Phoenix
TRAIN	37 mins **$10**	20–30 mins **$5**	30 mins **$2**
TAXI	30–45 mins **$60**	15–30 mins **$25**	15 mins **$17–25**
BUS	60–70 mins **$10**	30 mins **$8–10**	30 mins **$2**

ESTA VISA WAIVER

Visitors from the UK, Australia, New Zealand and many EU countries don't need visas for stays of less than 90 days, though they must get approval from the Electronic System for Travel Authorization (ESTA).

CANADIAN VISITORS

Visitors from Canada need neither a visa nor ESTA approval for stays of less than 90 days. Citizens of other nations should check travel.state.gov.

CUSTOMS

US and Canadian citizens, and those with ESTA visa waivers, can complete the US customs declaration at an Automated Passport Control kiosk. For the question, 'US Street Address,' a hotel is fine.

MAIN AIRPORTS

Major airports include Denver, Reno, Las Vegas, Albuquerque, Salt Lake City and Phoenix. All have ATMs and currency exchange desks, and most have free wi-fi, although it's often limited to a few hours.

Getting Around

PULLED OVER BY POLICE

If you are pulled over by the police, do not get out of your car. Wait for the officer to approach your window. In the meantime, collect your license, proof of insurance and registration or rental agreement, and have them ready for the officer to inspect. When the officer arrives, they will usually stand a little behind your left shoulder, where they can see your hands.

DRIVING INFO

Drive on the right.

70

Speed limit is usually 70mph on interstates; 55–65mph on highways; 25–35mph in urban areas.

.08

Blood-alcohol limit is 0.08%.

Harley or RV

If you dream of cruising across the US on a Harley, try EagleRider (eaglerider.com). If a recreational vehicle (RV) is more your style, places such as usarvrentals.com and cruiseamerica.com can help. Rental and insurance fees for these vehicles are expensive.

Fly to Save Time

The US domestic air system is extensive and reliable, with dozens of competing airlines, hundreds of airports and thousands of flights daily. It's the way to go when you're in a hurry to get to the start of your drive.

Fueling Up

At many US gas stations, the automated pay screens ask for your ZIP code. For foreign travelers, or those with cards issued outside the US, pay inside before (or, if the attendant is feeling generous, after) fueling up.

Take the Train

Amtrak (amtrak.com) has an extensive rail system throughout the USA. They're a relaxing, social and scenic all-American experience, especially on some Southwestern routes, where double-decker trains boast spacious lounge cars with panoramic windows.

TRAVEL COSTS

Fuel
$3.37/gallon

EV charging
$0.40–0.70/kWh

Train LA–Las Vegas one way
$90

Greyhound bus LA–Las Vegas one way
$75

Accommodations

THE AIRBNB EFFECT

Airbnb may have revolutionized the way we travel, but the impact it has had upon local communities has at times been far from positive. In many towns across Southwest USA, rental vacancies have shrunk to record levels as many property owners shift from longer-term rentals to more lucrative short-term holiday services such as Airbnb. The rise of Airbnb listings has also pushed prices higher, and is fostering resentment among locals; you're especially likely to encounter this in Colorado. For an Airbnb alternative, local tourist offices often have lists of B&Bs and private homes for rent, or look for smaller motels and hotels.

HOW MUCH FOR A NIGHT IN A...

Campground and hostel dorm
$10-50

Double room in a midrange hotel
$75-200

Double room in a resort or top-end hotel
From $250

B&Bs

In Southwest USA, many B&Bs are high-end romantic retreats in restored historic homes that are run by personable, independent innkeepers who serve gourmet breakfasts. These B&Bs often take pains to evoke a theme – Victorian, rustic, Old West and so on – and amenities range from merely comfortable to indulgent. Rates normally top $120, and the best run to $200 to $300.

B&B Bookings

Some B&Bs have minimum-stay requirements, and most exclude young children. To start your search, try: B&B Inns Online (bbonline.com), Vrbo (vrbo.com), BnB Finder (bnbfinder.com) or Select Registry (selectregistry.com).

Campgrounds

First-come, first-served 'primitive' campgrounds offer no facilities (free to around $10 per night). 'Basic' sites usually provide toilets (flush or pit), drinking water, fire pits and picnic tables ($8 to $20). Campgrounds in national or state parks have facilities that include showers, barbecue grills and RV sites with hookups etc ($18 to $50).

Motels

Distinguishable from hotels by having rooms that open onto a parking lot, motels tend to cluster around interstate exits and on main routes into town. Some remain smaller, less-expensive 'mom-and-pop' operations; breakfast is rarely included, and amenities might be a phone and TV (maybe with cable); most also have free wi-fi. Motels often have a few rooms with simple kitchenettes.

DUDE RANCHES

Dude ranches are a quintessentially Western take on accommodations. Across the Southwest you'll find anything from a working-ranch experience (chores and 5am wake-up calls included) to lavish resorts. While the centerpiece of dude-ranch vacations is horseback riding, many ranches feature swimming pools, fly-fishing, hiking, mountain biking, tennis, golf, skeet-shooting and cross-country skiing. For information contact the Dude Ranchers' Association (duderanch.org).

Cars

HOW MUCH TO RENT A...

Small car
$25–75 per day

Large car
$150 per day

EV
$40–500 per day

Car Rental

It's not unusual to arrive to pick up your prebooked vehicle only for the agent to try to sell you a whole list of additional services or upgrades. Make sure you know exactly what you're paying for. Tax on car rental varies by state and agency location; always ask for the total cost including all taxes and fees.

Most agencies charge more if you pick the car up in one place and drop it off in another, and usually only national agencies offer this option. Be careful about adding extra days or turning in a car early: extra days may be charged at a premium rate, or an early return may jeopardize any weekly or monthly discounts you originally arranged.

EVs

It's still unusual to rent an EV in the US, although hybrids are much more common (and more widely available). Some major national companies, including Avis, Budget and Hertz, offer 'green' fleets of hybrid or electric rental cars (eg Toyota Prius or Nissan Leafs), though you'll usually have to pay quite a bit more; remember, however, that you'll generally pay less to charge an EV than you would to fill a normal rental car's tank with gas. Because fleets are smaller, book your EV as early as possible to ensure you're not disappointed.

Some independent local agencies also offer hybrid-vehicle rentals. Try Green Motion USA (greenmotion.com) in Las Vegas.

OTHER GEAR

You'll usually pay extra for everything, from child-safety seats and bike racks to GPS devices and portable fridges. Most rental agencies have limited supplies of all extra gear, so if you're after something specific, reserve as early as you can.

LEFT: NOLICHUCKYJAKE/SHUTTERSTOCK ©, RIGHT: PICTOR PICTURES/SHUTTERSTOCK ©

Health & Safe Travel

THEFT

For the traveler it's not violent crime but petty theft that is the biggest concern. When possible, withdraw money from ATMs during the day, or in well-lit, busy areas at night. When driving, don't pick up hitchhikers, and lock valuables in the trunk of your car. In hotels, you can secure valuables in your room or hotel safe.

Hypothermia

If you're hiking at altitude (eg in the Colorado High Country), even in summer, weather conditions can change rapidly and without warning. Always carry waterproof garments and warm layers, and inform others of your route. Symptoms of hypothermia are exhaustion, numb skin (particularly of the toes and fingers), shivering, slurred speech, irrational or violent behavior, lethargy, stumbling, dizzy spells, muscle cramps and violent bursts of energy.

Natural Disasters

Most areas with predictable natural disturbances – tornadoes on the Great Plains and the South (including Texas), hurricanes in the Gulf and Atlantic Coasts – have an emergency siren system to alert communities to imminent danger. Hurricane season runs from June to November. Tornadoes are most likely from March to June. Wildfires are a growing peril during the summer months.

Heat Exhaustion

If hiking, take it easy as you acclimatize, especially on hot summer days and in the desert. One gallon of water per person per day minimum is recommended. Dehydration (lack of water) or salt deficiency can cause heat exhaustion, often characterized by heavy sweating, pale skin, fatigue, lethargy, headaches, nausea, vomiting, dizziness, muscle cramps and rapid, shallow breathing.

CAR BREAKDOWN

If your rental vehicle breaks down, your first call should be to the rental company (who should give you a 24-hour number to call). You should receive a replacement vehicle if your rental car is likely to be out of action for more than a few hours. The American Automobile Association (AAA; aaa.com) has reciprocal membership agreements with several international auto clubs (check with AAA and bring your membership card from home). This will only work if traveling in your own vehicle.

Responsible Travel

Climate Change

It's impossible to ignore the impact we have when traveling, and the importance of making changes where we can. Lonely Planet urges all travelers to engage with their travel carbon footprint. There are many carbon calculators online that allow travelers to estimate the carbon emissions generated by their journey; try resurgence.org/resources/carbon-calculator.html. Many airlines and booking sites offer travelers the option of offsetting the impact of greenhouse gas emissions by contributing to climate-friendly initiatives around the world. We continue to offset the carbon footprint of all Lonely Planet staff travel, while recognizing this is a mitigation more than a solution.

National Park Service

nps.gov
Information on how to travel the great outdoors responsibly.

Responsible Travel

responsibletravel.com/holidays/usa
Holiday ideas that leave a small footprint.

ROADSIDE ASSISTANCE

An ecofriendly alternative is Better World Club (betterworldclub.net), which donates 1% of revenue to assist environmental cleanup and offers ecologically sensitive choices. It will also cover you in a rental vehicle.

HELL'S BACKBONE GRILL

In Boulder, Utah, close to the Grand Staircase–Escalante National Monument, Hell's Backbone Grill is a poster child for what it calls organic, ethical and locally based destination restaurants. It also stood up to former US president Donald Trump.

GO LOCAL

Support sustainable businesses, such as those committed to using locally sourced ingredients and materials, and clean energy. Supporting small local businesses is another way you can help support local communities.

Nuts & Bolts

GOOD TO KNOW

Time zone
CST Central (GMT/UTC minus six hours): Houston; MST Mountain (GMT/UTC minus seven hours): Denver, Santa Fe, Phoenix; PST Pacific (GMT/UTC minus eight hours): Seattle, San Francisco

Country code
1

Emergency number
911

Population
51.9 million

CURRENCY: US DOLLAR ($)

Opening Hours

Banks 8:30am–4:30pm Monday–Thursday, to 5:30pm Friday (and possibly 9am–noon Saturday)

Post offices 9am–5pm Monday–Friday

Shopping malls 9am–9pm

Stores 9am–6pm Monday–Saturday, noon–5pm Sunday

Supermarkets 8am–8pm, some open 24 hours

Toilets

Most states have rest areas with free toilets along major highways; alternatively, as a paying customer you can seek out toilets at gas stations, coffee shops and restaurants.

ELECTRICITY 120V/60HZ

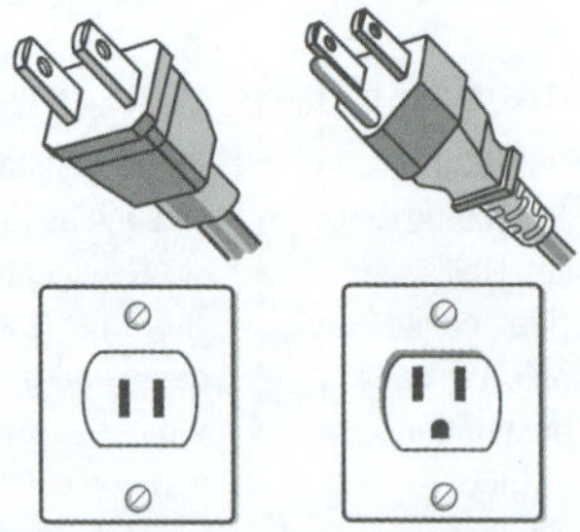

Type A
120V/60Hz

Type B
120V/60Hz

Weights & Measures

Weights are measured in ounces (oz), pounds (lb) and tons; liquids in fluid ounces (fl oz), pints (pt), quarts (qt) and gallons (gal); distance in feet (ft), yards (yd) and miles (mi).

Credit Cards

Major credit cards are almost universally accepted. In fact, it's near impossible to rent a car or make hotel reservations without one. It's highly recommended that you carry at least one credit card, if only for emergencies. Visa and MasterCard are the most widely accepted.

Payments

Some airlines require a US billing address. Note, too, that you may be asked to 'sign' for credit card purchases. It's normal for restaurant servers to take your card to a pay station to process. Mobile pay options (Apple Pay, Google Pay) are becoming increasingly common.

Tipping

Tipping is *not* optional; only withhold tips in cases of outrageously bad service. Suggested amounts: airport and hotel porters ($2 per bag); bartenders (15–20% per round); hotel housekeepers ($2–5 per night); restaurant servers (15–20%); taxi drivers (10–15%); valet parking attendants (at least $2 on return of the keys).

HOW MUCH FOR A...

Museum entry
free–$40

National park entry
$7–20 per person; $20–35 per vehicle

Coffee
$1.50–5

Local bus or train ticket
$2–5

Index

A

B

C

Map Pages 000

D

Map Pages 000

E

F

G

H

I

J

K

L

N

O

P

Q

R

S

THE WRITERS

This is the 5th edition of Lonely Planet's *Best Road Trips Southwest USA* guidebook, updated with new material by Anthony Ham. Writers on previous editions whose work also appears in this book are included below.

Anthony Ham

Anthony is a writer who travels the world in search of stories. His particular passions are the wildlife, wild places and wide-open spaces of the planet, from the Great Plains of the US and Outback Australia to the Amazon, Africa, and the Arctic. He writes for the New York Times among other magazines and newspapers around the world, and he has written two books of narrative nonfiction, *The Last Lions of Africa* and *The Man Who Loved Pink Dolphins*.

Contributing writers

Hugh McNaughtan, Amy C Balfour, Stephen Lioy, Carolyn McCarthy, Christopher Pitts, Ryan Ver Berkmoes, Benedict Walker

SEND US YOUR FEEDBACK

We love to hear from travelers – your comments keep us on our toes and help make our books better. Our well-travelled team reads every word on what you loved or loathed about this book. Although we cannot reply individually to your submissions, we always guarantee that your feedback goes straight to the appropriate writers, in time for the next edition. Each person who sends us information is thanked in the next edition.

Visit **lonelyplanet.com/contact** to submit your updates and suggestions or to ask for help. Our award-winning website also features inspirational travel stories and news.

Note: We may edit, reproduce and incorporate your comments in Lonely Planet products such as guidebooks, websites and digital products, so let us know if you are happy to have your name acknowledged. For a copy of our privacy policy visit **lonelyplanet.com/legal/intellectual-property**.

BEHIND THE SCENES

This book was produced by the following:

Commissioning Editor
Darren O'Connell

Production Editor
Sofie Andersen

Book Designer
Aomi Ito

Cartographer
Alison Lyall

Assisting Editors
Janet Austin, Gabrielle Innes, Fionnuala Twomey

Cover Researcher
Norma Brewer

Thanks to
Ronan Abayawickrema, Hannah Cartmel, Fergal Condon, Karen Henderson, Gabrielle Stefanos

Product Development
Amy Lynch, Marc Backwell, Katerina Pavkova, Fergal Condon, Ania Lenihan

ACKNOWLEDGMENTS

Cover photograph
Arches National Park, Utah, Andy Konieczny/Shutterstock ©